William Shakespeare

HAMLET

Edited by
David Bevington

David Scott Kastan,
James Hammersmith,
and Robert Kean Turner,
Associate Editors

With a Foreword by
Joseph Papp

BANTAM BOOKS
NEW YORK · TORONTO · LONDON · SYDNEY · AUCKLAND

HAMLET

*A Bantam Book / published by arrangement
with Scott, Foresman and Company*

PUBLISHING HISTORY

*Scott, Foresman edition published / January 1980
Bantam Classic edition, with newly edited text and substantially revised, edited, and
amplified notes, introductions, and other materials, published / February 1988
Valuable advice on staging matters has been provided by Richard Hosley.
Collations checked by Eric Rasmussen.
Additional editorial assistance by Claire McEachern.*

ISBN 0-553-21292-3

Published simultaneously in the United States and Canada

Bantam Books are published by Bantam Books, a division of Bantam Doubleday Dell
Publishing Group, Inc. Its trademark, consisting of the words "Bantam Books" and the
portrayal of a rooster, is Registered in U.S. Patent and Trademark Office and in other
countries. Marca Registrada. Bantam Books, 1540 Broadway, New York, New York
10036.

PRINTED IN THE UNITED STATES OF AMERICA

29   28   27   26   25

Contents

Foreword

It's hard to imagine, but Shakespeare wrote all of his plays with a quill pen, a goose feather whose hard end had to be sharpened frequently. How many times did he scrape the dull end to a point with his knife, dip it into the inkwell, and bring up, dripping wet, those wonderful words and ideas that are known all over the world?

In the age of word processors, typewriters, and ballpoint pens, we have almost forgotten the meaning of the word "blot." Yet when I went to school, in the 1930s, my classmates and I knew all too well what an inkblot from the metal-tipped pens we used would do to a nice clean page of a test paper, and we groaned whenever a splotch fell across the sheet. Most of us finished the school day with ink-stained fingers; those who were less careful also went home with ink-stained shirts, which were almost impossible to get clean.

When I think about how long it took me to write the simplest composition with a metal-tipped pen and ink, I can only marvel at how many plays Shakespeare scratched out with his goose-feather quill pen, year after year. Imagine him walking down one of the narrow cobblestoned streets of London, or perhaps drinking a pint of beer in his local alehouse. Suddenly his mind catches fire with an idea, or a sentence, or a previously elusive phrase. He is burning with impatience to write it down—but because he doesn't have a ballpoint pen or even a pencil in his pocket, he has to keep the idea in his head until he can get to his quill and parchment.

He rushes back to his lodgings on Silver Street, ignoring the vendors hawking brooms, the coaches clattering by, the piteous wails of beggars and prisoners. Bounding up the stairs, he snatches his quill and starts to write furiously, not even bothering to light a candle against the dusk. "To be, or not to be," he scrawls, "that is the—." But the quill point has gone dull, the letters have fattened out illegibly, and in the middle of writing one of the most famous passages in the history of dramatic literature, Shakespeare has to stop to sharpen his pen.

Taking a deep breath, he lights a candle now that it's dark, sits down, and begins again. By the time the candle has burned out and the noisy apprentices of his French Huguenot landlord have quieted down, Shakespeare has finished Act 3 of *Hamlet* with scarcely a blot.

Early the next morning, he hurries through the fog of a London summer morning to the rooms of his colleague Richard Burbage, the actor for whom the role of Hamlet is being written. He finds Burbage asleep and snoring loudly, sprawled across his straw mattress. Not only had the actor performed in *Henry V* the previous afternoon, but he had then gone out carousing all night with some friends who had come to the performance.

Shakespeare shakes his friend awake, until, bleary-eyed, Burbage sits up in his bed. "Dammit, Will," he grumbles, "can't you let an honest man sleep?" But the playwright, his eyes shining and the words tumbling out of his mouth, says, "Shut up and listen—tell me what you think of *this*!"

He begins to read to the still half-asleep Burbage, pacing around the room as he speaks. ". . . Whether 'tis nobler in the mind to suffer the slings and arrows of outrageous fortune—"

Burbage interrupts, suddenly wide awake, "That's excellent, very good, 'the slings and arrows of outrageous fortune,' yes, I think it will work quite well. . . ." He takes the parchment from Shakespeare and murmurs the lines to himself, slowly at first but with growing excitement.

The sun is just coming up, and the words of one of Shakespeare's most famous soliloquies are being uttered for the first time by the first actor ever to bring Hamlet to life. It must have been an exhilarating moment.

Shakespeare wrote most of his plays to be performed live by the actor Richard Burbage and the rest of the Lord Chamberlain's men (later the King's men). Today, however, our first encounter with the plays is usually in the form of the printed word. And there is no question that reading Shakespeare for the first time isn't easy. His plays aren't comic books or magazines or the dime-store detective novels I read when I was young. A lot of his sentences are complex. Many of his words are no longer used in our everyday speech. His profound thoughts are often condensed into poetry, which is not as straightforward as prose.

Yet when you hear the words spoken aloud, a lot of the language may strike you as unexpectedly modern. For Shakespeare's plays, like any dramatic work, weren't really meant to be read; they were meant to be spoken, seen, and performed. It's amazing how lines that are so troublesome in print can flow so naturally and easily when spoken.

I think it was precisely this music that first fascinated me. When I was growing up, Shakespeare was a stranger to me. I had no particular interest in him, for I was from a different cultural tradition. It never occurred to me that his plays might be more than just something to "get through" in school, like science or math or the physical education requirement we had to fulfill. My passions then were movies, radio, and vaudeville—certainly not Elizabethan drama.

I was, however, fascinated by words and language. Because I grew up in a home where Yiddish was spoken, and English was only a second language, I was acutely sensitive to the musical sounds of different languages and had an ear for lilt and cadence and rhythm in the spoken word. And so I loved reciting poems and speeches even as a very young child. In first grade I learned lots of short nature verses— "Who has seen the wind?," one of them began. My first foray into drama was playing the role of Scrooge in Charles Dickens's *A Christmas Carol* when I was eight years old. I liked summoning all the scorn and coldness I possessed and putting them into the words, "Bah, humbug!"

From there I moved on to longer and more famous poems and other works by writers of the 1930s. Then, in junior high school, I made my first acquaintance with Shakespeare through his play *Julius Caesar*. Our teacher, Miss McKay, assigned the class a passage to memorize from the opening scene of the play, the one that begins "Wherefore rejoice? What conquest brings he home?" The passage seemed so wonderfully theatrical and alive to me, and the experience of memorizing and reciting it was so much fun, that I went on to memorize another speech from the play on my own.

I chose Mark Antony's address to the crowd in Act 3,

scene 2, which struck me then as incredibly high drama.
Even today, when I speak the words, I feel the same thrill I
did that first time. There is the strong and athletic Antony
descending from the raised pulpit where he has been speaking, right into the midst of a crowded Roman square. Holding the torn and bloody cloak of the murdered Julius
Caesar in his hand, he begins to speak to the people of
Rome:

> If you have tears, prepare to shed them now.
> You all do know this mantle. I remember
> The first time ever Caesar put it on;
> 'Twas on a summer's evening in his tent,
> That day he overcame the Nervii.
> Look, in this place ran Cassius' dagger through.
> See what a rent the envious Casca made.
> Through this the well-belovèd Brutus stabbed,
> And as he plucked his cursèd steel away,
> Mark how the blood of Caesar followed it,
> As rushing out of doors to be resolved
> If Brutus so unkindly knocked or no;
> For Brutus, as you know, was Caesar's angel.
> Judge, O you gods, how dearly Caesar loved him!
> This was the most unkindest cut of all . . .

I'm not sure now that I even knew Shakespeare had written a lot of other plays, or that he was considered "time-
less," "universal," or "classic"—but I knew a good speech
when I heard one, and I found the splendid rhythms of
Antony's rhetoric as exciting as anything I'd ever come
across.

Fifty years later, I still feel that way. Hearing good actors
speak Shakespeare gracefully and naturally is a wonderful
experience, unlike any other I know. There's a satisfying
fullness to the spoken word that the printed page just can't
convey. This is why seeing the plays of Shakespeare performed live in a theater is the best way to appreciate them.
If you can't do that, listening to sound recordings or watch-
ing film versions of the plays is the next best thing.

But if you do start with the printed word, use the play as a
script. Be an actor yourself and say the lines out loud. Don't
worry too much at first about words you don't immediately
understand. Look them up in the footnotes or a dictionary,

but don't spend too much time on this. It is more profitable (and fun) to get the sense of a passage and sing it out. Speak naturally, almost as if you were talking to a friend, but be sure to enunciate the words properly. You'll be surprised at how much you understand simply by speaking the speech "trippingly on the tongue," as Hamlet advises the Players.

You might start, as I once did, with a speech from *Julius Caesar*, in which the tribune (city official) Marullus scolds the commoners for transferring their loyalties so quickly from the defeated and murdered general Pompey to the newly victorious Julius Caesar:

> Wherefore rejoice? What conquest brings he home?
> What tributaries follow him to Rome
> To grace in captive bonds his chariot wheels?
> You blocks, you stones, you worse than senseless
>   things!
> O you hard hearts, you cruel men of Rome,
> Knew you not Pompey? Many a time and oft
> Have you climbed up to walls and battlements,
> To towers and windows, yea, to chimney tops,
> Your infants in your arms, and there have sat
> The livelong day, with patient expectation,
> To see great Pompey pass the streets of Rome.

With the exception of one or two words like "wherefore" (which means "why," not "where"), "tributaries" (which means "captives"), and "patient expectation" (which means patient waiting), the meaning and emotions of this speech can be easily understood.

From here you can go on to dialogues or other more challenging scenes. Although you may stumble over unaccustomed phrases or unfamiliar words at first, and even fall flat when you're crossing some particularly rocky passages, pick yourself up and stay with it. Remember that it takes time to feel at home with anything new. Soon you'll come to recognize Shakespeare's unique sense of humor and way of saying things as easily as you recognize a friend's laughter.

And then it will just be a matter of choosing which one of Shakespeare's plays you want to tackle next. As a true fan of his, you'll find that you're constantly learning from his plays. It's a journey of discovery that you can continue for the rest of your life. For no matter how many times you read or see a particular play, there will always be something new there that you won't have noticed before.

Why do so many thousands of people get hooked on Shakespeare and develop a habit that lasts a lifetime? What can he really say to us today, in a world filled with inventions and problems he never could have imagined? And how do you get past his special language and difficult sentence structure to understand him?

The best way to answer these questions is to go see a live production. You might not know much about Shakespeare, or much about the theater, but when you watch actors performing one of his plays on the stage, it will soon become clear to you why people get so excited about a playwright who lived hundreds of years ago.

For the story—what's happening in the play—is the most accessible part of Shakespeare. In *A Midsummer Night's Dream*, for example, you can immediately understand the situation: a girl is chasing a guy who's chasing a girl who's chasing another guy. No wonder *A Midsummer Night's Dream* is one of the most popular of Shakespeare's plays: it's about one of the world's most popular pastimes—falling in love.

But the course of true love never did run smooth, as the young suitor Lysander says. Often in Shakespeare's comedies the girl whom the guy loves doesn't love him back, or she loves him but he loves someone else. In *The Two Gentlemen of Verona*, Julia loves Proteus, Proteus loves Sylvia, and Sylvia loves Valentine, who is Proteus's best friend. In the end, of course, true love prevails, but not without lots of complications along the way.

For in all of his plays—comedies, histories, and tragedies—Shakespeare is showing you human nature. His characters act and react in the most extraordinary ways—and sometimes in the most incomprehensible ways. People are always trying to find motivations for what a character does. They ask, "Why does Iago want to destroy Othello?"

The answer, to me, is very simple—because that's the way Iago is. That's just his nature. Shakespeare doesn't explain his characters; he sets them in motion—and away they go. He doesn't worry about whether they're likable or not. He's interested in interesting people, and his most fascinating characters are those who are unpredictable. If you lean back in your chair early on in one of his plays, thinking you've figured out what Iago or Shylock (in *The Merchant of Venice*) is up to, don't be too sure—because that great judge of human nature, Shakespeare, will surprise you every time.

He is just as wily in the way he structures a play. In *Macbeth*, a comic scene is suddenly introduced just after the bloodiest and most treacherous slaughter imaginable, of a guest and king by his host and subject, when in comes a drunk porter who has to go to the bathroom. Shakespeare is tickling your emotions by bringing a stand-up comic on-stage right on the heels of a savage murder.

It has taken me thirty years to understand even some of these things, and so I'm not suggesting that Shakespeare is immediately understandable. I've gotten to know him not through theory but through practice, the practice of the *living* Shakespeare—the playwright of the theater.

Of course the plays are a great achievement of dramatic literature, and they should be studied and analyzed in schools and universities. But you must always remember, when reading all the words *about* the playwright and his plays, that *Shakespeare's* words came first and that in the end there is nothing greater than a single actor on the stage speaking the lines of Shakespeare.

Everything important that I know about Shakespeare comes from the practical business of producing and directing his plays in the theater. The task of classifying, criticizing, and editing Shakespeare's printed works I happily leave to others. For me, his plays really do live on the stage, not on the page. That is what he wrote them for and that is how they are best appreciated.

Although Shakespeare lived and wrote hundreds of years ago, his name rolls off my tongue as if he were my brother. As a producer and director, I feel that there is a professional relationship between us that spans the centuries. As a human being, I feel that Shakespeare has enriched my understanding of life immeasurably. I hope you'll let him do the same for you.

❖

Hamlet has got just about all the ingredients of exciting, interesting theater—grand soliloquies, complex philosophizing, love relationships, family conflicts, ghosts, murder, revenge, swordplay, and a great death scene where bodies pile up on the stage. Young actors want to cut their teeth on the title role, and indeed, there is no more complex and challenging role for them, partly because of the weight of all the Hamlets who have gone before—among them Edwin Booth, the nineteenth-century American player, and Laurence Olivier, the great British actor of this century.

As I've been thinking about the play recently, it has struck me that *Hamlet* is a study of death and dying. Shakespeare's preoccupation is with life and death, and in his *Hamlet* he takes the popular form of the revenge tragedy and reduces it to its most basic elements. Death is the most recurrent theme in the play. From his first appearance onstage wearing the "inky cloak" of mourning and "customary suits of solemn black" that are "but the trappings and the suits of woe," Hamlet is fundamentally contemplating death. He sustains this preoccupation throughout the play, in his soliloquies—"To die, to sleep; / To sleep, perchance to dream. Ay, there's the rub, / For in that sleep of death what dreams may come, / When we have shuffled off this mortal coil, / Must give us pause."

In the end, death is the victor. Eight people die in the course of the play, the stage is littered with bodies in the last scene, and two entire families are wiped out, two bloodlines cut off forever. Yet this bloodbath at the end doesn't really solve anything, or answer the questions that plague Hamlet and perhaps plague us. To Hamlet, who has spent the entire play thinking about it and maybe even preparing for it, death comes too soon—as it always does:

> You that look pale and tremble at this chance,
> That are but mutes or audience to this act,
> Had I but time—as this fell sergeant, Death,
> Is strict in his arrest—O, I could tell you—

Yet in the midst of death, the wonder of the theater and the wonder of life persist. In his instructions to the Players, (3.2), Hamlet gives the greatest lesson in acting ever, better than anything modern theories or teachers can offer. He counsels restraint—"Nor do not saw the air too much with your hand, thus, but use all gently"—and decorum—"Suit the action to the word, the word to the action"—and reminds the Players that the purpose of acting, "both at the first and now, was and is to hold as 'twere the mirror up to nature."

Hamlet is a play *about* the theater, about the techniques of acting. In the entire middle section, beginning with the arrival of the traveling players in Act 2, scene 2, Shakespeare is reflecting on the uses and purposes of the theater by putting them inside the play itself. And Hamlet's method, like Shakespeare's, is to use theater to further his plot—"The play's the thing / Wherein I'll catch the conscience of the King"—to answer unanswerable questions, and ultimately, perhaps, to put off the death that haunts him.

JOSEPH PAPP

JOSEPH PAPP GRATEFULLY ACKNOWLEDGES THE HELP OF ELIZABETH KIRKLAND IN PREPARING THIS FOREWORD.

HAMLET

Introduction

A recurring motif in *Hamlet* is of a seemingly healthy exterior concealing an interior sickness. Mere pretense of virtue, as Hamlet warns his mother, "will but skin and film the ulcerous place, / Whiles rank corruption, mining all within, / Infects unseen" (3.4.154–156). Polonius confesses, when he is about to use his daughter as a decoy for Hamlet, that "with devotion's visage / And pious action we do sugar o'er / The devil himself"; and his observation elicits a more anguished mea culpa from Claudius in an aside: "How smart a lash that speech doth give my conscience! / The harlot's cheek, beautied with plastering art, / Is not more ugly to the thing that helps it / Than is my deed to my most painted word" (3.1.47–54).

This motif of concealed evil and disease continually reminds us that, in both a specific and a broader sense, "Something is rotten in the state of Denmark" (1.4.90). The specific source of contamination is a poison: the poison with which Claudius has killed Hamlet's father, the poison in the players' version of this same murder, and the two poisons (envenomed sword and poisoned drink) with which Claudius and Laertes plot to rid themselves of young Hamlet. More generally, the poison is an evil nature seeking to destroy humanity's better nature, as in the archetypal murder of Abel by Cain. "O, my offense is rank, it smells to heaven," laments Claudius, "It hath the primal eldest curse upon 't, / A brother's murder" (3.3.36–38). Hamlet's father and Claudius typify what is best and worst in humanity; one is the sun-god Hyperion, the other a satyr. Claudius is a "serpent" and a "mildewed ear, / Blasting his wholesome brother" (1.5.40; 3.4.65–66). Many a person, in Hamlet's view, is tragically destined to behold his or her better qualities corrupted by "some vicious mole of nature" over which the individual seems to have no control. "His virtues else, be they as pure as grace, / As infinite as man may undergo, / Shall in the general censure take corruption / From that particular fault." The "dram of evil" pollutes "all the noble substance" (1.4.24–37). Thus poison spreads outward to infect individual men, just as bad individuals can infect an entire court or nation.

Hamlet, his mind attuned to philosophical matters, is keenly and poetically aware of humanity's fallen condition. He is, moreover, a shrewd observer of the Danish court, one familiar with its ways and at the same time newly returned from abroad, looking at Denmark with a stranger's eyes. What particularly darkens his view of humanity, however, is not the general fact of corrupted human nature but rather Hamlet's knowledge of a dreadful secret. Even before he learns of his father's murder, Hamlet senses that there is something more deeply amiss than his mother's overhasty marriage to her deceased husband's brother. This is serious enough, to be sure, for it violates a taboo (parallel to the marriage of a widower to his deceased wife's sister, long regarded as incestuous by the English) and is thus understandably referred to as "incest" by Hamlet and his father's ghost. The appalling spectacle of Gertrude's "wicked speed, to post / With such dexterity to incestuous sheets" (1.2.156–157) overwhelms Hamlet with revulsion at carnal appetite and intensifies the emotional crisis any son would go through when forced to contemplate his father's death and his mother's remarriage. Still, the Ghost's revelation is of something far worse, something Hamlet has subconsciously feared and suspected. "O my prophetic soul! My uncle!" (1.5.42). Now Hamlet has confirming evidence for his intuition that the world itself is "an unweeded garden / That grows to seed. Things rank and gross in nature / Possess it merely" (1.2.135–137).

Something is indeed rotten in the state of Denmark. The monarch on whom the health and safety of the kingdom depend is a murderer. Yet few persons know his secret: Hamlet, Horatio only belatedly, Claudius himself, and ourselves as audience. Many ironies and misunderstandings of the play cannot be understood without a proper awareness of this gap between Hamlet's knowledge and most others' ignorance of the murder. For, according to their own lights, Polonius and the rest behave as courtiers normally behave, obeying and flattering a king whom they acknowledge as their legitimate ruler. Hamlet, for his part, is so obsessed with the secret murder that he overreacts to those around him, rejecting overtures of friendship and becoming embittered, callous, brutal, and even violent. His antisocial behavior gives the others good reason to fear him as a menace to the state. Nevertheless, we share with Hamlet a knowledge of the truth and know that he is right, whereas the others are at best unhappily deceived by their own blind complicity in evil.

Rosencrantz and Guildenstern, for instance, are boyhood friends of Hamlet but are now dependent on the favor of King Claudius. Despite their seeming concern for their one-time comrade, and Hamlet's initial pleasure in receiving them, they are faceless courtiers whose very names, like their personalities, are virtually interchangeable. "Thanks, Rosencrantz and gentle Guildenstern," says the King, and "Thanks, Guildenstern and gentle Rosencrantz," echoes the Queen (2.2.33–34). They cannot understand why Hamlet increasingly mocks their overtures of friendship, whereas Hamlet cannot stomach their subservience to the King. The secret murder divides Hamlet from them, since only he knows of it. As the confrontation between Hamlet and Claudius grows more deadly, Rosencrantz and Guildenstern, not knowing the true cause, can only interpret Hamlet's behavior as dangerous madness. The wild display he puts on during the performance of "The Murder of Gonzago" and the killing of Polonius are evidence of a treasonous threat to the crown, eliciting from them staunch assertions of the divine right of kings. "Most holy and religious fear it is / To keep those many many bodies safe / That live and feed upon Your Majesty," professes Guildenstern, and Rosencrantz reiterates the theme: "The cess of majesty / Dies not alone, but like a gulf doth draw / What's near it with it" (3.3.8–17). These sentiments of Elizabethan orthodoxy, similar to ones frequently heard in Shakespeare's history plays, are here undercut by a devastating irony, since they are spoken unwittingly in defense of a murderer. This irony pursues Rosencrantz and Guildenstern to their graves, for they are killed performing what they see as their duty to convey Hamlet safely to England. They are as ignorant of Claudius's secret orders for the murder of Hamlet in England as they are of Claudius's real reason for wishing to be rid of his stepson. That Hamlet should ingeniously

remove the secret commission from Rosencrantz and
Guildenstern's packet and substitute an order for their execution is ironically fitting, even though they are guiltless of
having plotted Hamlet's death. "Why, man, they did make
love to this employment," says Hamlet to Horatio. "They
are not near my conscience. Their defeat / Does by their
own insinuation grow" (5.2.57–59). They have condemned
themselves, in Hamlet's eyes, by interceding officiously in
deadly affairs of which they had no comprehension. Hamlet's judgment of them is harsh, and he himself appears
hardened and pitiless in his role as agent in their deaths,
but he is right that they have courted their own destiny.

Polonius, too, dies for meddling. It seems an unfair fate,
since he wishes no physical harm to Hamlet, and is only
trying to ingratiate himself with Claudius. Yet Polonius's
complicity in jaded court politics is deeper than his fatuous
parental sententiousness might lead one to suppose. His famous advice to his son, often quoted out of context as
though it were wise counsel, is in fact a worldly gospel of
self-interest and concern for appearances. Like his son,
Laertes, he cynically presumes that Hamlet's affection for
Ophelia cannot be serious, since princes are not free to
marry ladies of the court; accordingly, Polonius obliges his
daughter to return the love letters she so cherishes. Polonius's spies are everywhere, seeking to entrap Polonius's
own son in fleshly sin or to discover symptoms of Hamlet's
presumed lovesickness. Polonius may cut a ridiculous figure as a prattling busybody, but he is wily and even men-
acing in his intent. He has actually helped Claudius to the
throne and is an essential instrument of royal policy. His
ineffectuality and ignorance of the murder do not really excuse his guilty involvement.

Ophelia is more innocent than her father and brother,
and more truly affectionate toward Hamlet. She earns our
sympathy because she is caught between the conflicting
wills of the men who are supremely important to her—her
lover, her father, her brother. Obedient by instinct and
training to patriarchal instruction, she is unprepared to
cope with divided authority and so takes refuge in passivity. Nevertheless her pitiable story suggests that weak-
willed acquiescence is poisoned by the evil to which it

surrenders. However passively, Ophelia becomes an instrument through which Claudius attempts to spy on Hamlet. She is much like Gertrude, for the Queen has yielded to Claudius's importunity without ever knowing fully what awful price Claudius has paid for her and for the throne. The resemblance between Ophelia and Gertrude confirms Hamlet's tendency to generalize about feminine weakness—"frailty, thy name is woman" (1.2.146)—and prompts his misogynistic outburst against Ophelia when he concludes she, too, is spying on him. His rejection of love and friendship (except for Horatio's) seems paranoid in character and yet is at least partially justified by the fact that so many of the court are in fact conspiring to learn what he is up to.

Their oversimplification of his dilemma and their facile analyses vex Hamlet as much as their meddling. When they presume to diagnose his malady, the courtiers actually reveal more about themselves than about Hamlet—something we as readers and viewers might well bear in mind. Rosencrantz and Guildenstern think in political terms, reflecting their own ambitious natures, and Hamlet takes mordant delight in leading them on. "Sir, I lack advancement," he mockingly answers Rosencrantz's questioning as to the cause of his distemper. Rosencrantz is immediately taken in: "How can that be, when you have the voice of the King himself for your succession in Denmark?" (3.2.338–341). Actually Hamlet does hold a grudge against Claudius for having "Popped in between th' election and my hopes" (5.2.65) by using the Danish custom of "election" by the chief lords of the realm to deprive young Hamlet of the succession that would normally have been his. Nevertheless, it is a gross oversimplification to suppose that political frustration is the key to Hamlet's sorrow, and to speculate thus is presumptuous. "Why, look you now, how unworthy a thing you make of me!" Hamlet protests to Rosencrantz and Guildenstern. "You would play upon me, you would seem to know my stops, you would pluck out the heart of my mystery" (3.2.362–365). Yet the worst offender in these distortions of complex truth is Polonius, whose diagnosis of lovesickness appears to have been inspired by recollections of Polonius's own far-off youth. ("Truly in my

youth I suffered much extremity for love, very near this,"
2.2.189–191.) Polonius's fatuous complacency in his own
powers of analysis—"If circumstances lead me, I will find /
Where truth is hid, though it were hid indeed / Within the
center" (2.2.157–159)—reads like a parody of Hamlet's
struggle to discover what is true and what is not.

Thus, although Hamlet may seem to react with excessive
bitterness toward those who are set to watch over him, the
corruption he decries in Denmark is both real and universal. "The time is out of joint," he laments. "O cursèd spite /
That ever I was born to set it right!" (1.5.197–198). How is
he to proceed in setting things right? Ever since the nineteenth century it has been fashionable to discover reasons
for Hamlet's delaying his revenge. The basic Romantic approach is to find a defect, or tragic flaw, in Hamlet himself.
In Coleridge's words, Hamlet suffers from "an overbalance
in the contemplative faculty" and is "one who vacillates
from sensibility and procrastinates from thought, and loses
the power of action in the energy of resolve." More recent
psychological critics, such as Freud's disciple Ernest Jones,
still seek answers to the Romantics' question by explaining
Hamlet's failure of will. In Jones's interpretation, Hamlet
is the victim of an Oedipal trauma; he has longed uncon-
sciously to possess his mother and for that very reason cannot bring himself to punish the hated uncle who has
supplanted him in his incestuous and forbidden desire.
Such interpretations suggest, among other things, that
Hamlet continues to serve as a mirror in which analysts
who would pluck out the heart of his mystery see an image
of their own concerns—just as Rosencrantz and Guildenstern read politics, and Polonius lovesickness, into Hamlet's distress.

We can ask, however, not only whether the explanations
for Hamlet's supposed delay are valid but whether the
question they seek to answer is itself valid. Is the delay un-
necessary or excessive? The question did not even arise until the nineteenth century. Earlier audiences were evidently
satisfied that Hamlet must test the Ghost's credibility,
since apparitions can tell half-truths to deceive men, and
that once Hamlet has confirmed the Ghost's word, he proceeds as resolutely as his canny adversary allows. More re-

cent criticism, perhaps reflecting a modern absorption in existentialist philosophy, has proposed that Hamlet's dilemma is a matter not of personal failure but of the absurdity of action itself in a corrupt world. Does what Hamlet is asked to do make any sense, given the bestial nature of man and the impossibility of knowing what is right? In part it is a matter of style: Claudius's Denmark is crassly vulgar, and to combat this vulgarity on its own terms seems to require the sort of bad histrionics Hamlet derides in actors who mouth their lines or tear a passion to tatters. Hamlet's dilemma of action can best be studied in the play by comparing him with various characters who are obliged to act in situations similar to his own and who respond in meaningfully different ways.

Three young men—Hamlet, Laertes, and Fortinbras—are called upon to avenge their fathers' violent deaths. Ophelia, too, has lost a father by violent means, and her madness and death are another kind of reaction to such a loss. The responses of Laertes and Fortinbras offer implicit lessons to Hamlet, and in both cases the lesson seems to be of the futility of positive and forceful action. Laertes thinks he has received an unambiguous mandate to revenge, since Hamlet has undoubtedly slain Polonius and helped to deprive Ophelia of her sanity. Accordingly Laertes comes back to Denmark in a fury, stirring the rabble with his demagoguery and spouting Senecan rant about dismissing conscience "to the profoundest pit" in his quest for vengeance (4.5.135). When Claudius asks what Laertes would do to Hamlet "To show yourself in deed your father's son / More than in words," Laertes fires back: "To cut his throat i' the church" (4.7.126–127). This resolution is understandable. The pity is, however, that Laertes has only superficially identified the murderer in the case. He is too easily deceived by Claudius because he has accepted easy and fallacious conclusions, and so is doomed to become a pawn in Claudius's sly maneuverings. Too late he sees his error and must die for it, begging and receiving Hamlet's forgiveness. Before we accuse Hamlet of thinking too deliberately before acting, we must consider that Laertes does not think enough.

Fortinbras of Norway, as his name implies ("strong in

arms"), is one who believes in decisive action. At the beginning of the play we learn that his father has been slain in battle by old Hamlet, and that Fortinbras has collected an army to win back by force the territory fairly won by the Danes in that encounter. Like Hamlet, young Fortinbras does not succeed his father to the throne, but must now contend with an uncle-king. When this uncle, at Claudius's instigation, forbids Fortinbras to march against the Danes, and rewards him for his restraint with a huge annual income and a commission to fight the Poles instead, Fortinbras sagaciously welcomes the new opportunity. He pockets the money, marches against Poland, and waits for occasion to deliver Denmark as well into his hands. Clearly this is more of a success story than that of Laertes, and Hamlet does after all give his blessing to the "election" of Fortinbras to the Danish throne. Fortinbras is the man of the hour, the representative of a restored political stability. Yet Hamlet's admiration for this man on horseback is qualified by a profound reservation. The spectacle of Fortinbras marching against Poland "to gain a little patch of ground / That hath in it no profit but the name" prompts Hamlet to berate himself for inaction, but he cannot ignore the absurdity of the effort. "Two thousand souls and twenty thousand ducats / Will not debate the question of this straw." The soldiers will risk their very lives "Even for an eggshell" (4.4.19–54). It is only one step from this view of the vanity of ambitious striving to the speculation that great Caesar or Alexander, dead and turned to dust, may one day produce the loam or clay with which to stop the bunghole of a beer barrel. Fortinbras epitomizes the ongoing political order after Hamlet's death, but is that order of any consequence to us after we have imagined with Hamlet the futility of most human endeavor?

To ask such a question is to seek passive or self-abnegating answers to the riddle of life, and Hamlet is attuned to such inquiries. Even before he learns of his father's murder, he contemplates suicide, wishing "that the Everlasting had not fixed / His canon 'gainst self-slaughter" (1.2.131–132). As with the alternative of action, other characters serve as foils to Hamlet, revealing both the attractions and perils of withdrawal. Ophelia is destroyed by meekly acquiescing in others' desires. Whether she commits suicide is uncertain, but the very possibility reminds us that Hamlet has considered and reluctantly rejected this despairing path as forbidden by Christian teaching. He has also playacted at the madness to which Ophelia succumbs. Gertrude identifies herself with Ophelia and, like her, has surrendered her will to male aggressiveness. We suspect she knows little of the actual murder but dares not think how deeply she may be implicated. Her death may possibly be a suicide also, one of atonement. A more attractive alternative to decisive action for Hamlet is acting in the theater, and he is full of advice to the visiting players. The play they perform before Claudius at Hamlet's request and with some lines added by him, a play consciously archaic in style, offers to the Danish court a kind of heightened reflection of itself, a homiletic artifact rendering in conventional terms the taut anxieties and terrors of murder for the sake of ignoble passion. We are not surprised when, in his conversations with the players, Hamlet openly professes his admiration for the way in which art holds "the mirror up to nature, to show virtue her feature, scorn her own image, and the very age and body of the time his form and pressure" (3.2.22–24). Hamlet admires the dramatist's ability to transmute raw human feeling into tragic art, depicting and ordering reality as Shakespeare's play of *Hamlet* does for us. Yet playacting is also, Hamlet recognizes, a selfindulgent escape for him, a way of unpacking his heart with words, of verbalizing his situation without doing something to remedy it. Acting and talking remind him too much of Polonius, who was an actor in his youth and who continues to be, like Hamlet, an inveterate punster.

Of the passive responses in the play, the stoicism of Horatio is by far the most attractive to Hamlet. "More an antique Roman than a Dane" (5.2.343), Horatio is, as Hamlet praises him, immune to flattering or to opportunities for cheap self-advancement. He is "As one, in suffering all, that suffers nothing, / A man that Fortune's buffets and rewards / Hast ta'en with equal thanks" (3.2.65–67). Such a person has a sure defense against the worst that life can offer. Hamlet can trust and love Horatio as he can no one else. Yet even here there are limits, for Horatio's skeptical and Roman philosophy cuts him off from a Christian and metaphysical overview. "There are more things in heaven and earth, Horatio, / Than are dreamt of in your philosophy" (1.5.175–176). After they have beheld together the skulls of Yorick's graveyard, Horatio seemingly does not share with Hamlet the exulting Christian perception that, although human life is indeed vain, providence will reveal a pattern transcending human sorrow.

Hamlet's path must lie somewhere between the rash suddenness of Laertes or the canny resoluteness of Fortinbras on the one hand, and the passivity of Ophelia or Gertrude and the stoic resignation of Horatio on the other, but he alternates between action and inaction, finding neither satisfactory. The Ghost has commanded Hamlet to revenge, but has not explained how this is to be done; indeed, Gertrude is to be left passively to heaven and her conscience. If this method will suffice for her (and Christian wisdom taught that such a purgation was as thorough as it was sure), why not for Claudius? If Claudius must be killed, should it be while he is at his sin rather than at his prayers? The play is full of questions, stemming chiefly from the enigmatic commands of the Ghost. "Say, why is this? Wherefore? What should we do?" (1.4.57). Hamlet is not incapable of action. He shows unusual strength and cunning on the pirate ship, or in his duel with Laertes ("I shall win at the odds"; 5.2.209–210), or especially in his slaying of Polonius—an action hardly characterized by "thinking too precisely on th' event" (4.4.42). Here is forthright action of the sort Laertes espouses. Yet when the corpse behind his mother's arras turns out to be Polonius rather than Claudius, Hamlet knows he has offended heaven. Even if Polonius deserves what he got, Hamlet has made himself into a cruel "scourge" of providence who must himself suffer retribution as well as deal it out. Swift action has not accomplished what the Ghost commanded.

The Ghost in fact does not appear to speak for providence. His message is of revenge, a pagan concept basic to all primitive societies but at odds with Christian teaching. His wish that Claudius be sent to hell and that Gertrude be more gently treated is not the judgment of an impartial deity but the emotional reaction of a murdered man's restless spirit. This is not to say that Hamlet is being tempted to perform a damnable act, as he fears is possible, but that the Ghost's command cannot readily be reconciled with a complex and balanced view of justice. If Hamlet were to spring on Claudius in the fullness of his vice and cut his throat, we would pronounce Hamlet a murderer. What Hamlet believes he has learned instead is that he must become the instrument of providence according to *its* plans, not his own. After his return from England, he senses triumphantly that all will be for the best if he allows an unseen power to decide the time and place for his final act. Under these conditions, rash action will be right. "Rashly, / And praised be rashness for it—let us know / Our indiscretion sometimes serves us well / When our deep plots do pall, and that should learn us / There's a divinity that shapes our ends, / Rough-hew them how we will" (5.2.6–11). Passivity, too, is now a proper course, for Hamlet puts himself wholly at the disposal of providence. What had seemed so impossible when Hamlet tried to formulate his own design now proves elementary once he trusts to heaven's justice. Rashness and passivity are perfectly fused. Hamlet is revenged without having to commit premeditated murder and is relieved of his painful existence without having to commit suicide.

The circumstances of *Hamlet*'s catastrophe do indeed accomplish all that Hamlet desires, by a route so circuitous that no man could ever have foreseen or devised it. Polonius's death, as it turns out, was instrumental after all, for it led to Laertes's angry return to Denmark and the challenge to a duel. Every seemingly unrelated event has its place; "There is special providence in the fall of a sparrow" (5.2.217–218). Repeatedly the characters stress the role of seeming accident leading to just retribution. Horatio sums up a pattern "Of accidental judgments, casual slaughters . . . And, in this upshot, purposes mistook / Fall'n on th' inventors' heads" (5.2.384–387). Laertes confesses himself "a woodcock to mine own springe" (l. 309). As Hamlet had said earlier, of Rosencrantz and Guildenstern, " 'tis the sport to have the enginer / Hoist with his own petard" (3.4.213–214). Thus, too, Claudius's poisoned cup, intended for Hamlet, kills the Queen for whom Claudius had done such evil in order to acquire.

In its final resolution, *Hamlet* incorporates a broader conception of justice than its revenge formula seemed at first to make possible. Yet in its origins *Hamlet* is a revenge story, and these traditions have left some residual savagery in the play. In the *Historia Danica* of Saxo Grammaticus, 1180–1208, and in the rather free translation of Saxo into French by François de Belleforest, *Histoires Tragiques* (1576), Hamlet is cunning and bloodily resolute throughout. He kills an eavesdropper without a qualm during the interview with his mother and exchanges letters on his way to England with characteristic shrewdness. Ultimately he returns to Denmark, sets fire to his uncle's hall, slays its courtly inhabitants, and claims his rightful throne from a grateful people. The Ghost, absent in this account, may well have been supplied by Thomas Kyd, author of *The Spanish Tragedy* (c. 1587) and seemingly of a lost *Hamlet* play in existence by 1589. *The Spanish Tragedy* bears many resemblances to our *Hamlet* and suggests what the lost *Hamlet* may well have contained: a sensational murder, a Senecan Ghost demanding revenge, the avenger hampered by court intrigue, his resort to a feigned madness, his difficulty in authenticating the ghostly vision. A German version of *Hamlet*, called *Der bestrafte Brudermord* (1710), based seemingly on the older *Hamlet*, includes such details as the play within the play, the sparing of the King at his prayers in order to damn his soul, Ophelia's madness, the fencing match with poisoned swords and poisoned drink, and the final catastrophe of vengeance and death. Similarly, the early pirated first quarto of *Hamlet* (1603) offers some passages seemingly based on the older play by Kyd.

Although this evidence suggests that Shakespeare received most of the material for the plot intact, his transformation of that material was nonetheless immeasurable. To be sure, Kyd's *The Spanish Tragedy* contains many rhetorical passages on the inadequacy of human justice, but the overall effect is still sensational and the outcome is a triumph for the pagan spirit of revenge. So, too, with the many revenge plays of the 1590s and 1600s that Kyd's dramatic genius had inspired, including Shakespeare's own *Titus Andronicus* (c. 1589–1591). *Hamlet*, written in about 1599–1601 (it is not mentioned by Francis Meres in his *Palladis Tamia: Wit's Treasury*, in 1598, and was entered in the Stationers'

Register, the official record book of the London Company of Stationers [booksellers and printers], in 1602), is unparalleled in its philosophical richness. Its ending is truly cathartic, for Hamlet dies not as a bloodied avenger but as one who has affirmed the tragic dignity of man. His courage and faith, maintained in the face of great odds, atone for the dismal corruption in which Denmark has festered. His resolutely honest inquiries have taken him beyond the revulsion and doubt that express so eloquently, among other matters, the fearful response of Shakespeare's own generation to a seeming breakdown of established political, theological, and cosmological beliefs. Hamlet finally perceives that "if it be not now, yet it will come," and that "The readiness is all" (5.2.219–220). This discovery, this revelation of necessity and meaning in Hamlet's great reversal of fortune, enables him to confront the tragic circumstance of his life with understanding and heroism, and to demonstrate the triumph of the human spirit even in the moment of his catastrophe.

Such an assertion of the individual will does not lessen the tragic waste with which *Hamlet* ends. Hamlet is dead, the great promise of his life forever lost. Few others have survived. Justice has seemingly been fulfilled in the deaths of Claudius, Gertrude, Rosencrantz and Guildenstern, Polonius, Laertes, and perhaps even Ophelia, but in a wild and extravagant way, as though Justice herself, more vengeful than providential, were unceasingly hungry for victims. Hamlet, the minister of that justice, has likewise grown indifferent to the spilling of blood, even if he submits himself at last to the will of a force he recognizes as providential. Denmark faces the kind of political uncertainty with which the play began. However much Hamlet may admire Fortinbras's resolution, the prince of Norway seems an alien choice for Denmark, even an ironic one. Horatio sees so little point in outliving the catastrophe of this play that he would choose death were it not that he must draw his breath in pain to ensure that Hamlet's story is truly told. Still, that truth has been rescued from oblivion. Amid the ruin of the final scene we share the artist's vision, through which we struggle to interpret and give order to the tragedy of human existence.

Hamlet
in Performance

Most people who know their Shakespeare are surprised and disconcerted by the cutting of so much material when they see the otherwise admirable film of *Hamlet* by Laurence Olivier (1948): all of Fortinbras's role and the negotiations with Norway, all of Rosencrantz and Guildenstern, a good deal of Act 4, and still more. The supposed reason, that a film must cut heavily to make room for visual material and to be of an acceptable length, is of course true in the main, but it overlooks the long history of the play in production. Many of the same cuts prevailed from the Restoration until the later nineteenth century as a way not only of shortening a long play but of highlighting the role of Hamlet for the lead actor.

Even in its own day, *Hamlet* (with Richard Burbage in the title role) must have been heavily cut at times, especially in the fourth act; the so-called "bad" quarto of 1603, though garbled presumably by the actors who helped to prepare a stolen copy, appears to be the report of a shortened acting text. During the Restoration, the published edition of the version that diarist Samuel Pepys saw and enjoyed five times during the 1660s was offered to its readers with a warning: "This play being too long to be conveniently acted, such places as might be least prejudicial to the plot or sense are left out upon the stage." This *Hamlet*, prepared by William Davenant and acted by Thomas Betterton at intervals from 1661 until 1709, took out some 841 lines, including most of Fortinbras's part, Polonius's advice to Laertes and instructions to Reynaldo, much of Rosencrantz and Guildenstern, the scene between Hamlet and Fortinbras's captain (4.4), and other matters, though the appearance of Fortinbras at the end was retained. Betterton's successor, Robert Wilks (active in the part until 1732), went further by removing Fortinbras from Act 5 entirely, concluding the play instead with Horatio's farewell and eulogy to his sweet prince. This ending was the only one to be seen onstage from 1732 until 1897. An operatic version of *Ham-*

let in 1712 bore even less resemblance to Shakespeare's play, taking its inspiration chiefly from Saxo Grammaticus's *Historia Danica*, the twelfth-century narrative from which the history of Hamlet derives.

David Garrick used for a time a version of the Wilks text from which he also cut Hamlet's soliloquy in Act 3, scene 3, ("Now might I do it pat") and all mention of Hamlet's voyage to England. Then, in 1772, Garrick ventured to remove nearly all of the fifth act. In Garrick's *Hamlet* the protagonist never embarks for England at all, having been prevented from doing so by the arrival of Fortinbras. Laertes, hindered by a shipwreck, never gets to France. Laertes is a more estimable person than in Shakespeare's play, since he is entirely freed of the taint of plotting to kill Hamlet with a poisoned sword. Hamlet and Laertes fight, but without the poisoned sword; Claudius tries to intervene in the duel of the two young men and is slain by Hamlet, who then runs on Laertes's sword and falls, exchanging forgiveness with Laertes as he dies. Horatio, after attempting to kill Laertes in revenge, is persuaded by the dying Hamlet to accept the will of Heaven and to rule jointly with Laertes. The gravediggers are not needed since Ophelia's burial is omitted. Gertrude is not poisoned but, we are told, is in a trance and on the verge of madness from remorse. We do not hear of the execution of Rosencrantz and Guildenstern. Garrick's intention in all this novelty seems to have been to ennoble Hamlet by pairing him in the last scene with a worthy opponent, by reducing the bloodthirstiness of his killing of Claudius, and by omitting all mention of his part in the deaths of Rosencrantz and Guildenstern. Classical decorum was served by excising long gaps of time and travels into other lands, and by refusing to countenance the comedy of the gravediggers in a tragic play. Garrick restored the soliloquy, "How all occasions do inform against me" (4.4), again enhancing the role of the protagonist, along with some of Polonius's advice to his son.

Garrick called his alterations of *Hamlet* "the most imprudent thing" he had ever done. Although he was "sanguine" about the results, modern audiences are more likely to feel that the Romantic era was not an auspicious time for the play. In addition to Garrick's adaptations, German ac-

tors in England at the end of the century provided the play
a happy ending, with the Queen's illness warning Hamlet
in time. John Philip Kemble, acting the part at various
times from 1783 to 1817, cut the play back to a series of
well-known theatrical vignettes, prompting critic William
Hazlitt, while admiring Kemble's acting, to complain that
Hamlet is better not acted at all.

As if to confirm Hazlitt's worry about the often empty
theatricality of the nineteenth-century stage, a chief preoccupation of the time was to add pictorial splendor to stage
production. Actor-manager William Charles Macready, at
the Theatre Royal, Covent Garden, in 1838, won praise for
"a series of glorious pictures." Charles Kean, who in 1838
had a great success acting Hamlet at the Theatre Royal,
Drury Lane, lavished money and attention on the fortress of
Elsinore in his own production of the play at the Princess's
Theatre in 1850. With his customary passion for scenic
elaboration, he showed, among other scenes, a guard platform of the castle and then another part of the platform, the
royal court of Denmark and its handsome theater, the
Queen's "closet" or chamber, and the ancient burying
ground in the vicinity of the palace to which Ophelia was
borne with impressive if maimed rites. Nineteenth-century
illustrations of Shakespeare's plays testify to the age's interest in pictorially detailed reproductions of the play
within the play, Ophelia's mad scenes, and other emotion-
ally powerful moments in *Hamlet*. Ophelia became a favorite subject for the visual arts, in the theater and out of it,
perhaps because she was so well suited, like the Lady of
Shalott, for pre-Raphaelite interpretation. Pictorialism in
the theater thus accentuated the trend, already seen among
earlier actor-managers, toward highlighting the play's
great iconic moments at the expense of the rest of the text.
Ophelia became a leading role for actresses such as Julia
Bennett, Ellen and Kate Terry, and Helena Modjeska, especially in the latter part of the century.

Charles Fechter appears to have been the first, at the
Princess's Theatre in 1861 and then at the Lyceum Theatre
in 1864, to garb Hamlet, not in the velvet and lace of an
English aristocrat, but in Viking attire appropriate to
the play's Danish setting, which was matched with sur-

rounding sets in primitive and medieval decor. His Hamlet was flaxen-haired; Rosencrantz and Guildenstern were bearded Scandinavian warriors in coarse cross-gartered leggings. Much of the action took place in the large main hall of Elsinore. Edwin Booth in America and Henry Irving in England were the leading Hamlets of the late century. Booth appeared first in the role in 1853, in San Francisco, winning instant renown both in America and abroad. In 1861, in Manchester, England, he played Hamlet to Irving's Laertes. Three years later, Irving himself first played Hamlet, and he continued in the role until 1885. Irving chose a decor of the fifth or sixth century, though not rigorously so, and his costumes retained the attractiveness of Elizabethan dress. Hamlet's first encounter with his father's ghost was impressively set in a remote part of the battlements of the castle, amid massive rocks, with the soft light of the moon filtering onto the Ghost while hints of dawn appeared over the expanse of water to be seen in the background. The scenes on the battlements showed the illuminated windows of the palace in the distance. The funeral of Ophelia took place on a hill near the palace. Irving portrayed Hamlet as deeply affected by his love for Ophelia in a sentimental interpretation that gave prominence to Ellen Terry's Ophelia. Irving made little of Hamlet's voyage to England or his encounter with Fortinbras's captain, devoting most of Act 4 instead to Ophelia's mad scenes and ending the play with "The rest is silence." These descriptions suggest the extent to which the actor-managers of that age turned to favorite scenes for their theatrical effects, cutting much else to accommodate the ponderous scenery.

Beginning with Johnston Forbes-Robertson's restoration of the Fortinbras ending in 1897, as he was encouraged to do by George Bernard Shaw, twentieth-century directors have generally shown more respect for the play's text than did their predecessors. In 1881 at St. George's Hall, William Poel had already directed a group of amateur actors in a reading of the play based on the 1603 quarto, and in 1899 Frank Benson staged an uncut composite Folio-quarto text (something never acted in Shakespeare's day) at the Shakespeare Memorial Theatre in Stratford-upon-Avon. These were experimental performances and not rigorously fol-

lowed since, though Harcourt Williams directed John
Gielgud, in his first Hamlet, at the Old Vic in 1930 in a production without significant cuts. Tyrone Guthrie successfully produced the play in an uncut version, which starred
Laurence Olivier, at the Old Vic in 1937, and Olivier himself
directed an uncut *Hamlet* at London's National Theatre
starring Peter O'Toole in 1963. At the same time, directors
have turned away from the nineteenth-century sentimental
focus on Hamlet's delay and love melancholy to explore ironies and conflict. *Hamlet* in modern dress, beginning with
H. K. Ayliff at the Birmingham Repertory Theatre in 1925,
and followed by, among others, Tyrone Guthrie in 1938, in
another production at the Old Vic, explored the existential
challenges of the play in the context of Europe between two
world wars. Freudian interpretation played a major part in
Laurence Olivier's film version of 1948, as evidenced by the
camera's preoccupation with Gertrude's bedroom and by
the intimate scenes between mother and son. Olivier's cutting and rearranging of scenes owed much to eighteenth-
and nineteenth-century traditions, as we have seen, even
while his camera work found new ways to explore the mysterious and labyrinthine corridors of Elsinore Castle. Joseph Papp's *Hamlet* (Public Theater, New York, 1968) went
beyond Olivier in an iconoclastic and deliberately over-
stated psychological shocker, featuring a manacled Hamlet (Martin Sheen) in a coffinlike cradle at the feet of
Claudius's and Gertrude's bed. Grigori Kozintsev's Rus-
sian film version of 1964, using a cut text by Boris Pas-
ternak, found eloquent visual metaphors for Hamlet's
story in the recurring images of stone, iron, fire, sea, and
earth. Among the best Hamlets have been those of Richard
Burton (in 1964 at New York's Lunt-Fontanne Theater, directed by John Gielgud), Nicol Williamson (in 1969 at the
Roundhouse Theatre in London, directed by Tony Richard-
son), and Derek Jacobi (in 1979 at the Old Vic, directed by
Toby Robertson) portraying the protagonist as tough and serious, capable of great tenderness in friendship and love,
but faced with hard necessities and pursuing them with
fierce energy. Jacobi's *Hamlet* can be seen today in the generally excellent BBC Shakespeare television version, with a
strong supporting cast.

The melancholic, pale, introspective Hamlet of Kemble and the lovestruck prince of Irving have thus seldom been seen on the modern stage, though Olivier recalls the tradition of melancholy with his voice-over soliloquies, and John Gielgud's sonorously spectral voice excels in the meditations on suicide. Today the play is more apt to be satirical, even funny at times, presenting a mordant and disillusioned view of life at court, as in Peter Hall's 1965 production at Stratford-upon-Avon, or in Jonathan Miller's more austere *Hamlet* at London's Warehouse Theatre in 1982, both of which disturbingly portray a world in which, as Hall wrote, "politics are a game and a lie." Polonius, long regarded in the theater as little more than a "tedious old fool," as Hamlet calls him, can reveal in the performance of Felix Alymer or Hume Cronyn or Del Close a canniness in political survival that fits well with his matter-of-fact and philistine outlook. The scenes at court lend themselves to contemporary political analogies: Claudius can become the Great Communicator, adept at public relations gimmicks, the darling of television, while the creatures who bustle about him do their part to "sell" Claudius to a complacent court and a thoroughly skeptical Hamlet. As the outsider, Hamlet today is likely to be the rebel, a misfit, and justly so in view of what he sees in Denmark. Stacy Keach, in Gerald Freedman's *Hamlet* at New York's Delacorte Theater in 1972, was neither melancholy nor vulnerable; rather he was bitter, shrewd, and, as the drama critic of *The New York Times* wrote, "hell-bent for revenge."

As originally staged, *Hamlet* must have made good use of the handsome Globe Theatre, where it first appeared. Without scenery, the Globe offered its spectators an impressive evocation of an idea of order, with the heavens above, hell below the trapdoor, and on the main stage the ceremonial magnificence of the court of Denmark. Claudius's appearances are generally marked by ritual, by the presence of throne and crown, by an entourage of obsequious courtiers. Yet Claudius has vitiated all this seeming order by his secret murder, and Hamlet's presence is a continual reminder that all is not well in Denmark. Hamlet attires himself in black, acts strangely, insults the courtiers, makes fun of their ceremoniousness, and prefers to be alone or on the battlements with Horatio and the guard. The Ghost's appearances, too, betoken inversions of order; he reminds us of a greatness now lost to Denmark as he stalks on, usually through the stage doors, in armor and in the full light of day during an afternoon performance at the Globe. He also speaks from beneath the stage. The performance of Hamlet's "Mousetrap" play is a scene of rich panoply that is once again undercut by the secret act of murder now represented in a mimetic drama for the King who is also a murderer. The final scene of *Hamlet* is Claudius's most splendid moment of presiding over the court, until it is suddenly his last moment. The play's reflexive interest in the art of theater is everywhere evident, in Hamlet's instructions to the players and in his appraisal of himself as an actor, as he explores all that it might mean to "act." Shakespeare wrote *Hamlet* with his own theater very much in mind, and, paradoxically, precisely this has allowed it to remain so vibrantly alive in the modern theater.

The Playhouse

This early copy of a drawing by Johannes de Witt of the
Swan Theatre in London (c. 1596), made by his friend Arend
van Buchell, is the only surviving contemporary sketch of
the interior of a public theater in the 1590s.

From other contemporary evidence, including the stage directions and dialogue of Elizabethan plays, we can surmise that the various public theaters where Shakespeare's plays were produced (the Theatre, the Curtain, the Globe) resembled the Swan in many important particulars, though there must have been some variations as well. The public playhouses were essentially round, or polygonal, and open to the sky, forming an acting arena approximately 70 feet in diameter; they did not have a large curtain with which to open and close a scene, such as we see today in opera and some traditional theater. A platform measuring approximately 43 feet across and 27 feet deep, referred to in the de Witt drawing as the *proscaenium*, projected into the yard, *planities sive arena*. The roof, *tectum*, above the stage and supported by two pillars, could contain machinery for ascents and descents, as were required in several of Shakespeare's late plays. Above this roof was a hut, shown in the drawing with a flag flying atop it and a trumpeter at its door announcing the performance of a play. The underside of the stage roof, called the heavens, was usually richly decorated with symbolic figures of the sun, the moon, and the constellations. The platform stage stood at a height of 5½ feet or so above the yard, providing room under the stage for underworldly effects. A trapdoor, which is not visible in this drawing, gave access to the space below.

The structure at the back of the platform (labeled *mimorum aedes*), known as the tiring-house because it was the actors' attiring (dressing) space, featured at least two doors, as shown here. Some theaters seem to have also had a discovery space, or curtained recessed alcove, perhaps between the two doors—in which Falstaff could have hidden from the sheriff (*1 Henry IV*, 2.4) or Polonius could have eavesdropped on Hamlet and his mother (*Hamlet*, 3.4). This discovery space probably gave the actors a means of access to and from the tiring-house. Curtains may also have been hung in front of the stage doors on occasion. The de Witt drawing shows a gallery above the doors that extends across the back and evidently contains spectators. On occasions when action "above" demanded the use of this space, as when Juliet appears at her "window" (*Romeo and Juliet*, 2.2 and 3.5), the gallery seems to have been used by the actors, but large scenes there were impractical.

The three-tiered auditorium is perhaps best described by Thomas Platter, a visitor to London in 1599 who saw on that occasion Shakespeare's *Julius Caesar* performed at the Globe:

> The playhouses are so constructed that they play on a raised platform, so that everyone has a good view. There are different galleries and places [*orchestra, sedilia, porticus*], however, where the seating is better and more comfortable and therefore more expensive. For whoever cares to stand below only pays one English penny, but if he wishes to sit, he enters by another door [*ingressus*] and pays another penny, while if he desires to sit in the most comfortable seats, which are cushioned, where he not only sees everything well but can also be seen, then he pays yet another English penny at another door. And during the performance food and drink are carried round the audience, so that for what one cares to pay one may also have refreshment.

Scenery was not used, though the theater building itself was handsome enough to invoke a feeling of order and hierarchy that lent itself to the splendor and pageantry onstage. Portable properties, such as thrones, stools, tables, and beds, could be carried or thrust on as needed. In the scene pictured here by de Witt, a lady on a bench, attended perhaps by her waiting-gentlewoman, receives the address of a male figure. If Shakespeare had written *Twelfth Night* by 1596 for performance at the Swan, we could imagine Malvolio appearing like this as he bows before the Countess Olivia and her gentlewoman, Maria.

HAMLET

[*Dramatis Personae*

GHOST *of Hamlet, the former King of Denmark*
CLAUDIUS, *King of Denmark, the former King's brother*
GERTRUDE, *Queen of Denmark, widow of the former King and now wife of Claudius*
HAMLET, *Prince of Denmark, son of the late King and of Gertrude*

POLONIUS, *councillor to the King*
LAERTES, *his son*
OPHELIA, *his daughter*
REYNALDO, *his servant*

HORATIO, *Hamlet's friend and fellow student*

VOLTIMAND,
CORNELIUS,
ROSENCRANTZ,
GUILDENSTERN, } *members of the Danish court*
OSRIC,
A GENTLEMAN,
A LORD,

BERNARDO,
FRANCISCO, } *officers and soldiers on watch*
MARCELLUS,

FORTINBRAS, *Prince of Norway*
CAPTAIN *in his army*

Three or Four PLAYERS, *taking the roles of* PROLOGUE, PLAYER KING, PLAYER QUEEN, *and* LUCIANUS
Two MESSENGERS
FIRST SAILOR
Two CLOWNS, *a gravedigger and his companion*
PRIEST
FIRST AMBASSADOR *from England*

Lords, Soldiers, Attendants, Guards, other Players, Followers of Laertes, other Sailors, another Ambassador or Ambassadors from England

SCENE: *Denmark*]

1.1 *Enter Bernardo and Francisco, two sentinels,*
[meeting].

BERNARDO Who's there?

FRANCISCO
Nay, answer me. Stand and unfold yourself.   2

BERNARDO Long live the King!

FRANCISCO Bernardo?

BERNARDO He.

FRANCISCO
You come most carefully upon your hour.

BERNARDO
'Tis now struck twelve. Get thee to bed, Francisco.

FRANCISCO
For this relief much thanks. 'Tis bitter cold,
And I am sick at heart.

BERNARDO Have you had quiet guard?

FRANCISCO Not a mouse stirring.

BERNARDO Well, good night.
If you do meet Horatio and Marcellus,
The rivals of my watch, bid them make haste.   14

Enter Horatio and Marcellus.

FRANCISCO
I think I hear them.—Stand, ho! Who is there?

HORATIO Friends to this ground.   16

MARCELLUS And liegemen to the Dane.   17

FRANCISCO Give you good night.   18

MARCELLUS
O, farewell, honest soldier. Who hath relieved you?

FRANCISCO
Bernardo hath my place. Give you good night.

Exit Francisco.

MARCELLUS Holla! Bernardo!

BERNARDO Say, what, is Horatio there?

HORATIO A piece of him.

1.1. Location: Elsinore castle. A guard platform.
2 me (Francisco emphasizes that *he* is the sentry currently on watch.)
unfold yourself reveal your identity **14 rivals** partners **16 ground**
country, land **17 liegemen to the Dane** men sworn to serve the Danish
king **18 Give** i.e., may God give

BERNARDO
　Welcome, Horatio. Welcome, good Marcellus.
HORATIO
　What, has this thing appeared again tonight?
BERNARDO　I have seen nothing.
MARCELLUS
　Horatio says 'tis but our fantasy,　　　　　　　27
　And will not let belief take hold of him
　Touching this dreaded sight twice seen of us.
　Therefore I have entreated him along　　　　　30
　With us to watch the minutes of this night,　　31
　That if again this apparition come
　He may approve our eyes and speak to it.　　　33
HORATIO
　Tush, tush, 'twill not appear.
BERNARDO　　　　　　　　　　Sit down awhile,
　And let us once again assail your ears,
　That are so fortified against our story,
　What we have two nights seen.
HORATIO　　　　　　　　　　Well, sit we down,　　37
　And let us hear Bernardo speak of this.
BERNARDO　Last night of all,　　　　　　　39
　When yond same star that's westward from the pole　40
　Had made his course t' illume that part of heaven　41
　Where now it burns, Marcellus and myself,
　The bell then beating one—

　　　Enter Ghost.

MARCELLUS
　Peace, break thee off! Look where it comes again!
BERNARDO
　In the same figure like the King that's dead.
MARCELLUS
　Thou art a scholar. Speak to it, Horatio.　　　46
BERNARDO
　Looks 'a not like the King? Mark it, Horatio.　　47

---

27 fantasy imagination　**30 along** i.e., to come along　**31 watch** i.e.,
keep watch during　**33 approve** corroborate　**37 What** i.e., with what
39 Last . . . all i.e., this *very* last night. (Emphatic.)　**40 pole** polestar,
north star　**41 his** its.　**illume** illuminate　**46 scholar** one learned
enough to know how to question a ghost properly　**47 'a** he

HORATIO
Most like. It harrows me with fear and wonder.

BERNARDO
It would be spoke to.

MARCELLUS   Speak to it, Horatio.   49

HORATIO
What art thou that usurp'st this time of night,   50
Together with that fair and warlike form
In which the majesty of buried Denmark   52
Did sometime march? By heaven, I charge thee speak!   53

MARCELLUS
It is offended.

BERNARDO   See, it stalks away.

HORATIO
Stay! Speak, speak! I charge thee, speak! *Exit Ghost.*

MARCELLUS 'Tis gone and will not answer.

BERNARDO
How now, Horatio? You tremble and look pale.
Is not this something more than fantasy?
What think you on 't?   59

HORATIO
Before my God, I might not this believe
Without the sensible and true avouch   61
Of mine own eyes.

MARCELLUS   Is it not like the King?

HORATIO As thou art to thyself.
Such was the very armor he had on
When he the ambitious Norway combated.   65
So frowned he once when, in an angry parle,   66
He smote the sledded Polacks on the ice.   67
'Tis strange.

MARCELLUS
Thus twice before, and jump at this dead hour,   69
With martial stalk hath he gone by our watch.

HORATIO
In what particular thought to work I know not,   71

49 It . . . to (It was commonly believed that a ghost could not speak until spoken to.)   **50 usurp'st** wrongfully takes over   **52 buried Denmark** the buried King of Denmark   **53 sometime** formerly   **59 on 't** of it   **61 sensible** confirmed by the senses.   **avouch** warrant, evidence   **65 Norway** King of Norway   **66 parle** parley   **67 sledded** traveling on sleds.   **Polacks** Poles   **69 jump** exactly   **71 to work** i.e., to collect my thoughts and try to understand this

But in the gross and scope of mine opinion   72
This bodes some strange eruption to our state.

MARCELLUS

Good now, sit down, and tell me, he that knows,   74
Why this same strict and most observant watch
So nightly toils the subject of the land,   76
And why such daily cast of brazen cannon   77
And foreign mart for implements of war,   78
Why such impress of shipwrights, whose sore task   79
Does not divide the Sunday from the week.
What might be toward, that this sweaty haste   81
Doth make the night joint-laborer with the day?
Who is 't that can inform me?

HORATIO   That can I;
At least, the whisper goes so. Our last king,
Whose image even but now appeared to us,
Was, as you know, by Fortinbras of Norway,
Thereto pricked on by a most emulate pride,   87
Dared to the combat; in which our valiant Hamlet—
For so this side of our known world esteemed him—   89
Did slay this Fortinbras; who by a sealed compact   90
Well ratified by law and heraldry
Did forfeit, with his life, all those his lands
Which he stood seized of to the conqueror;   93
Against the which a moiety competent   94
Was gagèd by our king, which had returned   95
To the inheritance of Fortinbras
Had he been vanquisher, as, by the same covenant   97
And carriage of the article designed,   98
His fell to Hamlet. Now, sir, young Fortinbras,
Of unimprovèd mettle hot and full,   100

72 **gross and scope** general drift   74 **Good now** (An expression denoting
entreaty or expostulation.)   76 **toils** causes to toil.   **subject** subjects
77 **cast** casting   78 **mart** buying and selling   79 **impress** impressment,
conscription   81 **toward** in preparation   87 **Thereto . . . pride** (Refers
to old Fortinbras, not the Danish King.)   **pricked on** incited.
emulate emulous, ambitious   89 **this . . . world** i.e., all Europe, the
Western world   90 **sealed** certified, confirmed   93 **seized** possessed
94 **Against the** in return for.   **moiety competent** sufficient portion
95 **gagèd** engaged, pledged   97 **covenant** i.e., the *sealed compact* of
l. 90   98 **carriage** import, bearing.   **article designed** article or clause
drawn up or prearranged   100 **unimprovèd** unrestrained, undisciplined

Hath in the skirts of Norway here and there   101
Sharked up a list of lawless resolutes   102
For food and diet to some enterprise   103
That hath a stomach in 't, which is no other—   104
As it doth well appear unto our state—
But to recover of us, by strong hand
And terms compulsatory, those foresaid lands
So by his father lost. And this, I take it,
Is the main motive of our preparations,
The source of this our watch, and the chief head   110
Of this posthaste and rummage in the land.   111

BERNARDO
I think it be no other but e'en so.
Well may it sort that this portentous figure   113
Comes armèd through our watch so like the King
That was and is the question of these wars.   115

HORATIO
A mote it is to trouble the mind's eye.   116
In the most high and palmy state of Rome,   117
A little ere the mightiest Julius fell,
The graves stood tenantless and the sheeted dead   119
Did squeak and gibber in the Roman streets;
As stars with trains of fire and dews of blood,   121
Disasters in the sun; and the moist star   122
Upon whose influence Neptune's empire stands   123
Was sick almost to doomsday with eclipse.   124
And even the like precurse of feared events,   125
As harbingers preceding still the fates   126
And prologue to the omen coming on,   127
Have heaven and earth together demonstrated
Unto our climatures and countrymen.   129

101 skirts outlying regions, outskirts   **102 Sharked up** got together in irregular fashion. **list** i.e., troop. **resolutes** desperadoes   **103 For food and diet** i.e., they are to serve as *food*, or means, *to some enterprise* **104 stomach** (1) a spirit of daring (2) an appetite that is fed by the *lawless resolutes*   **110 head** source   **111 rummage** bustle, commotion   **113 sort** suit   **115 question** focus of contention   **116 mote** speck of dust **117 palmy** flourishing   **119 sheeted** shrouded   **121 As** (This abrupt transition suggests that matter is possibly omitted between ll. 120 and 121.)   **122 Disasters** unfavorable signs or aspects. **moist star** i.e., moon, governing tides   **123 Neptune** god of the sea.   **stands** depends **124 sick . . . doomsday** (See Matthew 24:29 and Revelation 6:12.) **125 precurse** heralding, foreshadowing   **126 harbingers** forerunners. **still** continually   **127 omen** calamitous event   **129 climatures** regions

Enter Ghost.

But soft, behold! Lo, where it comes again!   130
I'll cross it, though it blast me. (*It spreads his arms.*)
   Stay, illusion!   131
If thou hast any sound or use of voice,
Speak to me!
If there be any good thing to be done
That may to thee do ease and grace to me,
Speak to me!
If thou art privy to thy country's fate,
Which, happily, foreknowing may avoid,   138
O, speak!
Or if thou hast uphoarded in thy life
Extorted treasure in the womb of earth,
For which, they say, you spirits oft walk in death,
Speak of it! (*The cock crows.*) Stay and speak!—
   Stop it, Marcellus.

MARCELLUS
Shall I strike at it with my partisan?   144
HORATIO   Do, if it will not stand.   [*They strike at it.*]
BERNARDO   'Tis here!
HORATIO   'Tis here!   [*Exit Ghost.*]
MARCELLUS   'Tis gone.
   We do it wrong, being so majestical,
   To offer it the show of violence,
   For it is as the air invulnerable,
   And our vain blows malicious mockery.

BERNARDO
It was about to speak when the cock crew.

HORATIO
   And then it started like a guilty thing
   Upon a fearful summons. I have heard
   The cock, that is the trumpet to the morn,   156
   Doth with his lofty and shrill-sounding throat
   Awake the god of day, and at his warning,
   Whether in sea or fire, in earth or air,
   Th' extravagant and erring spirit hies   160

130 **soft** i.e., enough, break off   131 **cross** stand in its path, confront.
blast wither, strike with a curse   **s.d. his** its   138 **happily** haply, perchance   144 **partisan** long-handled spear   156 **trumpet** trumpeter
160 **extravagant and erring** wandering beyond bounds. (The words have
similar meaning.)

To his confine; and of the truth herein
This present object made probation.   162

MARCELLUS

It faded on the crowing of the cock.
Some say that ever 'gainst that season comes   164
Wherein our Savior's birth is celebrated,
This bird of dawning singeth all night long,
And then, they say, no spirit dare stir abroad;
The nights are wholesome, then no planets strike,   168
No fairy takes, nor witch hath power to charm,   169
So hallowed and so gracious is that time.   170

HORATIO

So have I heard and do in part believe it.
But, look, the morn in russet mantle clad
Walks o'er the dew of yon high eastward hill.
Break we our watch up, and by my advice
Let us impart what we have seen tonight
Unto young Hamlet; for upon my life,
This spirit, dumb to us, will speak to him.
Do you consent we shall acquaint him with it,
As needful in our loves, fitting our duty?

MARCELLUS

Let's do 't, I pray, and I this morning know
Where we shall find him most conveniently.

Exeunt.

✤

1.2   *Flourish. Enter Claudius, King of Denmark,*
         Gertrude the Queen, [the] Council, as Polonius
         and his son Laertes, Hamlet, cum aliis
         [including Voltimand and Cornelius].

KING

Though yet of Hamlet our dear brother's death
The memory be green, and that it us befitted
To bear our hearts in grief and our whole kingdom

162 probation proof   **164 'gainst** just before   **168 strike** destroy by evil
influence   **169 takes** bewitches   **170 gracious** full of grace

1.2. Location: The castle.
s.d. as i.e., such as, including.   **cum aliis** with others   **1 our** my. (The
royal "we"; also in the following lines.)

To be contracted in one brow of woe,
Yet so far hath discretion fought with nature
That we with wisest sorrow think on him
Together with remembrance of ourselves.
Therefore our sometime sister, now our queen,   8
Th' imperial jointress to this warlike state,   9
Have we, as 'twere with a defeated joy—
With an auspicious and a dropping eye,   11
With mirth in funeral and with dirge in marriage,
In equal scale weighing delight and dole—   13
Taken to wife. Nor have we herein barred
Your better wisdoms, which have freely gone
With this affair along. For all, our thanks.
Now follows that you know young Fortinbras,   17
Holding a weak supposal of our worth,   18
Or thinking by our late dear brother's death
Our state to be disjoint and out of frame,
Colleaguèd with this dream of his advantage,   21
He hath not failed to pester us with message
Importing the surrender of those lands   23
Lost by his father, with all bonds of law,   24
To our most valiant brother. So much for him.
Now for ourself and for this time of meeting.
Thus much the business is: we have here writ
To Norway, uncle of young Fortinbras—
Who, impotent and bedrid, scarcely hears   29
Of this his nephew's purpose—to suppress
His further gait herein, in that the levies,   31
The lists, and full proportions are all made   32
Out of his subject; and we here dispatch   33
You, good Cornelius, and you, Voltimand,
For bearers of this greeting to old Norway,
Giving to you no further personal power
To business with the King more than the scope

---

8 sometime former **9 jointress** woman possessing property with her
husband **11 With . . . eye** with one eye smiling and the other weeping
13 dole grief **17 know** be informed (that) **18 weak supposal** low
estimate **21 Colleaguèd with** joined to, allied with. **dream . . . advantage** illusory hope of success. (His only ally is this hope.) **23 Importing**
pertaining to **24 bonds** contracts **29 impotent** helpless **31 His** i.e.,
Fortinbras's. **gait** proceeding **31–33 in that . . . subject** since the
levying of troops and supplies is drawn entirely from the King of Norway's own subjects

Of these dilated articles allow. [*He gives a paper.*] 38
Farewell, and let your haste commend your duty. 39

CORNELIUS, VOLTIMAND
In that, and all things, will we show our duty.

KING
We doubt it nothing. Heartily farewell. 41
              [*Exeunt Voltimand and Cornelius.*]
And now, Laertes, what's the news with you?
You told us of some suit; what is 't, Laertes?
You cannot speak of reason to the Dane 44
And lose your voice. What wouldst thou beg, Laertes, 45
That shall not be my offer, not thy asking?
The head is not more native to the heart, 47
The hand more instrumental to the mouth, 48
Than is the throne of Denmark to thy father.
What wouldst thou have, Laertes?

LAERTES   My dread lord,
Your leave and favor to return to France, 51
From whence though willingly I came to Denmark
To show my duty in your coronation,
Yet now I must confess, that duty done,
My thoughts and wishes bend again toward France
And bow them to your gracious leave and pardon. 56

KING
Have you your father's leave? What says Polonius?

POLONIUS
H'ath, my lord, wrung from me my slow leave 58
By laborsome petition, and at last
Upon his will I sealed my hard consent. 60
I do beseech you, give him leave to go.

KING
Take thy fair hour, Laertes. Time be thine, 62
And thy best graces spend it at thy will! 63

---

38 dilated set out at length **39 commend** recommend to friendly
remembrance. (Their haste will impress the King with their attention to
duty.) **41 nothing** not at all **44 the Dane** the Danish king **45 lose
your voice** waste your speech **47 native** closely connected, related
48 instrumental serviceable **51 leave and favor** kind permission
56 leave and pardon permission to depart **58 H'ath** he has **60 sealed**
(as if sealing a legal document). **hard** reluctant **62 Take thy fair hour**
enjoy your time of youth **63 And . . . will** and may your finest qualities
guide the way you choose to spend your time

But now, my cousin Hamlet, and my son—   64
HAMLET
A little more than kin, and less than kind.   65
KING
How is it that the clouds still hang on you?
HAMLET
Not so, my lord. I am too much in the sun.   67
QUEEN
Good Hamlet, cast thy nighted color off,   68
And let thine eye look like a friend on Denmark.   69
Do not forever with thy vailèd lids   70
Seek for thy noble father in the dust.
Thou know'st 'tis common, all that lives must die,   72
Passing through nature to eternity.
HAMLET
Ay, madam, it is common.
QUEEN   If it be,
Why seems it so particular with thee?   75
HAMLET
Seems, madam? Nay, it is. I know not "seems."
'Tis not alone my inky cloak, good Mother,
Nor customary suits of solemn black,   78
Nor windy suspiration of forced breath,   79
No, nor the fruitful river in the eye,   80
Nor the dejected havior of the visage,   81
Together with all forms, moods, shapes of grief,   82
That can denote me truly. These indeed seem,
For they are actions that a man might play.
But I have that within which passes show;
These but the trappings and the suits of woe.

---

64 cousin any kin not of the immediate family   **65 A little . . . kind** i.e.,
closer than an ordinary nephew (since I am stepson), and yet more
separated in natural feeling (with pun on *kind* meaning "affectionate"
and "natural," "lawful." This line is often read as an aside, but it need
not be. The King chooses perhaps not to respond to Hamlet's cryptic
and bitter remark.)   **67 the sun** i.e., the sunshine of the King's royal
favor (with pun on *son*)   **68 nighted color** (1) mourning garments of
black (2) dark melancholy   **69 Denmark** the King of Denmark
70 vailèd lids lowered eyes   **72 common** of universal occurrence. (But
Hamlet plays on the sense of "vulgar" in l. 74.)   **75 particular** personal   **78 customary** (1) socially conventional (2) habitual with me
79 suspiration sighing   **80 fruitful** abundant   **81 havior** expression
82 moods outward expressions of feeling

KING

'Tis sweet and commendable in your nature, Hamlet,
To give these mourning duties to your father.
But you must know your father lost a father,
That father lost, lost his, and the survivor bound
In filial obligation for some term
To do obsequious sorrow. But to persever   92
In obstinate condolement is a course   93
Of impious stubbornness. 'Tis unmanly grief.
It shows a will most incorrect to heaven,
A heart unfortified, a mind impatient,   96
An understanding simple and unschooled.   97
For what we know must be and is as common
As any the most vulgar thing to sense,   99
Why should we in our peevish opposition
Take it to heart? Fie, 'tis a fault to heaven,
A fault against the dead, a fault to nature,
To reason most absurd, whose common theme
Is death of fathers, and who still hath cried,   104
From the first corpse till he that died today,   105
"This must be so." We pray you, throw to earth
This unprevailing woe and think of us   107
As of a father; for let the world take note,
You are the most immediate to our throne,   109
And with no less nobility of love
Than that which dearest father bears his son
Do I impart toward you. For your intent   112
In going back to school in Wittenberg,   113
It is most retrograde to our desire,   114
And we beseech you bend you to remain   115
Here in the cheer and comfort of our eye,
Our chiefest courtier, cousin, and our son.

QUEEN

Let not thy mother lose her prayers, Hamlet.
I pray thee, stay with us, go not to Wittenberg.

---

92 obsequious suited to obsequies or funerals.   **persever** persevere
93 condolement sorrowing   **96 unfortified** i.e., against adversity
97 simple ignorant   **99 As . . . sense** as the most ordinary experience
104 still always   **105 the first corpse** (Abel's)   **107 unprevailing** unavailing   **109 most immediate** next in succession   **112 impart toward** i.e., bestow my affection on.   **For** as for   **113 to school** i.e., to your studies.   **Wittenberg** famous German university founded in 1502
114 retrograde contrary   **115 bend you** incline yourself

HAMLET

   I shall in all my best obey you, madam.   120

KING

   Why, 'tis a loving and a fair reply.
   Be as ourself in Denmark. Madam, come.
   This gentle and unforced accord of Hamlet
   Sits smiling to my heart, in grace whereof   124
   No jocund health that Denmark drinks today   125
   But the great cannon to the clouds shall tell,
   And the King's rouse the heaven shall bruit again,   127
   Respeaking earthly thunder. Come away.   128
                  Flourish. Exeunt all but Hamlet.

HAMLET

   O, that this too too sullied flesh would melt,   129
   Thaw, and resolve itself into a dew!
   Or that the Everlasting had not fixed
   His canon 'gainst self-slaughter! O God, God,   132
   How weary, stale, flat, and unprofitable
   Seem to me all the uses of this world!   134
   Fie on 't, ah fie! 'Tis an unweeded garden
   That grows to seed. Things rank and gross in nature
   Possess it merely. That it should come to this!   137
   But two months dead—nay, not so much, not two.
   So excellent a king, that was to this   139
   Hyperion to a satyr, so loving to my mother   140
   That he might not beteem the winds of heaven   141
   Visit her face too roughly. Heaven and earth,
   Must I remember? Why, she would hang on him
   As if increase of appetite had grown
   By what it fed on, and yet within a month—
   Let me not think on 't; frailty, thy name is woman!—
   A little month, or ere those shoes were old   147
   With which she followed my poor father's body,

---

120 in all my best to the best of my ability   **124 to** i.e., at.   **grace** thanksgiving   **125 jocund** merry   **127 rouse** drinking of a draft of liquor. **bruit again** loudly echo   **128 thunder** i.e., of trumpet and kettledrum, sounded when the King drinks; see 1.4.8–12   **129 sullied** defiled. (The early quartos read *sallied*, the Folio *solid*.)   **132 canon** law   **134 all the uses** the whole routine   **137 merely** completely   **139 to** in comparison to   **140 Hyperion** Titan sun-god, father of Helios.   **satyr** a lecherous creature of classical mythology, half-human but with a goat's legs, tail, ears, and horns   **141 beteem** allow   **147 or ere** even before

Like Niobe, all tears, why she, even she—   149
O God, a beast, that wants discourse of reason,   150
Would have mourned longer—married with my uncle,
My father's brother, but no more like my father
Than I to Hercules. Within a month,
Ere yet the salt of most unrighteous tears
Had left the flushing in her gallèd eyes,   155
She married. O, most wicked speed, to post
With such dexterity to incestuous sheets!   157
It is not, nor it cannot come to good.
But break, my heart, for I must hold my tongue.

Enter Horatio, Marcellus, and Bernardo.

HORATIO
Hail to your lordship!
HAMLET   I am glad to see you well.
Horatio!—or I do forget myself.
HORATIO
The same, my lord, and your poor servant ever.
HAMLET
Sir, my good friend; I'll change that name with you.   163
And what make you from Wittenberg, Horatio?—   164
Marcellus.
MARCELLUS   My good lord.
HAMLET
I am very glad to see you. [*To Bernardo.*] Good even, sir.—
But what in faith make you from Wittenberg?
HORATIO
A truant disposition, good my lord.
HAMLET
I would not hear your enemy say so,
Nor shall you do my ear that violence
To make it truster of your own report
Against yourself. I know you are no truant.

149 **Niobe** Tantalus' daughter, Queen of Thebes, who boasted that she
had more sons and daughters than Leto; for this, Apollo and Artemis,
children of Leto, slew her fourteen children. She was turned by Zeus
into a stone that continually dropped tears.   150 **wants . . . reason** lacks
the faculty of reason   155 **gallèd** irritated, inflamed   157 **incestuous** (In
Shakespeare's day, the marriage of a man like Claudius to his deceased
brother's wife was considered incestuous.)   163 **change** exchange (i.e.,
the name of friend)   164 **make** do

But what is your affair in Elsinore?
We'll teach you to drink deep ere you depart.

HORATIO
My lord, I came to see your father's funeral.

HAMLET
I prithee, do not mock me, fellow student;
I think it was to see my mother's wedding.

HORATIO
Indeed, my lord, it followed hard upon.   179

HAMLET
Thrift, thrift, Horatio! The funeral baked meats   180
Did coldly furnish forth the marriage tables.   181
Would I had met my dearest foe in heaven   182
Or ever I had seen that day, Horatio!   183
My father!—Methinks I see my father.

HORATIO
Where, my lord?

HAMLET   In my mind's eye, Horatio.

HORATIO
I saw him once. 'A was a goodly king.   186

HAMLET
'A was a man. Take him for all in all,
I shall not look upon his like again.

HORATIO
My lord, I think I saw him yesternight.

HAMLET   Saw? Who?

HORATIO   My lord, the King your father.

HAMLET   The King my father?

HORATIO
Season your admiration for a while   193
With an attent ear till I may deliver,   194
Upon the witness of these gentlemen,
This marvel to you.

HAMLET   For God's love, let me hear!

HORATIO
Two nights together had these gentlemen,
Marcellus and Bernardo, on their watch,
In the dead waste and middle of the night,

179 hard close   **180 baked meats** meat pies   **181 coldly** i.e., as cold
leftovers   **182 dearest** closest (and therefore deadliest)   **183 Or ever**
before   **186 'A** he   **193 Season your admiration** restrain your astonishment   **194 attent** attentive

Been thus encountered. A figure like your father,
Armèd at point exactly, cap-à-pie,   201
Appears before them, and with solemn march
Goes slow and stately by them. Thrice he walked
By their oppressed and fear-surprisèd eyes
Within his truncheon's length, whilst they, distilled   205
Almost to jelly with the act of fear,   206
Stand dumb and speak not to him. This to me
In dreadful secrecy impart they did,
And I with them the third night kept the watch,
Where, as they had delivered, both in time,
Form of the thing, each word made true and good,
The apparition comes. I knew your father;
These hands are not more like.

HAMLET   But where was this?

MARCELLUS
My lord, upon the platform where we watch.

HAMLET
Did you not speak to it?

HORATIO   My lord, I did,
But answer made it none. Yet once methought
It lifted up its head and did address   217
Itself to motion, like as it would speak;   218
But even then the morning cock crew loud,   219
And at the sound it shrunk in haste away
And vanished from our sight.

HAMLET   'Tis very strange.

HORATIO
As I do live, my honored lord, 'tis true,
And we did think it writ down in our duty
To let you know of it.

HAMLET
Indeed, indeed, sirs. But this troubles me.
Hold you the watch tonight?

ALL   We do, my lord.

HAMLET   Armed, say you?

ALL   Armed, my lord.

HAMLET   From top to toe?

201 at point correctly in every detail.   **cap-à-pie** from head to foot
205 truncheon officer's staff.   **distilled** dissolved   **206 act** action,
operation   **217–218 did . . . speak** began to move as though it were
about to speak   **219 even then** at that very instant

ALL   My lord, from head to foot.

HAMLET   Then saw you not his face?

HORATIO

   O, yes, my lord, he wore his beaver up.   232

HAMLET   What looked he, frowningly?   233

HORATIO

   A countenance more in sorrow than in anger.

HAMLET   Pale or red?

HORATIO   Nay, very pale.

HAMLET   And fixed his eyes upon you?

HORATIO   Most constantly.

HAMLET   I would I had been there.

HORATIO   It would have much amazed you.

HAMLET   Very like, very like. Stayed it long?

HORATIO

   While one with moderate haste might tell a hundred.   242

MARCELLUS, BERNARDO   Longer, longer.

HORATIO   Not when I saw 't.

HAMLET   His beard was grizzled—no?   245

HORATIO

   It was, as I have seen it in his life,
   A sable silvered.

HAMLET   I will watch tonight.   247
   Perchance 'twill walk again.

HORATIO   I warrant it will.

HAMLET

   If it assume my noble father's person,
   I'll speak to it though hell itself should gape
   And bid me hold my peace. I pray you all,
   If you have hitherto concealed this sight,
   Let it be tenable in your silence still,   253
   And whatsoever else shall hap tonight,
   Give it an understanding but no tongue.
   I will requite your loves. So, fare you well.
   Upon the platform twixt eleven and twelve
   I'll visit you.

ALL   Our duty to your honor.

232 beaver visor on the helmet   **233 What** how   **242 tell** count
245 grizzled gray   **247 sable silvered** black mixed with white
253 tenable held tightly

HAMLET
　Your loves, as mine to you. Farewell.
　　　　　　　　　　　Exeunt [all but Hamlet].
　My father's spirit in arms! All is not well.
　I doubt some foul play. Would the night were come!   261
　Till then sit still, my soul. Foul deeds will rise,
　Though all the earth o'erwhelm them, to men's eyes.
　　　　　　　　　　　　　　　　　Exit.

✦

1.3　*Enter Laertes and Ophelia, his sister.*

LAERTES
　My necessaries are embarked. Farewell.
　And, sister, as the winds give benefit
　And convoy is assistant, do not sleep   3
　But let me hear from you.
OPHELIA　　　　　　　　　Do you doubt that?
LAERTES
　For Hamlet, and the trifling of his favor,
　Hold it a fashion and a toy in blood,   6
　A violet in the youth of primy nature,   7
　Forward, not permanent, sweet, not lasting,   8
　The perfume and suppliance of a minute—   9
　No more.
OPHELIA　　No more but so?
LAERTES　　　　　　　　Think it no more.
　For nature crescent does not grow alone   11
　In thews and bulk, but as this temple waxes   12
　The inward service of the mind and soul
　Grows wide withal. Perhaps he loves you now,   14
　And now no soil nor cautel doth besmirch   15
　The virtue of his will; but you must fear,   16

---

261 doubt suspect

1.3. Location: Polonius's chambers.
3 convoy is assistant means of conveyance are available　**6 toy in blood**
passing amorous fancy　**7 primy** in its prime, springtime　**8 Forward**
precocious　**9 suppliance** supply, filler　**11 crescent** growing, waxing
12 thews bodily strength.　**temple** i.e., body　**14 Grows wide withal**
grows along with it　**15 soil** blemish.　**cautel** deceit　**16 will** desire

His greatness weighed, his will is not his own.   17
For he himself is subject to his birth.
He may not, as unvalued persons do,
Carve for himself, for on his choice depends   20
The safety and health of this whole state,
And therefore must his choice be circumscribed
Unto the voice and yielding of that body   23
Whereof he is the head. Then if he says he loves you,
It fits your wisdom so far to believe it
As he in his particular act and place   26
May give his saying deed, which is no further   27
Than the main voice of Denmark goes withal.   28
Then weigh what loss your honor may sustain
If with too credent ear you list his songs,   30
Or lose your heart, or your chaste treasure open
To his unmastered importunity.
Fear it, Ophelia, fear it, my dear sister,
And keep you in the rear of your affection,   34
Out of the shot and danger of desire.   35
The chariest maid is prodigal enough   36
If she unmask her beauty to the moon.   37
Virtue itself scapes not calumnious strokes.
The canker galls the infants of the spring   39
Too oft before their buttons be disclosed,   40
And in the morn and liquid dew of youth   41
Contagious blastments are most imminent.   42
Be wary then; best safety lies in fear.
Youth to itself rebels, though none else near.   44

OPHELIA
I shall the effect of this good lesson keep
As watchman to my heart. But, good my brother,
Do not, as some ungracious pastors do,   47

17 His greatness weighed considering his high position   **20 Carve** i.e.,
choose   **23 voice and yielding** assent, approval   **26 in . . . place** in his
particular restricted circumstances   **27 deed** effect   **28 main voice**
general assent.   **withal** along with   **30 credent** credulous.   **list** listen
to   **34 keep . . . affection** don't advance as far as your affection might
lead you. (A military metaphor.)   **35 shot** range   **36 chariest** most
scrupulously modest   **37 If she unmask** if she does no more than show
her beauty.   **moon** (Symbol of chastity.)   **39 canker galls** cankerworm
destroys   **40 buttons** buds.   **disclosed** opened   **41 liquid dew** i.e., time
when dew is fresh and bright   **42 blastments** blights   **44 Youth . . .
rebels** youth is inherently rebellious   **47 ungracious** ungodly

Show me the steep and thorny way to heaven,
Whiles like a puffed and reckless libertine   49
Himself the primrose path of dalliance treads,
And recks not his own rede.

Enter Polonius.

LAERTES   O, fear me not.   51
I stay too long. But here my father comes.
A double blessing is a double grace;   53
Occasion smiles upon a second leave.   54

POLONIUS
Yet here, Laertes? Aboard, aboard, for shame!
The wind sits in the shoulder of your sail,
And you are stayed for. There—my blessing with thee!
And these few precepts in thy memory
Look thou character. Give thy thoughts no tongue,   59
Nor any unproportioned thought his act.   60
Be thou familiar, but by no means vulgar.   61
Those friends thou hast, and their adoption tried,   62
Grapple them unto thy soul with hoops of steel,
But do not dull thy palm with entertainment   64
Of each new-hatched, unfledged courage. Beware   65
Of entrance to a quarrel, but being in,
Bear 't that th' opposèd may beware of thee.   67
Give every man thy ear, but few thy voice;
Take each man's censure, but reserve thy judgment.   69
Costly thy habit as thy purse can buy,   70
But not expressed in fancy; rich, not gaudy,   71
For the apparel oft proclaims the man,
And they in France of the best rank and station
Are of a most select and generous chief in that.   74
Neither a borrower nor a lender be,

---

49 puffed bloated, or swollen with pride   **51 recks** heeds.   **rede** counsel   **53 double** (Laertes has already bidden his father good-bye.)
54 Occasion . . . leave happy is the circumstance that provides a second leave-taking. (The goddess Occasion, or Opportunity, smiles.)   **59 Look** be sure that.   **character** inscribe   **60 unproportioned** badly calculated, intemperate.   **his** its   **61 familiar** sociable.   **vulgar** common   **62 tried** tested   **64 dull thy palm** i.e., shake hands so often as to make the gesture meaningless   **65 courage** young man of spirit   **67 Bear 't** that manage it so that   **69 censure** opinion, judgment   **70 habit** clothing   **71 fancy** excessive ornament, decadent fashion   **74 Are . . . that** i.e., are of a most refined and well-bred preeminence in choosing what to wear

For loan oft loses both itself and friend,
And borrowing dulls the edge of husbandry.   77
This above all: to thine own self be true,
And it must follow, as the night the day,
Thou canst not then be false to any man.
Farewell. My blessing season this in thee!   81

LAERTES
Most humbly do I take my leave, my lord.

POLONIUS
The time invests you. Go, your servants tend.   83

LAERTES
Farewell, Ophelia, and remember well
What I have said to you.

OPHELIA   'Tis in my memory locked,
And you yourself shall keep the key of it.

LAERTES   Farewell.   *Exit Laertes.*

POLONIUS
What is 't, Ophelia, he hath said to you?

OPHELIA
So please you, something touching the Lord Hamlet.

POLONIUS   Marry, well bethought.   91
'Tis told me he hath very oft of late
Given private time to you, and you yourself
Have of your audience been most free and bounteous.
If it be so—as so 'tis put on me,   95
And that in way of caution—I must tell you
You do not understand yourself so clearly
As it behooves my daughter and your honor.   98
What is between you? Give me up the truth.

OPHELIA
He hath, my lord, of late made many tenders   100
Of his affection to me.

POLONIUS
Affection? Pooh! You speak like a green girl,
Unsifted in such perilous circumstance.   103
Do you believe his tenders, as you call them?

---

77 husbandry thrift **81 season** mature **83 invests** besieges, presses
upon. **tend** attend, wait **91 Marry** i.e., by the Virgin Mary. (A mild
oath.) **95 put on** impressed on, told to **98 behooves** befits
100 tenders offers **103 Unsifted** i.e., untried

OPHELIA
  I do not know, my lord, what I should think.

POLONIUS
  Marry, I will teach you. Think yourself a baby
  That you have ta'en these tenders for true pay   107
  Which are not sterling. Tender yourself more dearly, 108
  Or—not to crack the wind of the poor phrase,   109
  Running it thus—you'll tender me a fool.   110

OPHELIA
  My lord, he hath importuned me with love
  In honorable fashion.

POLONIUS
  Ay, fashion you may call it. Go to, go to.   113

OPHELIA
  And hath given countenance to his speech, my lord,   114
  With almost all the holy vows of heaven.

POLONIUS
  Ay, springes to catch woodcocks. I do know,   116
  When the blood burns, how prodigal the soul   117
  Lends the tongue vows. These blazes, daughter,
  Giving more light than heat, extinct in both
  Even in their promise as it is a-making,   120
  You must not take for fire. From this time
  Be something scanter of your maiden presence.   122
  Set your entreatments at a higher rate   123
  Than a command to parle. For Lord Hamlet,   124
  Believe so much in him that he is young,   125
  And with a larger tether may he walk
  Than may be given you. In few, Ophelia,   127

107 tenders (with added meaning here of "promises to pay")
108 sterling legal currency.   **Tender** hold, look after, offer   **109 crack
the wind** i.e., run it until it is broken-winded   **110 tender me a fool**
(1) show yourself to me as a fool (2) show me up as a fool (3) present
me with a grandchild. (*Fool* was a term of endearment for a child.)
113 fashion mere form, pretense.   **Go to** (An expression of impatience.)   **114 countenance** credit, confirmation   **116 springes** snares.
woodcocks birds easily caught; here used to connote gullibility
117 prodigal i.e., prodigally   **120 it** i.e., the promise   **122 something**
somewhat   **123 entreatments** negotiations for surrender. (A military
term.)   **124 parle** discuss terms with the enemy. (Polonius urges his
daughter, in the metaphor of military language, not to meet with Hamlet and consider giving in to him merely because he requests an interview.)   **125 so . . . him** this much concerning him   **127 In few** briefly

Do not believe his vows, for they are brokers,   128
Not of that dye which their investments show,   129
But mere implorators of unholy suits,   130
Breathing like sanctified and pious bawds   131
The better to beguile. This is for all: 132
I would not, in plain terms, from this time forth
Have you so slander any moment leisure   134
As to give words or talk with the Lord Hamlet.
Look to 't, I charge you. Come your ways.   136
OPHELIA   I shall obey, my lord.   *Exeunt.*

❖

1.4   *Enter Hamlet, Horatio, and Marcellus.*

HAMLET
The air bites shrewdly; it is very cold.   1
HORATIO
It is a nipping and an eager air.   2
HAMLET
What hour now?
HORATIO   I think it lacks of twelve.   3
MARCELLUS
No, it is struck.
HORATIO   Indeed? I heard it not.
It then draws near the season   5
Wherein the spirit held his wont to walk.   6
          A flourish of trumpets, and two pieces go off
                                          [*within*].
What does this mean, my lord?
HAMLET
The King doth wake tonight and takes his rouse,   8

128 brokers go-betweens, procurers   **129 dye** color or sort.   **invest-ments** clothes. (The vows are not what they seem.)   **130 mere implo-rators** out and out solicitors   **131 Breathing** speaking   **132 for all** once for all, in sum   **134 slander** abuse, misuse.   **moment** moment's   **136 Come your ways** come along

1.4. Location: The guard platform.
1 shrewdly keenly, sharply   **2 eager** biting   **3 lacks of** is just short of   **5 season** time   **6 held his wont** was accustomed   **s.d. pieces** i.e., of ordnance, cannon   **8 wake** stay awake and hold revel.   **rouse** ca-rouse, drinking bout

Keeps wassail, and the swaggering upspring reels;	9
And as he drains his drafts of Rhenish down,	10
The kettledrum and trumpet thus bray out	
The triumph of his pledge.	
HORATIO Is it a custom?	12
HAMLET Ay, marry, is 't,	
But to my mind, though I am native here	
And to the manner born, it is a custom	15
More honored in the breach than the observance.	16
This heavy-headed revel east and west	17
Makes us traduced and taxed of other nations.	18
They clepe us drunkards, and with swinish phrase	19
Soil our addition; and indeed it takes	20
From our achievements, though performed at height,	21
The pith and marrow of our attribute.	22
So, oft it chances in particular men,	
That for some vicious mole of nature in them,	24
As in their birth—wherein they are not guilty,	
Since nature cannot choose his origin—	26
By their o'ergrowth of some complexion,	27
Oft breaking down the pales and forts of reason,	28
Or by some habit that too much o'erleavens	29
The form of plausive manners, that these men	30
Carrying, I say, the stamp of one defect,	
Being nature's livery or fortune's star,	32
His virtues else, be they as pure as grace,	33
As infinite as man may undergo,	34
Shall in the general censure take corruption	35

9 **wassail** carousal. **upspring** wild German dance. **reels** dances
10 **Rhenish** Rhine wine   12 **the triumph . . . pledge** i.e., his feat in
draining the wine in a single draft   15 **manner** custom (of drinking)
16 **More . . . observance** better neglected than followed   17 **east and
west** i.e., everywhere   18 **taxed of** censured by   19 **clepe** call. **with
swinish phrase** i.e., by calling us swine   20 **addition** reputation   21 **at
height** outstandingly   22 **The pith . . . attribute** the essence of the
reputation that others attribute to us   24 **for** on account of. **mole of
nature** natural blemish in one's constitution   26 **his** its   27 **their
o'ergrowth . . . complexion** the excessive growth in individuals of
some natural trait   28 **pales** palings, fences (as of a fortification)
29 **o'erleavens** induces a change throughout (as yeast works in dough)
30 **plausive** pleasing   32 **nature's livery** sign of one's servitude to
nature. **fortune's star** the destiny that chance brings   33 **His virtues
else** i.e., the other qualities of *these men* (l. 30)   34 **may undergo** can
sustain   35 **general censure** general opinion that people have of him

From that particular fault. The dram of evil   36
Doth all the noble substance often dout   37
To his own scandal.

    Enter Ghost.

HORATIO   Look, my lord, it comes!   38
HAMLET

Angels and ministers of grace defend us!
Be thou a spirit of health or goblin damned,   40
Bring with thee airs from heaven or blasts from hell, 41
Be thy intents wicked or charitable,   42
Thou com'st in such a questionable shape   43
That I will speak to thee. I'll call thee Hamlet,
King, Father, royal Dane. O, answer me!
Let me not burst in ignorance, but tell
Why thy canonized bones, hearsèd in death,   47
Have burst their cerements; why the sepulcher   48
Wherein we saw thee quietly inurned   49
Hath oped his ponderous and marble jaws
To cast thee up again. What may this mean,
That thou, dead corpse, again in complete steel,   52
Revisits thus the glimpses of the moon,   53
Making night hideous, and we fools of nature   54
So horridly to shake our disposition   55
With thoughts beyond the reaches of our souls?
Say, why is this? Wherefore? What should we do?
           [The Ghost] beckons [Hamlet].

HORATIO

It beckons you to go away with it,
As if it some impartment did desire   59
To you alone.

36–38 The dram . . . scandal i.e., the small drop of evil blots out or
works against the noble substance of the whole and brings it into
disrepute. To *dout* is to blot out. (A famous crux.) **38 To . . . scandal**
i.e., with consequent ruin or disgrace to that man **40 Be thou** i.e.,
whether you are. **spirit of health** good angel **41 Bring** i.e., whether
you bring **42 Be thy intents** i.e., whether your intents are **43 questionable** inviting question **47 canonized** buried according to the canons
of the church. **hearsèd** coffined **48 cerements** grave-clothes
49 inurned entombed **52 complete steel** full armor **53 glimpses of the
moon** pale and uncertain moonlight **54 fools of nature** mere men,
limited to natural knowledge and subject to the caprices of nature
55 So . . . disposition to distress our mental composure so violently
59 impartment communication

MARCELLUS   Look with what courteous action
  It wafts you to a more removèd ground.
  But do not go with it.
HORATIO   No, by no means.
HAMLET
  It will not speak. Then I will follow it.
HORATIO
  Do not, my lord!
HAMLET   Why, what should be the fear?
  I do not set my life at a pin's fee,   65
  And for my soul, what can it do to that,
  Being a thing immortal as itself?
  It waves me forth again. I'll follow it.
HORATIO
  What if it tempt you toward the flood, my lord,   69
  Or to the dreadful summit of the cliff
  That beetles o'er his base into the sea,   71
  And there assume some other horrible form
  Which might deprive your sovereignty of reason   73
  And draw you into madness? Think of it.
  The very place puts toys of desperation,   75
  Without more motive, into every brain
  That looks so many fathoms to the sea
  And hears it roar beneath.
HAMLET
  It wafts me still.—Go on, I'll follow thee.
MARCELLUS
  You shall not go, my lord.   [*They try to stop him.*]
HAMLET   Hold off your hands!
HORATIO
  Be ruled. You shall not go.
HAMLET   My fate cries out,   81
  And makes each petty artery in this body   82
  As hardy as the Nemean lion's nerve.   83
  Still am I called. Unhand me, gentlemen.

65 fee value **69 flood** sea **71 beetles o'er** overhangs threateningly (like bushy eyebrows). **his** its **73 deprive . . . reason** take away the rule of reason over your mind **75 toys of desperation** fancies of desperate acts, i.e., suicide **81 My fate cries out** my destiny summons me **82 petty** weak. **artery** (through which the vital spirits were thought to have been conveyed) **83 Nemean lion** one of the monsters slain by Hercules in his twelve labors. **nerve** sinew

By heaven, I'll make a ghost of him that lets me!   85
I say, away!—Go on, I'll follow thee.

Exeunt Ghost and Hamlet.

HORATIO
He waxes desperate with imagination.

MARCELLUS
Let's follow. 'Tis not fit thus to obey him.

HORATIO
Have after. To what issue will this come?   89

MARCELLUS
Something is rotten in the state of Denmark.

HORATIO
Heaven will direct it.

MARCELLUS   Nay, let's follow him.   *Exeunt.* 91

❖

1.5   *Enter Ghost and Hamlet.*

HAMLET
Whither wilt thou lead me? Speak. I'll go no further.

GHOST
Mark me.

HAMLET   I will.

GHOST   My hour is almost come,
When I to sulfurous and tormenting flames
Must render up myself.

HAMLET   Alas, poor ghost!

GHOST
Pity me not, but lend thy serious hearing
To what I shall unfold.

HAMLET   Speak. I am bound to hear.   7

GHOST
So art thou to revenge, when thou shalt hear.

HAMLET   What?

GHOST   I am thy father's spirit,
Doomed for a certain term to walk the night,

---

85 lets hinder   **89 Have after** let's go after him.   **issue** outcome
91 it i.e., the outcome

1.5. Location: The battlements of the castle.
7 bound (1) ready (2) obligated by duty and fate. (The Ghost, in l. 8,
answers in the second sense.)

And for the day confined to fast in fires, 12
Till the foul crimes done in my days of nature 13
Are burnt and purged away. But that I am forbid 14
To tell the secrets of my prison house,
I could a tale unfold whose lightest word
Would harrow up thy soul, freeze thy young blood, 17
Make thy two eyes like stars start from their spheres, 18
Thy knotted and combinèd locks to part, 19
And each particular hair to stand on end
Like quills upon the fretful porpentine. 21
But this eternal blazon must not be 22
To ears of flesh and blood. List, list, O, list!
If thou didst ever thy dear father love—

HAMLET O God!

GHOST
Revenge his foul and most unnatural murder.

HAMLET Murder?

GHOST
Murder most foul, as in the best it is, 28
But this most foul, strange, and unnatural.

HAMLET
Haste me to know 't, that I, with wings as swift
As meditation or the thoughts of love
May sweep to my revenge.

GHOST   I find thee apt;
And duller shouldst thou be than the fat weed 33
That roots itself in ease on Lethe wharf, 34
Wouldst thou not stir in this. Now, Hamlet, hear.
'Tis given out that, sleeping in my orchard, 36
A serpent stung me. So the whole ear of Denmark
Is by a forgèd process of my death 38
Rankly abused. But know, thou noble youth, 39
The serpent that did sting thy father's life
Now wears his crown.

---

12 fast do penance   **13 crimes** sins   **14 But that** were it not that   **17 harrow up** lacerate, tear   **18 spheres** i.e., eye-sockets, here compared to the orbits or transparent revolving spheres in which, according to Ptolemaic astronomy, the heavenly bodies were fixed   **19 knotted . . . locks** i.e., hair neatly arranged and confined   **21 porpentine** porcupine   **22 eternal blazon** revelation of the secrets of eternity   **28 in the best** even at best   **33 shouldst thou be** you would have to be.   **fat** torpid, lethargic   **34 Lethe** the river of forgetfulness in Hades.   **wharf** bank   **36 orchard** garden   **38 forgèd process** falsified account   **39 abused** deceived

HAMLET O, my prophetic soul! My uncle!

GHOST

Ay, that incestuous, that adulterate beast, 43
With witchcraft of his wit, with traitorous gifts— 44
O wicked wit and gifts, that have the power
So to seduce!—won to his shameful lust
The will of my most seeming-virtuous queen.
O Hamlet, what a falling off was there!
From me, whose love was of that dignity
That it went hand in hand even with the vow 50
I made to her in marriage, and to decline
Upon a wretch whose natural gifts were poor
To those of mine! 53
But virtue, as it never will be moved, 54
Though lewdness court it in a shape of heaven, 55
So lust, though to a radiant angel linked,
Will sate itself in a celestial bed 57
And prey on garbage.
But soft, methinks I scent the morning air.
Brief let me be. Sleeping within my orchard,
My custom always of the afternoon,
Upon my secure hour thy uncle stole, 62
With juice of cursèd hebona in a vial, 63
And in the porches of my ears did pour 64
The leprous distillment, whose effect 65
Holds such an enmity with blood of man
That swift as quicksilver it courses through
The natural gates and alleys of the body,
And with a sudden vigor it doth posset 69
And curd, like eager droppings into milk, 70
The thin and wholesome blood. So did it mine,
And a most instant tetter barked about, 72

43 **adulterate** adulterous 44 **gifts** (1) talents (2) presents 50 **even with the vow** with the very vow 53 **To** compared to 54 **virtue, as it** as virtue 55 **shape of heaven** heavenly form 57 **sate . . . bed** i.e., cease to find sexual pleasure in a virtuously lawful marriage 62 **secure** confident, unsuspicious 63 **hebona** a poison. (The word seems to be a form of *ebony*, though it is thought perhaps to be related to *henbane*, a poison, or to *ebenus*, yew.) 64 **porches of my ears** ears as a porch or entrance of the body 65 **leprous distillment** distillation causing leprosy-like disfigurement 69 **posset** coagulate, curdle 70 **eager** sour, acid 72 **tetter** eruption of scabs. **barked** covered with a rough covering, like bark on a tree

Most lazar-like, with vile and loathsome crust,   73
All my smooth body.
Thus was I, sleeping, by a brother's hand
Of life, of crown, of queen at once dispatched,   76
Cut off even in the blossoms of my sin,
Unhouseled, disappointed, unaneled,   78
No reckoning made, but sent to my account   79
With all my imperfections on my head.
O, horrible! O, horrible, most horrible!
If thou hast nature in thee, bear it not.   82
Let not the royal bed of Denmark be
A couch for luxury and damnèd incest.   84
But, howsoever thou pursues this act,
Taint not thy mind nor let thy soul contrive
Against thy mother aught. Leave her to heaven
And to those thorns that in her bosom lodge,
To prick and sting her. Fare thee well at once.
The glowworm shows the matin to be near,   90
And 'gins to pale his uneffectual fire.   91
Adieu, adieu, adieu! Remember me.   [*Exit.*]

HAMLET

O all you host of heaven! O earth! What else?
And shall I couple hell? O, fie! Hold, hold, my heart,   94
And you, my sinews, grow not instant old,   95
But bear me stiffly up. Remember thee?
Ay, thou poor ghost, whiles memory holds a seat
In this distracted globe. Remember thee?   98
Yea, from the table of my memory   99
I'll wipe away all trivial fond records,   100
All saws of books, all forms, all pressures past   101
That youth and observation copied there,
And thy commandment all alone shall live
Within the book and volume of my brain,

73 lazar-like leper-like   **76 dispatched** suddenly deprived   **78 Unhouseled** without having received the Sacrament.   **disappointed** un-
ready (spiritually) for the last journey.   **unaneled** without having received extreme unction   **79 reckoning** settling of accounts   **82 nature**
i.e., the promptings of a son   **84 luxury** lechery   **90 matin** i.e., morning   **91 uneffectual fire** light rendered ineffectual by the approach of
bright day   **94 couple** add.   **Hold** hold together   **95 instant** instantly
98 globe (1) head (2) world   **99 table** tablet, slate   **100 fond** foolish
101 saws wise sayings.   **forms** shapes or images copied onto the slate;
general ideas.   **pressures** impressions stamped

Unmixed with baser matter. Yes, by heaven!
O most pernicious woman!
O villain, villain, smiling, damnèd villain!
My tables—meet it is I set it down   108
That one may smile, and smile, and be a villain.
At least I am sure it may be so in Denmark.

                                        [*Writing.*]

So, uncle, there you are. Now to my word: 111
It is "Adieu, adieu! Remember me."
I have sworn 't.

         Enter Horatio and Marcellus.

HORATIO   My lord, my lord!
MARCELLUS   Lord Hamlet!
HORATIO   Heavens secure him!   116
HAMLET   So be it.
MARCELLUS   Hillo, ho, ho, my lord!
HAMLET   Hillo, ho, ho, boy! Come, bird, come.   119
MARCELLUS   How is 't, my noble lord?
HORATIO   What news, my lord?
HAMLET   O, wonderful!
HORATIO   Good my lord, tell it.
HAMLET   No, you will reveal it.
HORATIO   Not I, my lord, by heaven.
MARCELLUS   Nor I, my lord.
HAMLET
How say you, then, would heart of man once think it? 127
But you'll be secret?
HORATIO, MARCELLUS   Ay, by heaven, my lord.
HAMLET
There's never a villain dwelling in all Denmark
But he's an arrant knave.   130
HORATIO
There needs no ghost, my lord, come from the grave
To tell us this.
HAMLET   Why, right, you are in the right.

---

108 tables writing tablets.   **meet it is** it is fitting   **111 there you are** i.e.,
there, I've written that down against you   **116 secure him** keep him
safe   **119 Hillo . . . come** (A falconer's call to a hawk in air. Hamlet
mocks the hallooing as though it were a part of hawking.)   **127 once**
ever   **130 arrant** thoroughgoing

And so, without more circumstance at all,   133
I hold it fit that we shake hands and part,
You as your business and desire shall point you—
For every man hath business and desire,
Such as it is—and for my own poor part,
Look you, I'll go pray.

HORATIO
These are but wild and whirling words, my lord.

HAMLET
I am sorry they offend you, heartily;
Yes, faith, heartily.

HORATIO   There's no offense, my lord.

HAMLET
Yes, by Saint Patrick, but there is, Horatio,   142
And much offense too. Touching this vision here,   143
It is an honest ghost, that let me tell you.   144
For your desire to know what is between us,
O'ermaster 't as you may. And now, good friends,
As you are friends, scholars, and soldiers,
Give me one poor request.

HORATIO   What is 't, my lord? We will.

HAMLET
Never make known what you have seen tonight.

HORATIO, MARCELLUS   My lord, we will not.

HAMLET   Nay, but swear 't.

HORATIO   In faith, my lord, not I.   153

MARCELLUS   Nor I, my lord, in faith.

HAMLET   Upon my sword.   [*He holds out his sword.*]   155

MARCELLUS   We have sworn, my lord, already.   156

HAMLET   Indeed, upon my sword, indeed.

GHOST (*Cries under the stage*)   Swear.

HAMLET
Ha, ha, boy, sayst thou so? Art thou there, truepenny?   159

---

83 circumstance ceremony, elaboration   142 Saint Patrick (The
keeper of Purgatory and patron saint of all blunders and confusion.)
143 offense (Hamlet deliberately changes Horatio's "no offense taken"
"an offense against all decency.")   144 an honest ghost i.e., a real
ghost and not an evil spirit   153 In faith . . . I i.e., I swear not to tell
what I have seen. (Horatio is not refusing to swear.)   155 sword i.e., the
hilt in the form of a cross   156 We . . . already i.e., we swore *in faith*
159 truepenny honest old fellow

Come on, you hear this fellow in the cellarage.
Consent to swear.

HORATIO   Propose the oath, my lord.

HAMLET
Never to speak of this that you have seen,
Swear by my sword.

GHOST [*Beneath*]   Swear.   [*They swear.*]

HAMLET
Hic et ubique? Then we'll shift our ground.   1
                         [*He moves to another spot.*]
Come hither, gentlemen,
And lay your hands again upon my sword.
Swear by my sword
Never to speak of this that you have heard.

GHOST [*Beneath*]   Swear by his sword.   [*They swear.*]

HAMLET
Well said, old mole. Canst work i' th' earth so fast?
A worthy pioner! Once more remove, good friends.   1
                         [*He moves again.*]

HORATIO
O day and night, but this is wondrous strange!

HAMLET
And therefore as a stranger give it welcome.   1
There are more things in heaven and earth, Horatio,
Than are dreamt of in your philosophy.   1
But come;
Here, as before, never, so help you mercy,   1
How strange or odd soe'er I bear myself—
As I perchance hereafter shall think meet
To put an antic disposition on—   1
That you, at such times seeing me, never shall,
With arms encumbered thus, or this headshake,   1

---

164 s.d. They swear (Seemingly they swear here, and at ll. 170 and 190,
as they lay their hands on Hamlet's sword. Triple oaths would have
particular force; these three oaths deal with what they have seen, what
they have heard, and what they promise about Hamlet's *antic disposition*.)   **165 Hic et ubique** here and everywhere. (Latin.)   **172 pioner** foot
soldier assigned to dig tunnels and excavations   **174 as a stranger** i.e.,
since it is a stranger and hence needing your hospitality   **176 your
philosophy** i.e., this subject called "natural philosophy" or "science"
that people talk about   **178 so help you mercy** i.e., as you hope for
God's mercy when you are judged   **181 antic** fantastic   **183 encumbered** folded or entwined

Or by pronouncing of some doubtful phrase
As "Well, we know," or "We could, an if we would,"   185
Or "If we list to speak," or "There be, an if they might,"   186
Or such ambiguous giving out, to note   187
That you know aught of me—this do swear,   188
So grace and mercy at your most need help you.
GHOST [Beneath]   Swear.   [They swear.]

HAMLET
Rest, rest, perturbèd spirit! So, gentlemen,
With all my love I do commend me to you;   192
And what so poor a man as Hamlet is
May do t' express his love and friending to you,   194
God willing, shall not lack. Let us go in together,   195
And still your fingers on your lips, I pray.   196
The time is out of joint. O cursèd spite   197
That ever I was born to set it right!
                    [They wait for him to leave first.]
Nay, come, let's go together.   Exeunt. 199

✦

185 an if if   186 list wished.   There . . . might i.e., there are people here
(we, in fact) who could tell news if we were at liberty to do so   187 giving out intimation, promulgating.   note draw attention to the fact
188 aught i.e., something secret   192 do . . . you entrust myself to you
194 friending friendliness   195 lack be lacking   196 still always
197 The time i.e., the state of affairs.   spite i.e., the spite of Fortune
199 let's go together (Probably they wait for him to leave first, but he
refuses this ceremoniousness.)

2.1   *Enter old Polonius with his man [Reynaldo].*

POLONIUS
  Give him this money and these notes, Reynaldo.
                            [He gives money and papers.]
REYNALDO   I will, my lord.
POLONIUS
  You shall do marvelous wisely, good Reynaldo,   3
  Before you visit him, to make inquire   4
  Of his behavior.
REYNALDO   My lord, I did intend it.
POLONIUS
  Marry, well said, very well said. Look you, sir,
  Inquire me first what Danskers are in Paris,   7
  And how, and who, what means, and where they keep, 8
  What company, at what expense; and finding
  By this encompassment and drift of question   10
  That they do know my son, come you more nearer 11
  Than your particular demands will touch it.   12
  Take you, as 'twere, some distant knowledge of him, 13
  As thus, "I know his father and his friends,
  And in part him." Do you mark this, Reynaldo?
REYNALDO   Ay, very well, my lord.
POLONIUS
  "And in part him, but," you may say, "not well.
  But if 't be he I mean, he's very wild,
  Addicted so and so," and there put on him   19
  What forgeries you please—marry, none so rank   20
  As may dishonor him, take heed of that,
  But, sir, such wanton, wild, and usual slips   22
  As are companions noted and most known
  To youth and liberty.
REYNALDO   As gaming, my lord.

2.1. Location: Polonius' chambers.
3 marvelous marvelously **4 inquire** inquiry **7 Danskers** Danes
8 what means what wealth (they have). **keep** dwell **10 encompassment** roundabout talking. **drift** gradual approach or course
11–12 come . . . it i.e., you will find out more this way than by asking
pointed questions (*particular demands*) **13 Take you** assume, pretend
19 put on impute to **20 forgeries** invented tales. **rank** gross
22 wanton sportive, unrestrained

POLONIUS   Ay, or drinking, fencing, swearing,
  Quarreling, drabbing—you may go so far.   27
REYNALDO   My lord, that would dishonor him.
POLONIUS
  Faith, no, as you may season it in the charge.   29
  You must not put another scandal on him
  That he is open to incontinency;   31
  That's not my meaning. But breathe his faults so
    quaintly   32
  That they may seem the taints of liberty,   33
  The flash and outbreak of a fiery mind,
  A savageness in unreclaimèd blood,   35
  Of general assault.   36
REYNALDO   But, my good lord—
POLONIUS
  Wherefore should you do this?
REYNALDO   Ay, my lord, I would know that.
POLONIUS   Marry, sir, here's my drift,
  And I believe it is a fetch of warrant.   41
  You laying these slight sullies on my son,
  As 'twere a thing a little soiled wi' the working,   43
  Mark you,
  Your party in converse, him you would sound,   45
  Having ever seen in the prenominate crimes   46
  The youth you breathe of guilty, be assured   47
  He closes with you in this consequence: 48
  "Good sir," or so, or "friend," or "gentleman,"
  According to the phrase or the addition   50
  Of man and country.
REYNALDO   Very good, my lord.
POLONIUS   And then, sir, does 'a this—'a does—what was I
  about to say? By the Mass, I was about to say something.
  Where did I leave?

27 drabbing keeping company with loose women   **29 season** temper, soften
31 incontinency habitual sexual excess   **32 quaintly** artfully, subtly
33 taints of liberty faults resulting from free living   **35–36 A savageness
. . . assault** a wildness in untamed youth that assails all indiscriminately
41 fetch of warrant legitimate trick   **43 soiled wi' the working** soiled by
handling while it is being made   **45 converse** conversation.   **sound** i.e.,
sound out   **46 Having ever** if he has ever.   **prenominate crimes** before-
mentioned offenses   **47 breathe** speak   **48 closes . . . consequence**
follows your lead in some fashion as follows   **50 addition** title

REYNALDO   At "closes in the consequence."
POLONIUS
   At "closes in the consequence," ay, marry.
   He closes thus: "I know the gentleman,
   I saw him yesterday," or "th' other day,"
   Or then, or then, with such or such, "and as you say,
   There was 'a gaming,' " "there o'ertook in 's rouse,"   60
   "There falling out at tennis," or perchance   61
   "I saw him enter such a house of sale,"
   Videlicet a brothel, or so forth. See you now,   63
   Your bait of falsehood takes this carp of truth;   64
   And thus do we of wisdom and of reach,   65
   With windlasses and with assays of bias,   66
   By indirections find directions out.   67
   So by my former lecture and advice
   Shall you my son. You have me, have you not?   69
REYNALDO
   My lord, I have.
POLONIUS   God b' wi' ye; fare ye well.   70
REYNALDO   Good my lord.
POLONIUS
   Observe his inclination in yourself.   72
REYNALDO   I shall, my lord.
POLONIUS   And let him ply his music.   74
REYNALDO   Well, my lord.
POLONIUS
   Farewell.   *Exit Reynaldo.*

      Enter Ophelia.

            How now, Ophelia, what's the matter?
OPHELIA
   O my lord, my lord, I have been so affrighted!
POLONIUS   With what, i' the name of God?

---

60 o'ertook in 's rouse overcome by drink   **61 falling out** quarreling
63 Videlicet namely   **64 carp** a fish   **65 reach** capacity, ability
66 windlasses i.e., circuitous paths. (Literally, circuits made to head off
the game in hunting.)   **assays of bias** attempts through indirection (like
the curving path of the bowling ball which is biased or weighted to one
side)   **67 directions** i.e., the way things really are   **69 have** understand   **70 b' wi'** be with   **72 in yourself** in your own person (as well as
by asking questions)   **74 let him ply** see that he continues to study

OPHELIA

My lord, as I was sewing in my closet,   79
Lord Hamlet, with his doublet all unbraced,   80
No hat upon his head, his stockings fouled,
Ungartered, and down-gyvèd to his ankle,   82
Pale as his shirt, his knees knocking each other,
And with a look so piteous in purport   84
As if he had been loosèd out of hell
To speak of horrors—he comes before me.

POLONIUS

Mad for thy love?

OPHELIA   My lord, I do not know,
But truly I do fear it.

POLONIUS   What said he?

OPHELIA

He took me by the wrist and held me hard.
Then goes he to the length of all his arm,
And with his other hand thus o'er his brow
He falls to such perusal of my face
As 'a would draw it. Long stayed he so.   93
At last, a little shaking of mine arm
And thrice his head thus waving up and down,
He raised a sigh so piteous and profound
As it did seem to shatter all his bulk   97
And end his being. That done, he lets me go,
And with his head over his shoulder turned
He seemed to find his way without his eyes,
For out o' doors he went without their helps,
And to the last bended their light on me.

POLONIUS

Come, go with me. I will go seek the King.
This is the very ecstasy of love,   104
Whose violent property fordoes itself   105
And leads the will to desperate undertakings
As oft as any passion under heaven
That does afflict our natures. I am sorry.
What, have you given him any hard words of late?

---

79 closet private chamber **80 doublet** close-fitting jacket. **unbraced**
unfastened **82 down-gyvèd** fallen to the ankles (like gyves or fetters)
84 in purport in what it expressed **93 As** as if (also in l. 97) **97 bulk**
body **104 ecstasy** madness **105 property** nature. **fordoes** destroys

OPHELIA
No, my good lord, but as you did command
I did repel his letters and denied
His access to me.
POLONIUS   That hath made him mad.
I am sorry that with better heed and judgment
I had not quoted him. I feared he did but trifle   114
And meant to wrack thee. But beshrew my jealousy!   115
By heaven, it is as proper to our age   116
To cast beyond ourselves in our opinions   117
As it is common for the younger sort
To lack discretion. Come, go we to the King.
This must be known, which, being kept close, might
    move   120
More grief to hide than hate to utter love.   121
Come.   *Exeunt.*

✤

2.2   *Flourish. Enter King and Queen, Rosencrantz,*
          and Guildenstern [with others].

KING
Welcome, dear Rosencrantz and Guildenstern.
Moreover that we much did long to see you,   2
The need we have to use you did provoke
Our hasty sending. Something have you heard
Of Hamlet's transformation—so call it,
Sith nor th' exterior nor the inward man   6
Resembles that it was. What it should be,   7
More than his father's death, that thus hath put him
So much from th' understanding of himself,
I cannot dream of. I entreat you both

114 **quoted** observed   115 **wrack** i.e., ruin, seduce.   **beshrew my jealousy** a plague upon my suspicious nature   116 **proper ... age** characteristic of us (old) men   117 **cast beyond** overshoot, miscalculate
120 **close** secret   120–121 **might ... love** i.e., might cause more grief
(because of what Hamlet might do) by hiding the knowledge of Hamlet's strange behavior to Ophelia than unpleasantness by telling it

2.2. Location: The castle.
2 **Moreover that** besides the fact that   6 **Sith** since.   **nor ... nor** neither
... nor   7 **that** what

That, being of so young days brought up with him,   11
And sith so neighbored to his youth and havior,   12
That you vouchsafe your rest here in our court   13
Some little time, so by your companies
To draw him on to pleasures, and to gather
So much as from occasion you may glean,   16
Whether aught to us unknown afflicts him thus
That, opened, lies within our remedy.   18

QUEEN
Good gentlemen, he hath much talked of you,
And sure I am two men there is not living
To whom he more adheres. If it will please you
To show us so much gentry and good will   22
As to expend your time with us awhile
For the supply and profit of our hope,   24
Your visitation shall receive such thanks
As fits a king's remembrance.

ROSENCRANTZ   Both Your Majesties   26
Might, by the sovereign power you have of us,   27
Put your dread pleasures more into command   28
Than to entreaty.

GUILDENSTERN   But we both obey,
And here give up ourselves in the full bent   30
To lay our service freely at your feet,
To be commanded.

KING
Thanks, Rosencrantz and gentle Guildenstern.

QUEEN
Thanks, Guildenstern and gentle Rosencrantz.
And I beseech you instantly to visit
My too much changèd son. Go, some of you,
And bring these gentlemen where Hamlet is.

GUILDENSTERN
Heavens make our presence and our practices   38
Pleasant and helpful to him!

11 of . . . days from such early youth   12 And sith so neighbored to i.e., and since you are (or, and since that time you are) intimately acquainted with. havior demeanor   13 vouchsafe your rest please to stay   16 occasion opportunity   18 opened being revealed   22 gentry courtesy   24 supply . . . hope aid and furtherance of what we hope for   26 As fits . . . remembrance i.e., as would be a fitting gift of a king who rewards true service   27 of over   28 dread inspiring awe   30 in . . . bent to the utmost degree of our capacity   38 practices doings •

QUEEN   Ay, amen!
                    Exeunt Rosencrantz and Guildenstern [with
                                        some attendants].

  Enter Polonius.

POLONIUS
 Th' ambassadors from Norway, my good lord,
 Are joyfully returned.
KING
 Thou still hast been the father of good news.   42
POLONIUS
 Have I, my lord? I assure my good liege
 I hold my duty, as I hold my soul,   44
 Both to my God and to my gracious king;
 And I do think, or else this brain of mine
 Hunts not the trail of policy so sure   47
 As it hath used to do, that I have found
 The very cause of Hamlet's lunacy.
KING
 O, speak of that! That do I long to hear.
POLONIUS
 Give first admittance to th' ambassadors.
 My news shall be the fruit to that great feast.   52
KING
 Thyself do grace to them and bring them in.
        [Exit Polonius.]
 He tells me, my dear Gertrude, he hath found
 The head and source of all your son's distemper.
QUEEN
 I doubt it is no other but the main,   56
 His father's death and our o'erhasty marriage.

  Enter Ambassadors [Voltimand and Cornelius,
  with Polonius].

KING
 Well, we shall sift him.—Welcome, my good friends!   58
 Say, Voltimand, what from our brother Norway?   59

---

42 still always **44 hold** maintain. **as** as firmly as **47 policy** state-
craft **52 fruit** dessert **56 doubt** fear, suspect. **main** chief point,
principal concern **58 sift him** i.e., question Polonius closely
59 brother i.e., fellow king

VOLTIMAND
Most fair return of greetings and desires.   60
Upon our first, he sent out to suppress   61
His nephew's levies, which to him appeared
To be a preparation 'gainst the Polack,
But, better looked into, he truly found
It was against Your Highness. Whereat grieved
That so his sickness, age, and impotence   66
Was falsely borne in hand, sends out arrests   67
On Fortinbras, which he, in brief, obeys,
Receives rebuke from Norway, and in fine   69
Makes vow before his uncle never more
To give th' assay of arms against Your Majesty.   71
Whereon old Norway, overcome with joy,
Gives him three thousand crowns in annual fee
And his commission to employ those soldiers,
So levied as before, against the Polack,
With an entreaty, herein further shown,
                              [*Giving a paper*]
That it might please you to give quiet pass
Through your dominions for this enterprise
On such regards of safety and allowance   79
As therein are set down.
KING   It likes us well,   80
And at our more considered time we'll read,   81
Answer, and think upon this business.
Meantime we thank you for your well-took labor.
Go to your rest; at night we'll feast together.
Most welcome home!   *Exeunt Ambassadors.*
POLONIUS   This business is well ended.
My liege, and madam, to expostulate   86
What majesty should be, what duty is,
Why day is day, night night, and time is time,
Were nothing but to waste night, day, and time.

---

60 desires good wishes **61 Upon our first** at our first words on the business **66 impotence** helplessness **67 borne in hand** deluded, taken advantage of. **arrests** orders to desist **69 in fine** in conclusion **71 give th' assay** make trial of strength, challenge **79 On . . . allowance** i.e., with such considerations or conditions for the safety of Denmark and terms of permission for Fortinbras **80 likes** pleases **81 considered** suitable for deliberation **86 expostulate** expound, inquire into

Therefore, since brevity is the soul of wit,   90
And tediousness the limbs and outward flourishes,
I will be brief. Your noble son is mad.
Mad call I it, for, to define true madness,
What is 't but to be nothing else but mad?
But let that go.
QUEEN   More matter, with less art.
POLONIUS
Madam, I swear I use no art at all.
That he's mad, 'tis true; 'tis true 'tis pity,
And pity 'tis 'tis true—a foolish figure,   98
But farewell it, for I will use no art.
Mad let us grant him, then, and now remains
That we find out the cause of this effect,
Or rather say, the cause of this defect,
For this effect defective comes by cause.   103
Thus it remains, and the remainder thus.
Perpend.   105
I have a daughter—have while she is mine—
Who, in her duty and obedience, mark,
Hath given me this. Now gather and surmise.   108
[He reads the letter.] "To the celestial and my soul's idol,
the most beautified Ophelia"—
That's an ill phrase, a vile phrase; "beautified" is a vile
phrase. But you shall hear. Thus: [He reads.]
"In her excellent white bosom, these, etc."   113
QUEEN   Came this from Hamlet to her?
POLONIUS
Good madam, stay awhile. I will be faithful.   115
                    [He reads.]
          "Doubt thou the stars are fire,
              Doubt that the sun doth move,
          Doubt truth to be a liar,   118
              But never doubt I love.
O dear Ophelia, I am ill at these numbers. I have not   120

90 **wit** sound sense or judgment, intellectual keenness   98 **figure** figure
of speech   103 **For . . . cause** i.e., for this defective behavior, this madness, has a cause   105 **Perpend** consider   108 **gather and surmise** draw
your own conclusions   113 **In . . . bosom** (The letter is poetically ad-
dressed to her heart.)   **these** i.e., the letter   115 **stay** wait.   **faithful** i.e.,
in reading the letter accurately   118 **Doubt** suspect   120 **ill . . . numbers** unskilled at writing verses

art to reckon my groans. But that I love thee best, O 121
most best, believe it. Adieu.
           Thine evermore, most dear lady, whilst this
                          machine is to him, Hamlet." 124
This in obedience hath my daughter shown me,
And, more above, hath his solicitings,   126
As they fell out by time, by means, and place,   127
All given to mine ear.
KING   But how hath she   128
Received his love?
POLONIUS   What do you think of me?
KING
As of a man faithful and honorable.
POLONIUS
I would fain prove so. But what might you think,   131
When I had seen this hot love on the wing—
As I perceived it, I must tell you that,
Before my daughter told me—what might you,
Or my dear Majesty your queen here, think,
If I had played the desk or table book,   136
Or given my heart a winking, mute and dumb,   137
Or looked upon this love with idle sight?   138
What might you think? No, I went round to work,   139
And my young mistress thus I did bespeak: 140
"Lord Hamlet is a prince out of thy star;   141
This must not be." And then I prescripts gave her   142
That she should lock herself from his resort,   143
Admit no messengers, receive no tokens.
Which done, she took the fruits of my advice;
And he, repellèd—a short tale to make—
Fell into a sadness, then into a fast,
Thence to a watch, thence into a weakness,   148
Thence to a lightness, and by this declension   149

121 **reckon** (1) count (2) number metrically, scan   124 **machine** i.e.,
body   126 **more above** moreover   127 **fell out** occurred.   **by** according
to   128 **given . . . ear** i.e., told me about   131 **fain** gladly   136 **played
. . . table book** i.e., remained shut up, concealing the information; or,
acted as a go-between, provided communication   137 **given . . . winking**
closed the eyes of my heart to this   138 **with idle sight** complacently or
incomprehendingly   139 **round** roundly, plainly   140 **bespeak** address   141 **out of thy star** above your sphere, position   142 **prescripts**
orders   143 **his resort** his visits   148 **watch** state of sleeplessness
149 **lightness** lightheadedness.   **declension** decline, deterioration

Into the madness wherein now he raves
And all we mourn for.

KING [*To Queen*]   Do you think 'tis this?   151

QUEEN   It may be, very like.

POLONIUS
Hath there been such a time—I would fain know that—
That I have positively said " 'Tis so,"
When it proved otherwise?

KING   Not that I know.

POLONIUS
Take this from this, if this be otherwise.   156
If circumstances lead me, I will find
Where truth is hid, though it were hid indeed
Within the center.

KING   How may we try it further?   159

POLONIUS
You know sometimes he walks four hours together
Here in the lobby.

QUEEN   So he does indeed.

POLONIUS
At such a time I'll loose my daughter to him.   162
Be you and I behind an arras then.   163
Mark the encounter. If he love her not
And be not from his reason fallen thereon,   165
Let me be no assistant for a state,
But keep a farm and carters.

KING   We will try it.

Enter Hamlet [reading on a book].

QUEEN
But look where sadly the poor wretch comes reading.   168

POLONIUS
Away, I do beseech you both, away.

---

151 all i.e., into everything that   **156 Take this from this** (The actor
gestures, indicating that he means his head from his shoulders, or his
staff of office or chain from his hands or neck, or something similar.)
159 center middle point of the earth (which is also the center of the
Ptolemaic universe).   **try** test, judge   **162 loose** (as one might release an
animal that is being mated)   **163 arras** hanging, tapestry   **165 thereon**
on that account   **168 sadly** seriously

I'll board him presently. O, give me leave.   170
      Exeunt King and Queen [with attendants].
How does my good Lord Hamlet?

HAMLET   Well, God-a-mercy.   172

POLONIUS   Do you know me, my lord?

HAMLET   Excellent well. You are a fishmonger.   174

POLONIUS   Not I, my lord.

HAMLET   Then I would you were so honest a man.

POLONIUS   Honest, my lord?

HAMLET   Ay, sir. To be honest, as this world goes, is to be one man picked out of ten thousand.

POLONIUS   That's very true, my lord.

HAMLET   For if the sun breed maggots in a dead dog, being a good kissing carrion—Have you a daughter?   182

POLONIUS   I have, my lord.

HAMLET   Let her not walk i' the sun. Conception is a   184 blessing, but as your daughter may conceive, friend, look to 't.

POLONIUS *[Aside]*   How say you by that? Still harping on my daughter. Yet he knew me not at first; 'a said I   188 was a fishmonger. 'A is far gone. And truly in my youth I suffered much extremity for love, very near this. I'll speak to him again.—What do you read, my lord?

HAMLET   Words, words, words.

POLONIUS   What is the matter, my lord?   194

HAMLET   Between who?

POLONIUS   I mean, the matter that you read, my lord.

HAMLET   Slanders, sir; for the satirical rogue says here that old men have gray beards, that their faces are wrinkled, their eyes purging thick amber and plum-tree   199 gum, and that they have a plentiful lack of wit, to-   200

---

170 board accost.   **presently** at once.   **give me leave** i.e., excuse me. (Said to those he hurries offstage, including the King and Queen.)
172 God-a-mercy i.e., thank you   **174 fishmonger** fish merchant   **182 a good kissing carrion** i.e., a good piece of flesh for kissing, or for the sun to kiss   **184 i' the sun** (with additional implication of the sunshine of princely favors).   **Conception** (1) understanding (2) pregnancy   **188 'a** he   **194 matter** substance. (But Hamlet plays on the sense of "basis for a dispute.")   **199 purging** discharging.   **amber** i.e., resin, like the resinous *plum-tree gum*   **200 wit** understanding

gether with most weak hams. All which, sir, though I
most powerfully and potently believe, yet I hold it not
honesty to have it thus set down, for yourself, sir, shall 203
grow old as I am, if like a crab you could go backward. 204

POLONIUS [*Aside*] Though this be madness, yet there is
method in 't.—Will you walk out of the air, my lord? 206

HAMLET Into my grave.

POLONIUS Indeed, that's out of the air. [*Aside*.] How
pregnant sometimes his replies are! A happiness that 209
often madness hits on, which reason and sanity could
not so prosperously be delivered of. I will leave him 211
and suddenly contrive the means of meeting between 212
him and my daughter.—My honorable lord, I will
most humbly take my leave of you.

HAMLET You cannot, sir, take from me anything that I
will more willingly part withal—except my life, except 216
my life, except my life.

Enter Guildenstern and Rosencrantz.

POLONIUS Fare you well, my lord.

HAMLET These tedious old fools!   219

POLONIUS You go to seek the Lord Hamlet. There he is.

ROSENCRANTZ [*To Polonius*] God save you, sir!

                                    [*Exit Polonius.*]

GUILDENSTERN My honored lord!

ROSENCRANTZ My most dear lord!

HAMLET My excellent good friends! How dost thou,
Guildenstern? Ah, Rosencrantz! Good lads, how do
you both?

ROSENCRANTZ
As the indifferent children of the earth.   227

GUILDENSTERN
Happy in that we are not overhappy.
On Fortune's cap we are not the very button.

---

203 honesty decency, decorum **204 old** as old **206 out of the air** (The
open air was considered dangerous for sick people.) **209 pregnant**
quick-witted, full of meaning. **happiness** felicity of expression
211 prosperously successfully **212 suddenly** immediately **216 withal**
with **219 old fools** i.e., old men like Polonius **227 indifferent** ordinary,
at neither extreme of fortune or misfortune

HAMLET Nor the soles of her shoe?

ROSENCRANTZ Neither, my lord.

HAMLET Then you live about her waist, or in the middle of her favors?   233

GUILDENSTERN Faith, her privates we.   234

HAMLET In the secret parts of Fortune? O, most true, she is a strumpet. What news?   236

ROSENCRANTZ None, my lord, but the world's grown honest.

HAMLET Then is doomsday near. But your news is not true. Let me question more in particular. What have you, my good friends, deserved at the hands of Fortune that she sends you to prison hither?

GUILDENSTERN Prison, my lord?

HAMLET Denmark's a prison.

ROSENCRANTZ Then is the world one.

HAMLET A goodly one, in which there are many con-   246
fines, wards, and dungeons, Denmark being one o' the   247
worst.

ROSENCRANTZ We think not so, my lord.

HAMLET Why then 'tis none to you, for there is nothing either good or bad but thinking makes it so. To me it is a prison.

ROSENCRANTZ Why then, your ambition makes it one. 'Tis too narrow for your mind.

HAMLET O God, I could be bounded in a nutshell and count myself a king of infinite space, were it not that I have bad dreams.

GUILDENSTERN Which dreams indeed are ambition, for the very substance of the ambitious is merely the   259
shadow of a dream.

HAMLET A dream itself is but a shadow.

ROSENCRANTZ Truly, and I hold ambition of so airy and light a quality that it is but a shadow's shadow.

---

233 favors i.e., sexual favors   **234 her privates we** i.e., (1) we are sexually intimate with Fortune, the fickle goddess who bestows her favors indiscriminately (2) we are her ordinary citizens   **236 strumpet** prostitute. (A common epithet for indiscriminate Fortune; see l. 493 below.)
246–247 confines places of confinement   **247 wards** cells   **259 the very
. . . ambitious** that seemingly very substantial thing that the ambitious pursue

HAMLET   Then are our beggars bodies, and our mon- 264
archs and outstretched heroes the beggars' shadows. 265
Shall we to the court? For, by my fay, I cannot reason. 266
ROSENCRANTZ, GUILDENSTERN   We'll wait upon you.   267
HAMLET   No such matter. I will not sort you with the 268
rest of my servants, for, to speak to you like an honest
man, I am most dreadfully attended. But, in the 270
beaten way of friendship, what make you at Elsinore? 271
ROSENCRANTZ   To visit you, my lord, no other occasion.
HAMLET   Beggar that I am, I am even poor in thanks;
but I thank you, and sure, dear friends, my thanks are
too dear a halfpenny. Were you not sent for? Is it your 275
own inclining? Is it a free visitation? Come, come, deal 276
justly with me. Come, come; nay, speak.
GUILDENSTERN   What should we say, my lord?
HAMLET   Anything but to the purpose. You were sent 279
for, and there is a kind of confession in your looks which
your modesties have not craft enough to color. I know 281
the good King and Queen have sent for you.
ROSENCRANTZ   To what end, my lord?
HAMLET   That you must teach me. But let me conjure 284
you, by the rights of our fellowship, by the conso- 285
nancy of our youth, by the obligation of our ever-pre- 286
served love, and by what more dear a better proposer 287
could charge you withal, be even and direct with me 288
whether you were sent for or no.
ROSENCRANTZ [Aside to Guildenstern]   What say you?
HAMLET [Aside]   Nay, then, I have an eye of you.—If 291
you love me, hold not off.   292

264 bodies i.e., solid substances rather than shadows (since beggars are
not ambitious)   **265 outstretched** (1) far-reaching in their ambition (2) elon-
gated as shadows   **266 fay** faith   **267 wait upon** accompany, attend. (But
Hamlet uses the phrase in the sense of providing menial service.)
268 sort class, categorize   **270 dreadfully attended** waited upon in
slovenly fashion   **271 beaten way** familiar path, tried-and-true course.
make do   **275 dear a halfpenny** expensive at the price of a halfpenny,
i.e., of little worth   **276 free** voluntary   **279 Anything but to the purpose** anything except a straightforward answer. (Said ironically.)
281 modesties sense of shame.   **color** disguise   **284 conjure** adjure,
entreat   **285–286 the consonancy of our youth** our closeness in
our younger days   **287 better proposer** more skillful propounder
288 charge urge.   **even** straight, honest   **291 of** on   **292 hold not
off** don't hold back

GUILDENSTERN My lord, we were sent for.

HAMLET I will tell you why; so shall my anticipation 294
prevent your discovery, and your secrecy to the King 295
and Queen molt no feather. I have of late—but 296
wherefore I know not—lost all my mirth, forgone all
custom of exercises; and indeed it goes so heavily with
my disposition that this goodly frame, the earth,
seems to me a sterile promontory; this most excellent
canopy, the air, look you, this brave o'erhanging fir- 301
mament, this majestical roof fretted with golden fire, 302.
why, it appeareth nothing to me but a foul and pesti-
lent congregation of vapors. What a piece of work is a 304
man! How noble in reason, how infinite in faculties,
in form and moving how express and admirable, in 306
action how like an angel, in apprehension how like a 307
god! The beauty of the world, the paragon of animals!
And yet, to me, what is this quintessence of dust? 309
Man delights not me—no, nor woman neither,
though by your smiling you seem to say so.

ROSENCRANTZ My lord, there was no such stuff in my
thoughts.

HAMLET Why did you laugh then, when I said man
delights not me?

ROSENCRANTZ To think, my lord, if you delight not in
man, what Lenten entertainment the players shall re- 317
ceive from you. We coted them on the way, and hither 318
are they coming to offer you service.

HAMLET He that plays the king shall be welcome; His
Majesty shall have tribute of me. The adventurous 321
knight shall use his foil and target, the lover shall not 322

294–295 so . . . discovery in that way my saying it first will spare you
from revealing the truth   **296 molt no feather** i.e., not diminish in the
least   **301 brave** splendid   **302 fretted** adorned (with fretwork, as in a
vaulted ceiling)   **304 congregation** mass.   **piece of work** masterpiece
306 express well-framed, exact, expressive (?)   **307 apprehension** power
of comprehending   **309 quintessence** the fifth essence of ancient philosophy, beyond earth, water, air, and fire, supposed to be the substance of
the heavenly bodies and to be latent in all things   **317 Lenten entertainment** meager reception (appropriate to Lent)   **318 coted** overtook and
passed by   **321 shall . . . of me** will receive my tribute of praise
322 foil and target sword and shield

sigh gratis, the humorous man shall end his part in 323
peace, the clown shall make those laugh whose lungs 324
are tickle o' the sear, and the lady shall say her mind 325
freely, or the blank verse shall halt for 't. What players 326
are they?

ROSENCRANTZ Even those you were wont to take such
delight in, the tragedians of the city.

HAMLET How chances it they travel? Their residence, 330
both in reputation and profit, was better both ways.

ROSENCRANTZ I think their inhibition comes by the 332
means of the late innovation.   333

HAMLET Do they hold the same estimation they did
when I was in the city? Are they so followed?

ROSENCRANTZ No, indeed are they not.

HAMLET How comes it? Do they grow rusty?   337

ROSENCRANTZ Nay, their endeavor keeps in the wonted 338
pace. But there is, sir, an aerie of children, little eyases, 339
that cry out on the top of question and are most tyran- 340
nically clapped for 't. These are now the fashion, and 341
so berattle the common stages—so they call them— 342
that many wearing rapiers are afraid of goose quills 343
and dare scarce come thither.

HAMLET What, are they children? Who maintains 'em?
How are they escoted? Will they pursue the quality no 346
longer than they can sing? Will they not say after- 347

323 **gratis** for nothing. **humorous man** eccentric character, dominated
by one trait or "humor" 323–324 **in peace** i.e., with full license
325 **tickle o' the sear** easy on the trigger, ready to laugh easily. (A *sear* is
part of a gunlock.) 326 **halt** limp 330 **residence** remaining in one
place, i.e., in the city 332 **inhibition** formal prohibition (from acting
plays in the city) 333 **late** recent. **innovation** i.e., the new fashion in
satirical plays performed by boy actors in the "private" theaters; or
possibly a political uprising; or the strict limitations set on the theaters
in London in 1600 337–362 **How . . . load too** (The passage, omitted
from the early quartos, alludes to the so-called War of the Theaters,
1599–1602, the rivalry between the children's companies and the adult
actors.) 338 **keeps** continues. **wonted** usual 339 **aerie** nest. **eyases**
young hawks 340 **cry . . . question** speak shrilly, dominating the controversy (in decrying the public theaters) 340–341 **tyrannically** outra-
geously 342 **berattle** berate, clamor against. **common stages** public
theaters 343 **many wearing rapiers** i.e., many men of fashion, afraid to
patronize the common players for fear of being satirized by the poets
writing for the boy actors. **goose quills** i.e., pens of satirists
346 **escoted** maintained. **quality** (acting) profession 346–347 **no
longer . . . sing** i.e., only until their voices change

wards, if they should grow themselves to common 348
players—as it is most like, if their means are no bet- 349
ter—their writers do them wrong to make them ex- 350
claim against their own succession? 351

ROSENCRANTZ Faith, there has been much to-do on 352
both sides, and the nation holds it no sin to tar them 353
to controversy. There was for a while no money bid
for argument unless the poet and the player went to 355
cuffs in the question. 356

HAMLET Is 't possible?

GUILDENSTERN O, there has been much throwing about
of brains.

HAMLET Do the boys carry it away? 360

ROSENCRANTZ Ay, that they do, my lord—Hercules 361
and his load too. 362

HAMLET It is not very strange; for my uncle is King of
Denmark, and those that would make mouths at him 364
while my father lived give twenty, forty, fifty, a
hundred ducats apiece for his picture in little. 'Sblood, 366
there is something in this more than natural, if philos- 367
ophy could find it out. 368

                    A flourish [*of trumpets within*].

GUILDENSTERN There are the players.

HAMLET Gentlemen, you are welcome to Elsinore. Your
hands, come then. Th' appurtenance of welcome is 371
fashion and ceremony. Let me comply with you in this 372
garb, lest my extent to the players, which, I tell you, 373
must show fairly outwards, should more appear like 374
entertainment than yours. You are welcome. But my 375
uncle-father and aunt-mother are deceived.

---

348 common regular, adult **349 like** likely **349–350 if ... better** if
they find no better way to support themselves **351 succession** i.e.,
future careers **352 to-do** ado **353 tar** set on (as dogs) **355 argument**
plot for a play **355–356 went ... question** came to blows in the play
itself **360 carry it away** i.e., win the day **361–362 Hercules ... load**
(Thought to be an allusion to the sign of the Globe Theatre, which was
Hercules bearing the world on his shoulder.) **364 mouths** faces
366 ducats gold coins. **in little** in miniature. **'Sblood** by God's
(Christ's) blood **367–368 philosophy** i.e., scientific inquiry
371 appurtenance proper accompaniment **372 comply** observe the
formalities of courtesy **373 garb** i.e., manner. **my extent** that which I
extend, i.e., my polite behavior **374 show fairly outwards** show every
evidence of cordiality **375 entertainment** a (warm) reception

GUILDENSTERN   In what, my dear lord?

HAMLET   I am but mad north-north-west. When the wind is southerly I know a hawk from a handsaw.

Enter Polonius.

POLONIUS   Well be with you, gentlemen!

HAMLET   Hark you, Guildenstern, and you too; at each ear a hearer. That great baby you see there is not yet out of his swaddling clouts.

ROSENCRANTZ   Haply he is the second time come to them, for they say an old man is twice a child.

HAMLET   I will prophesy he comes to tell me of the players; mark it.—You say right, sir, o' Monday morning, 'twas then indeed.

POLONIUS   My lord, I have news to tell you.

HAMLET   My lord, I have news to tell you. When Roscius was an actor in Rome—

POLONIUS   The actors are come hither, my lord.

HAMLET   Buzz, buzz!

POLONIUS   Upon my honor—

HAMLET   Then came each actor on his ass.

POLONIUS   The best actors in the world, either for tragedy, comedy, history, pastoral, pastoral-comical, historical-pastoral, tragical-historical, tragical-comical-historical-pastoral, scene individable, or poem unlimited. Seneca cannot be too heavy, nor Plautus too light. For the law of writ and the liberty, these are the only men.

HAMLET   O Jephthah, judge of Israel, what a treasure hadst thou!

378 north-north-west i.e., only partly, at times   **379 hawk, handsaw** i.e., two very different things, though also perhaps meaning a mattock (or *hack*) and a carpenter's cutting tool respectively; also birds, with a play on *hernshaw* or heron   **383 swaddling clouts** cloths in which to wrap a newborn baby   **384 Haply** perhaps   **390–391 Roscius** a famous Roman actor who died in 62 B.C.   **393 Buzz** (An interjection used to denote stale news.)   **399 scene individable** a play observing the unity of place; or perhaps one that is unclassifiable   **399–400 poem unlimited** a play disregarding the unities of time and place; one that is all-inclusive   **400 Seneca** writer of Latin tragedies.   **Plautus** writer of Latin comedy   **401 law . . . liberty** dramatic composition both according to rules and without rules, i.e., "classical" and "romantic" dramas.   **these** i.e., the actors   **403 Jephthah . . . Israel** (Jephthah had to sacrifice his daughter; see Judges 11. Hamlet goes on to quote from a ballad on the theme.)

POLONIUS　What a treasure had he, my lord?

HAMLET　Why,

"One fair daughter, and no more,
　The which he lovèd passing well."　　　　　408

POLONIUS [*Aside*]　Still on my daughter.

HAMLET　Am I not i' the right, old Jephthah?

POLONIUS　If you call me Jephthah, my lord, I have a
daughter that I love passing well.

HAMLET　Nay, that follows not.

POLONIUS　What follows then, my lord?

HAMLET　Why,

"As by lot, God wot,"　　　　　　　　　416

and then, you know,

"It came to pass, as most like it was"—　418

the first row of the pious chanson will show you more,　419
for look where my abridgment comes.　　　　　420

Enter the Players.

You are welcome, masters; welcome, all. I am glad to
see thee well. Welcome, good friends. O, old friend!
Why, thy face is valanced since I saw thee last. Com'st　423
thou to beard me in Denmark? What, my young lady　424
and mistress! By 'r Lady, your ladyship is nearer to　425
heaven than when I saw you last, by the altitude of a
chopine. Pray God your voice, like a piece of uncur-　427
rent gold, be not cracked within the ring. Masters, you　428
are all welcome. We'll e'en to 't like French falconers,　429
fly at anything we see. We'll have a speech straight.　430
Come, give us a taste of your quality. Come, a passion-　431
ate speech.

FIRST PLAYER　What speech, my good lord?

---

408 passing surpassingly　**416 lot** chance.　**wot** knows　**418 like** likely,
probable　**419 row** stanza.　**chanson** ballad, song　**420 my abridgment**
something that cuts short my conversation; also, a diversion　**423 valanced** fringed (with a beard)　**424 beard** confront, challenge (with
obvious pun).　**young lady** i.e., boy playing women's parts　**425 By 'r
Lady** by Our Lady　**427 chopine** thick-soled shoe of Italian fashion
427–428 uncurrent not passable as lawful coinage　**428 cracked . . . ring**
i.e., changed from adolescent to male voice, no longer suitable for women's
roles. (Coins featured rings enclosing the sovereign's head; if the coin
was cracked within this ring, it was unfit for currency.)　**429 e'en to 't**
go at it　**430 straight** at once　**431 quality** professional skill

HAMLET I heard thee speak me a speech once, but it
was never acted, or if it was, not above once, for the
play, I remember, pleased not the million; 'twas cav- 436
iar to the general. But it was—as I received it, and 437
others, whose judgments in such matters cried in the 438
top of mine—an excellent play, well digested in the 439
scenes, set down with as much modesty as cunning. I 440
remember one said there were no sallets in the lines to 441
make the matter savory, nor no matter in the phrase
that might indict the author of affectation, but called it 443
an honest method, as wholesome as sweet, and by
very much more handsome than fine. One speech in 't 445
I chiefly loved: 'twas Aeneas' tale to Dido, and there-
about of it especially when he speaks of Priam's 447
slaughter. If it live in your memory, begin at this line: 448
let me see, let me see—

    "The rugged Pyrrhus, like th' Hyrcanian beast"— 450
'Tis not so. It begins with Pyrrhus:
    "The rugged Pyrrhus, he whose sable arms, 452
      Black as his purpose, did the night resemble
      When he lay couchèd in the ominous horse, 454
      Hath now this dread and black complexion smeared
      With heraldry more dismal. Head to foot 456
      Now is he total gules, horridly tricked 457
      With blood of fathers, mothers, daughters, sons,
      Baked and impasted with the parching streets, 459

436–437 caviar to the general caviar to the multitude, i.e., a choice dish
too elegant for coarse tastes **438–439 cried in the top of** i.e., spoke
with greater authority than **439 digested** arranged, ordered
440 modesty moderation, restraint. **cunning** skill **441 sallets** i.e.,
something savory, spicy improprieties **443 indict** convict **445 fine**
elaborately ornamented, showy **447–448 Priam's slaughter** the slaying
of the ruler of Troy, when the Greeks finally took the city **450 Pyrrhus**
a Greek hero in the Trojan War, also known as Neoptolemus, son of
Achilles—another avenging son. **Hyrcanian beast** i.e., tiger. (On the
death of Priam, see Virgil, *Aeneid*, 2.506–558; compare the whole speech
with Marlowe's *Dido Queen of Carthage*, 2.1.214 ff. On the *Hyrcanian*
tiger, see *Aeneid*, 4.366–367. Hyrcania is on the Caspian Sea.) **452 sable**
black (for reasons of camouflage during the episode of the Trojan
horse) **454 couchèd** concealed. **ominous horse** Trojan horse, by which
the Greeks gained access to Troy **456 dismal** ill-omened **457 gules**
red. (A heraldic term.) **tricked** adorned, decorated **459 impasted**
crusted, like a thick paste. **with . . . streets** by the parching heat of the
streets (because of the fires everywhere)

       That lend a tyrannous and a damnèd light
       To their lord's murder. Roasted in wrath and fire,   461
       And thus o'ersizèd with coagulate gore,   462
       With eyes like carbuncles, the hellish Pyrrhus   463
       Old grandsire Priam seeks."
  So proceed you.

POLONIUS 'Fore God, my lord, well spoken, with good
accent and good discretion.

FIRST PLAYER   "Anon he finds him
       Striking too short at Greeks. His antique sword,
       Rebellious to his arm, lies where it falls,
       Repugnant to command. Unequal matched,   471
       Pyrrhus at Priam drives, in rage strikes wide,
       But with the whiff and wind of his fell sword   473
       Th' unnervèd father falls. Then senseless Ilium,   474
       Seeming to feel this blow, with flaming top
       Stoops to his base, and with a hideous crash   476
       Takes prisoner Pyrrhus' ear. For, lo! His sword,
       Which was declining on the milky head   478
       Of reverend Priam, seemed i' th' air to stick.
       So as a painted tyrant Pyrrhus stood,   480
       And, like a neutral to his will and matter,   481
       Did nothing.
       But as we often see against some storm   483
       A silence in the heavens, the rack stand still,   484
       The bold winds speechless, and the orb below   485
       As hush as death, anon the dreadful thunder
       Doth rend the region, so, after Pyrrhus' pause,   487
       Arousèd vengeance sets him new a-work,
       And never did the Cyclops' hammers fall   489
       On Mars's armor forged for proof eterne   490
       With less remorse than Pyrrhus' bleeding sword   491
       Now falls on Priam.

---

461 their lord's i.e., Priam's   **462 o'ersizèd** covered as with size or glue
463 carbuncles large fiery-red precious stones thought to emit their own
light   **471 Repugnant** disobedient, resistant   **473 fell** cruel   **474 unnervèd**
strengthless.   **senseless Ilium** inanimate citadel of Troy   **476 his** its
478 declining descending.   **milky** white-haired   **480 painted** i.e., painted in
a picture   **481 like . . . matter** i.e., as though suspended between his
intention and its fulfillment   **483 against** just before   **484 rack** mass of
clouds   **485 orb** globe, earth   **487 region** sky   **489 Cyclops** giant armor-
makers in the smithy of Vulcan   **490 proof eterne** eternal resistance to
assault   **491 remorse** pity

Out, out, thou strumpet Fortune! All you gods
In general synod take away her power!   494
Break all the spokes and fellies from her wheel,   495
And bowl the round nave down the hill of heaven   496
As low as to the fiends!"

POLONIUS   This is too long.

HAMLET   It shall to the barber's with your beard.—Prithee, say on. He's for a jig or a tale of bawdry, or he   500
sleeps. Say on; come to Hecuba.   501

FIRST PLAYER
     "But who, ah woe! had seen the mobl̀èd queen"—   502

HAMLET   "The mobl̀èd queen"?

POLONIUS   That's good. "Mobl̀èd queen" is good.

FIRST PLAYER
     "Run barefoot up and down, threat'ning the flames
     With bisson rheum, a clout upon that head   506
     Where late the diadem stood, and, for a robe,   507
     About her lank and all o'erteemèd loins   508
     A blanket, in the alarm of fear caught up—
     Who this had seen, with tongue in venom steeped,
     'Gainst Fortune's state would treason have
          pronounced.   511
     But if the gods themselves did see her then
     When she saw Pyrrhus make malicious sport
     In mincing with his sword her husband's limbs,
     The instant burst of clamor that she made,
     Unless things mortal move them not at all,
     Would have made milch the burning eyes of heaven,   517
     And passion in the gods."   518

POLONIUS   Look whe'er he has not turned his color and   519
has tears in 's eyes. Prithee, no more.

HAMLET   'Tis well. I'll have thee speak out the rest of
this soon.—Good my lord, will you see the players well

---

494 synod assembly   495 fellies pieces of wood forming the rim of a
wheel   496 nave hub   500 jig comic song and dance often given at the
end of a play   501 Hecuba wife of Priam   502 who . . . had anyone who
had (also in l. 510).   mobl̀èd muffled   506 bisson rheum blinding
tears.   clout cloth   507 late lately   508 o'erteemèd worn out with
bearing children   511 state rule, managing.   pronounced proclaimed
517 milch milky, moist with tears   518 passion overpowering emotion
519 whe'er whether

bestowed? Do you hear, let them be well used, for they 523
are the abstract and brief chronicles of the time. After 524
your death you were better have a bad epitaph than
their ill report while you live.

POLONIUS   My lord, I will use them according to their
desert.

HAMLET   God's bodikin, man, much better. Use every 529
man after his desert, and who shall scape whipping?
Use them after your own honor and dignity. The less
they deserve, the more merit is in your bounty. Take
them in.

POLONIUS   Come, sirs.

HAMLET   Follow him, friends. We'll hear a play tomor-
row. [*As they start to leave, Hamlet detains the First
Player.*] Dost thou hear me, old friend? Can you play
The Murder of Gonzago?

FIRST PLAYER   Ay, my lord.

HAMLET   We'll ha 't tomorrow night. You could, for 540
a need, study a speech of some dozen or sixteen lines 541
which I would set down and insert in 't, could you
not?

FIRST PLAYER   Ay, my lord.

HAMLET   Very well. Follow that lord, and look you mock 545
him not. (*Exeunt Polonius and Players.*) My good friends,
I'll leave you till night. You are welcome to Elsinore.

ROSENCRANTZ   Good my lord!

>   *Exeunt* [*Rosencrantz and Guildenstern*].

HAMLET
Ay, so, goodbye to you.—Now I am alone.
O, what a rogue and peasant slave am I!
Is it not monstrous that this player here,
But in a fiction, in a dream of passion,   552
Could force his soul so to his own conceit   553
That from her working all his visage wanned,   554
Tears in his eyes, distraction in his aspect,

---

523 bestowed lodged   **524 abstract** summary account   **529 God's
bodikin** by God's (Christ's) little body, *bodykin*. (Not to be confused with
bodkin, dagger.)   **540 ha 't** have it   **541 study** memorize   **545 mock**
mimic derisively   **552 But** merely   **553 to** in accord with.   **conceit**
conception   **554 from her working** as a result of, or in response to, his
soul's activity.   **wanned** grew pale

A broken voice, and his whole function suiting 556
With forms to his conceit? And all for nothing! 557
For Hecuba!
What's Hecuba to him, or he to Hecuba,
That he should weep for her? What would he do
Had he the motive and the cue for passion
That I have? He would drown the stage with tears
And cleave the general ear with horrid speech, 563
Make mad the guilty and appall the free, 564
Confound the ignorant, and amaze indeed
The very faculties of eyes and ears. Yet I,
A dull and muddy-mettled rascal, peak 567
Like John-a-dreams, unpregnant of my cause, 568
And can say nothing—no, not for a king
Upon whose property and most dear life 570
A damned defeat was made. Am I a coward? 571
Who calls me villain? Breaks my pate across?
Plucks off my beard and blows it in my face?
Tweaks me by the nose? Gives me the lie i' the throat 574
As deep as to the lungs? Who does me this?
Ha, 'swounds, I should take it; for it cannot be 576
But I am pigeon-livered and lack gall 577
To make oppression bitter, or ere this 578
I should ha' fatted all the region kites 579
With this slave's offal. Bloody, bawdy villain!
Remorseless, treacherous, lecherous, kindless villain! 581
O, vengeance!
Why, what an ass am I! This is most brave, 583
That I, the son of a dear father murdered,
Prompted to my revenge by heaven and hell,
Must like a whore unpack my heart with words

556–557 his whole . . . conceit all his bodily powers responding with
actions to suit his thought   **563 the general ear** everyone's ear.   **horrid**
horrible   **564 appall** (Literally, make pale.)   **free** innocent   **567 muddy-
mettled** dull-spirited.   **peak** mope, pine   **568 John-a-dreams** a sleepy,
dreaming idler.   **unpregnant of** not quickened by   **570 property** i.e., the
crown; perhaps also character, quality   **571 defeat** destruction
574 Gives me the lie calls me a liar   **576 'swounds** by his (Christ's)
wounds   **577 pigeon-livered** (The pigeon or dove was popularly supposed to be mild because it secreted no gall.)   **578 To . . . bitter** to make
tyranny bitter to itself   **579 region kites** kites (birds of prey) of the air
581 Remorseless pitiless.   **kindless** unnatural   **583 brave** fine, admirable. (Said ironically.)

And fall a-cursing, like a very drab,   587
A scullion! Fie upon 't, foh! About, my brain!   588
Hum, I have heard
That guilty creatures sitting at a play
Have by the very cunning of the scene   591
Been struck so to the soul that presently   592
They have proclaimed their malefactions;
For murder, though it have no tongue, will speak
With most miraculous organ. I'll have these players
Play something like the murder of my father
Before mine uncle. I'll observe his looks;
I'll tent him to the quick. If 'a do blench,   598
I know my course. The spirit that I have seen
May be the devil, and the devil hath power
T' assume a pleasing shape; yea, and perhaps,
Out of my weakness and my melancholy,
As he is very potent with such spirits,   603
Abuses me to damn me. I'll have grounds   604
More relative than this. The play's the thing   605
Wherein I'll catch the conscience of the King.   *Exit.*

✤

587 drab prostitute **588 scullion** menial kitchen servant (apt to be foulmouthed). **About** about it, to work **591 cunning** art, skill. **scene** dramatic presentation **592 presently** at once **598 tent** probe. **blench** quail, flinch **603 spirits** humors (of melancholy) **604 Abuses** deludes **605 relative** cogent, pertinent

3.1 *Enter King, Queen, Polonius, Ophelia,*
Rosencrantz, Guildenstern, lords.

KING
 And can you by no drift of conference   1
 Get from him why he puts on this confusion,
 Grating so harshly all his days of quiet
 With turbulent and dangerous lunacy?

ROSENCRANTZ
 He does confess he feels himself distracted,
 But from what cause 'a will by no means speak.

GUILDENSTERN
 Nor do we find him forward to be sounded,   7
 But with a crafty madness keeps aloof
 When we would bring him on to some confession
 Of his true state.

QUEEN   Did he receive you well?

ROSENCRANTZ   Most like a gentleman.

GUILDENSTERN
 But with much forcing of his disposition.   12

ROSENCRANTZ
 Niggard of question, but of our demands   13
 Most free in his reply.

QUEEN   Did you assay him   14
 To any pastime?

ROSENCRANTZ
 Madam, it so fell out that certain players
 We o'erraught on the way. Of these we told him,   17
 And there did seem in him a kind of joy
 To hear of it. They are here about the court,
 And, as I think, they have already order
 This night to play before him.

POLONIUS   'Tis most true,
 And he beseeched me to entreat Your Majesties
 To hear and see the matter.

KING
 With all my heart, and it doth much content me
 To hear him so inclined.

3.1. Location: The castle.
1 drift of conference directing of conversation   **7 forward** willing.
sounded questioned   **12 disposition** inclination   **13 question** conversation   **14 assay** try to win   **17 o'erraught** overtook and passed

Good gentlemen, give him a further edge　　　　26
And drive his purpose into these delights.

POLONIUS

ROSENCRANTZ
We shall, my lord.
　　　　　　　Exeunt Rosencrantz and Guildenstern.
KING　　　　　　　Sweet Gertrude, leave us too,
For we have closely sent for Hamlet hither,　　　　29
That he, as 'twere by accident, may here
Affront Ophelia.　　　　31
Her father and myself, lawful espials,　　　　32
Will so bestow ourselves that seeing, unseen,
We may of their encounter frankly judge,
And gather by him, as he is behaved,
If 't be th' affliction of his love or no
That thus he suffers for.
QUEEN　　　　　　　　I shall obey you.
And for your part, Ophelia, I do wish
That your good beauties be the happy cause
Of Hamlet's wildness. So shall I hope your virtues
Will bring him to his wonted way again,
To both your honors.
OPHELIA　　　　　　　Madam, I wish it may.
　　　　　　　　　　[Exit Queen.]

POLONIUS
Ophelia, walk you here.—Gracious, so please you,　　　43
We will bestow ourselves. *[To Ophelia.]* Read on this
　book,　　　　　　　*[Giving her a book]*　44
That show of such an exercise may color　　　　45
Your loneliness. We are oft to blame in this—　　46
'Tis too much proved—that with devotion's visage　　47
And pious action we do sugar o'er
The devil himself.
KING *[Aside]*　O, 'tis too true!
How smart a lash that speech doth give my conscience!
The harlot's cheek, beautied with plastering art,
Is not more ugly to the thing that helps it　　　53

26 edge incitement　**29 closely** privately　**31 Affront** confront, meet
32 espials spies　**43 Gracious** Your Grace (i.e., the King)　**44 bestow**
conceal　**45 exercise** act of devotion. (The book she reads is one of
devotion.)　**color** give a plausible appearance to　**46 loneliness** being
alone　**47 too much proved** too often shown to be true, too often prac-
ticed　**53 to** compared to.　**the thing** i.e., the cosmetic

Than is my deed to my most painted word.
O heavy burden!

POLONIUS
I hear him coming. Let's withdraw, my lord.   56

[The King and Polonius withdraw.]

Enter Hamlet. [Ophelia pretends to read a book.]

HAMLET
To be, or not to be, that is the question:
Whether 'tis nobler in the mind to suffer
The slings and arrows of outrageous fortune,   59
Or to take arms against a sea of troubles
And by opposing end them. To die, to sleep—
No more—and by a sleep to say we end
The heartache and the thousand natural shocks
That flesh is heir to. 'Tis a consummation
Devoutly to be wished. To die, to sleep;
To sleep, perchance to dream. Ay, there's the rub,   66
For in that sleep of death what dreams may come,
When we have shuffled off this mortal coil,   68
Must give us pause. There's the respect   69
That makes calamity of so long life.   70
For who would bear the whips and scorns of time,   71
Th' oppressor's wrong, the proud man's contumely,   72
The pangs of disprized love, the law's delay,   73
The insolence of office, and the spurns   74
That patient merit of th' unworthy takes,   75
When he himself might his quietus make   76
With a bare bodkin? Who would fardels bear,   77
To grunt and sweat under a weary life,
But that the dread of something after death,
The undiscovered country from whose bourn   80
No traveler returns, puzzles the will,

56 s.d. withdraw (The King and Polonius may retire behind an arras.
The stage directions specify that they "enter" again near the end of the
scene.)   **59 slings** missiles   **66 rub** (Literally, an obstacle in the game of
bowls.)   **68 shuffled** sloughed, cast.   **coil** turmoil   **69 respect** consideration   **70 of . . . life** so long-lived (also suggesting that long life is itself
a calamity)   **71 time** the world we live in   **72 contumely** insolent
abuse   **73 disprized** unvalued   **74 office** officialdom.   **spurns** insults
75 of . . . takes receives from unworthy persons   **76 quietus** acquittance; here, death   **77 a bare** merely a.   **bodkin** dagger.   **fardels** bur-
dens   **80 bourn** boundary

And makes us rather bear those ills we have
Than fly to others that we know not of?
Thus conscience does make cowards of us all;
And thus the native hue of resolution   85
Is sicklied o'er with the pale cast of thought,   86
And enterprises of great pitch and moment   87
With this regard their currents turn awry   88
And lose the name of action.—Soft you now,   89
The fair Ophelia. Nymph, in thy orisons   90
Be all my sins remembered.

OPHELIA   Good my lord.
How does your honor for this many a day?

HAMLET
I humbly thank you; well, well, well.

OPHELIA
My lord, I have remembrances of yours,
That I have longèd long to redeliver.
I pray you, now receive them.   [*She offers tokens.*]

HAMLET
No, not I. I never gave you aught.

OPHELIA
My honored lord, you know right well you did,
And with them words of so sweet breath composed
As made the things more rich. Their perfume lost,
Take these again, for to the noble mind
Rich gifts wax poor when givers prove unkind.
There, my lord.   [*She gives tokens.*]

HAMLET   Ha, ha! Are you honest?   104

OPHELIA   My lord?

HAMLET   Are you fair?   106

OPHELIA   What means your lordship?

HAMLET   That if you be honest and fair, your honesty   108
should admit no discourse to your beauty.   109

OPHELIA   Could beauty, my lord, have better commerce   110
than with honesty?

85 native hue natural color, complexion   **86 cast** tinge, shade of color
87 pitch height (as of a falcon's flight).   **moment** importance   **88 regard**
respect, consideration.   **currents** courses   **89 Soft you** i.e., wait a minute,
gently   **90 orisons** prayers   **104 honest** (1) truthful (2) chaste   **106 fair**
(1) beautiful (2) just, honorable   **108 your honesty** your chastity
109 discourse to familiar dealings with   **110 commerce** dealings,
intercourse

HAMLET Ay, truly, for the power of beauty will sooner
transform honesty from what it is to a bawd than the
force of honesty can translate beauty into his likeness. 114
This was sometime a paradox, but now the time gives 115
it proof. I did love you once.

OPHELIA Indeed, my lord, you made me believe so.

HAMLET You should not have believed me, for virtue
cannot so inoculate our old stock but we shall relish of 119
it. I loved you not. 120

OPHELIA I was the more deceived.

HAMLET Get thee to a nunnery. Why wouldst thou be a 122
breeder of sinners? I am myself indifferent honest, but 123
yet I could accuse me of such things that it were better
my mother had not borne me: I am very proud, re-
vengeful, ambitious, with more offenses at my beck 126
than I have thoughts to put them in, imagination to
give them shape, or time to act them in. What should
such fellows as I do crawling between earth and
heaven? We are arrant knaves all; believe none of us.
Go thy ways to a nunnery. Where's your father?

OPHELIA At home, my lord.

HAMLET Let the doors be shut upon him, that he may
play the fool nowhere but in 's own house. Farewell.

OPHELIA O, help him, you sweet heavens!

HAMLET If thou dost marry, I'll give thee this plague for
thy dowry: be thou as chaste as ice, as pure as snow,
thou shalt not escape calumny. Get thee to a nunnery,
farewell. Or, if thou wilt needs marry, marry a fool,
for wise men know well enough what monsters you 140
make of them. To a nunnery, go, and quickly too. Farewell.

OPHELIA Heavenly powers, restore him!

HAMLET I have heard of your paintings too, well
enough. God hath given you one face, and you make

---

114 his its   115 sometime formerly.   a paradox a view opposite to
commonly held opinion.   the time the present age   119 inoculate graft,
be engrafted to   119–120 but . . . it i.e., that we do not still have about
us a taste of the old stock, i.e., retain our sinfulness   122 nunnery
convent (with possibly an awareness that the word was also used derisively to denote a brothel)   123 indifferent honest reasonably virtuous   126 beck command   140 monsters (An allusion to the horns of a
cuckold.)   you i.e., you women

yourselves another. You jig, you amble, and you 146
lisp, you nickname God's creatures, and make your 147
wantonness your ignorance. Go to, I'll no more on 't; 148
it hath made me mad. I say we will have no more
marriage. Those that are married already—all but
one—shall live. The rest shall keep as they are. To a
nunnery, go.　　　　　　　　　　　　　　　*Exit.*

OPHELIA
O, what a noble mind is here o'erthrown!
The courtier's, soldier's, scholar's, eye, tongue, sword,
Th' expectancy and rose of the fair state,　　　　155
The glass of fashion and the mold of form,　　　　156
Th' observed of all observers, quite, quite down!　157
And I, of ladies most deject and wretched,
That sucked the honey of his music vows,
Now see that noble and most sovereign reason
Like sweet bells jangled out of tune and harsh,
That unmatched form and feature of blown youth　162
Blasted with ecstasy. O, woe is me,　　　　　　163
T' have seen what I have seen, see what I see!

　　　Enter King and Polonius.

KING
Love? His affections do not that way tend;　　　165
Nor what he spake, though it lacked form a little,
Was not like madness. There's something in his soul
O'er which his melancholy sits on brood,　　　　168
And I do doubt the hatch and the disclose　　　169
Will be some danger; which for to prevent,
I have in quick determination
Thus set it down: he shall with speed to England　172

146 **jig** i.e., dance and sing affectedly and wantonly. **amble** dance,
move coquettishly 147 **lisp** (A wanton affectation.) **nickname** find a
new name for, transform (as in using cosmetics) 147–148 **make . . .
ignorance** i.e., excuse your affectation on the grounds of your ignorance 148 **on 't** of it 155 **Th' expectancy . . . state** the hope and
ornament of the kingdom made fair (by him) 156 **The glass . . . form**
the mirror of true self-fashioning and the pattern of courtly behavior
157 **Th' observed . . . observers** i.e., the center of attention and honor in
the court 162 **blown** blooming 163 **Blasted** withered. **ecstasy** madness 165 **affections** emotions, feelings 168 **sits on brood** sits like a
bird on a nest, about to *hatch* mischief (l. 169) 169 **doubt** fear.
disclose disclosure, hatching 172 **set it down** resolved

For the demand of our neglected tribute.   173
Haply the seas and countries different
With variable objects shall expel   175
This something settled matter in his heart,   176
Whereon his brains still beating puts him thus   177
From fashion of himself. What think you on 't?   178

POLONIUS
It shall do well. But yet do I believe
The origin and commencement of his grief
Sprung from neglected love.—How now, Ophelia?
You need not tell us what Lord Hamlet said;
We heard it all.—My lord, do as you please,
But, if you hold it fit, after the play
Let his queen-mother all alone entreat him   185
To show his grief. Let her be round with him;   186
And I'll be placed, so please you, in the ear
Of all their conference. If she find him not,   188
To England send him, or confine him where
Your wisdom best shall think.

KING   It shall be so.
Madness in great ones must not unwatched go.
                                                        Exeunt

❖

3.2   *Enter Hamlet and three of the Players.*

HAMLET   Speak the speech, I pray you, as I pronounced
it to you, trippingly on the tongue. But if you mouth
it, as many of our players do, I had as lief the town   3
crier spoke my lines. Nor do not saw the air too much
with your hand, thus, but use all gently; for in the very
torrent, tempest, and, as I may say, whirlwind of your

173 **For . . . of** to demand   175 **variable objects** various sights and
surroundings to divert him   176 **This something . . . heart** the strange
unidentified matter settled in his heart   177 **still** continually
178 **From . . . himself** out of his natural manner   185 **queen-mother**
queen and mother, not widowed dowager   186 **round** blunt   188 **find
him not** fails to discover what is troubling him

3.2. Location: The castle.
3 **our players** (Indefinite use; i.e., players nowadays.)   **I had as lief** I
would just as soon

passion, you must acquire and beget a temperance
that may give it smoothness. O, it offends me to the
soul to hear a robustious periwig-pated fellow tear a 9
passion to tatters, to very rags, to split the ears of the
groundlings, who for the most part are capable of 11
nothing but inexplicable dumb shows and noise. I
would have such a fellow whipped for o'erdoing Ter- 13
magant. It out-Herods Herod. Pray you, avoid it.   14

FIRST PLAYER   I warrant your honor.

HAMLET   Be not too tame neither, but let your own discretion be your tutor. Suit the action to the word, the
word to the action, with this special observance, that
you o'erstep not the modesty of nature. For anything 19
so o'erdone is from the purpose of playing, whose 20
end, both at the first and now, was and is to hold as
'twere the mirror up to nature, to show virtue her
feature, scorn her own image, and the very age and 23
body of the time his form and pressure. Now this 24
overdone or come tardy off, though it makes the un- 25
skillful laugh, cannot but make the judicious grieve, 26
the censure of the which one must in your allowance 27
o'erweigh a whole theater of others. O, there be players that I have seen play, and heard others praise, and
that highly, not to speak it profanely, that, neither 30
having th' accent of Christians nor the gait of Chris- 31
tian, pagan, nor man, have so strutted and bellowed 32
that I have thought some of nature's journeymen had 33

---

9 robustious violent, boisterous.   **periwig-pated** wearing a wig
11 groundlings spectators who paid least and stood in the yard of the
theater.   **capable of** able to understand   **13–14 Termagant** a supposed
deity of the Mohammedans, not found in any English medieval play but
elsewhere portrayed as violent and blustering   **14 Herod** Herod of
Jewry. (A character in *The Slaughter of the Innocents* and other cycle
plays. The part was played with great noise and fury.)   **19 modesty**
restraint, moderation   **20 from** contrary to   **23 scorn** i.e., something
foolish and deserving of scorn   **23–24 the very . . . time** i.e., the present
state of affairs   **24 his** its.   **pressure** stamp, impressed character
25 come tardy off inadequately done   **25–26 the unskillful** those lacking in judgment   **27 the censure . . . one** the judgment of even one of
whom.   **your allowance** your scale of values   **30 not . . . profanely**
(Hamlet anticipates his idea in ll. 33–34 that some men were not made
by God at all.)   **31 Christians** i.e., ordinary decent folk   **32 nor man** i.e.,
nor any human being at all   **33 journeymen** laborers not yet masters in
their trade

made men and not made them well, they imitated humanity so abominably.   35
FIRST PLAYER   I hope we have reformed that indifferently   36
with us, sir.
HAMLET   O, reform it altogether. And let those that play
your clowns speak no more than is set down for them;
for there be of them that will themselves laugh, to set   40
on some quantity of barren spectators to laugh too,   41
though in the meantime some necessary question of
the play be then to be considered. That's villainous,
and shows a most pitiful ambition in the fool that uses
it. Go make you ready.   [*Exeunt Players.*]

    Enter Polonius, Guildenstern, and Rosencrantz.

How now, my lord, will the King hear this piece of
work?
POLONIUS   And the Queen too, and that presently.   48
HAMLET   Bid the players make haste.   [*Exit Polonius.*]
Will you two help to hasten them?
ROSENCRANTZ
Ay, my lord.   *Exeunt they two.*
HAMLET   What ho, Horatio!

    Enter Horatio.

HORATIO   Here, sweet lord, at your service.
HAMLET
Horatio, thou art e'en as just a man
As e'er my conversation coped withal.   54
HORATIO
O, my dear lord—
HAMLET   Nay, do not think I flatter,
For what advancement may I hope from thee
That no revenue hast but thy good spirits
To feed and clothe thee? Why should the poor be
   flattered?

---

35 abominably (Shakespeare's usual spelling, *abhominably*, suggests a
literal though etymologically incorrect meaning, "removed from human
nature.")   **36 indifferently** tolerably   **40 of them** i.e., some among
them   **41 barren** i.e., of wit   **48 presently** at once   **54 my ... withal** my
contact with people provided opportunity for encounter with

No, let the candied tongue lick absurd pomp,　　　59
And crook the pregnant hinges of the knee　　　60
Where thrift may follow fawning. Dost thou hear?　　61
Since my dear soul was mistress of her choice
And could of men distinguish her election,　　　63
Sh' hath sealed thee for herself, for thou hast been　64
As one, in suffering all, that suffers nothing,
A man that Fortune's buffets and rewards
Hast ta'en with equal thanks; and blest are those
Whose blood and judgment are so well commeddled　68
That they are not a pipe for Fortune's finger
To sound what stop she please. Give me that man　70
That is not passion's slave, and I will wear him
In my heart's core, ay, in my heart of heart,
As I do thee.—Something too much of this.—
There is a play tonight before the King.
One scene of it comes near the circumstance
Which I have told thee of my father's death.
I prithee, when thou seest that act afoot,
Even with the very comment of thy soul　　　78
Observe my uncle. If his occulted guilt　　　79
Do not itself unkennel in one speech,　　　80
It is a damnèd ghost that we have seen,　　　81
And my imaginations are as foul
As Vulcan's stithy. Give him heedful note,　　　83
For I mine eyes will rivet to his face,
And after we will both our judgments join
In censure of his seeming.
HORATIO　　　　　　　Well, my lord.　　　86
If 'a steal aught the whilst this play is playing　87
And scape detecting, I will pay the theft.

---

59 candied sugared, flattering　**60 pregnant** compliant　**61 thrift**
profit　**63 could . . . election** could make distinguishing choices among
men　**64 sealed thee** (Literally, as one would seal a legal document to
mark possession.)　**68 blood** passion.　**commeddled** commingled
70 stop hole in a wind instrument for controlling the sound　**78 very
. . . soul** i.e., your most penetrating observation and consideration
79 occulted hidden　**80 unkennel** (As one would say of a fox driven from
its lair.)　**81 damnèd** in league with Satan　**83 stithy** smithy, place of
stiths (anvils)　**86 censure of his seeming** judgment of his appearance or
behavior　**87 If 'a steal aught** i.e., if he hides anything

*[Flourish.] Enter trumpets and kettledrums,
King, Queen, Polonius, Ophelia, [Rosencrantz,
Guildenstern, and other lords, with guards
carrying torches].*

HAMLET   They are coming to the play. I must be idle. 89
Get you a place.   *[The King, Queen, and courtiers sit.]*

KING   How fares our cousin Hamlet?   91

HAMLET   Excellent, i' faith, of the chameleon's dish: I eat 92
the air, promise-crammed. You cannot feed capons so. 93

KING   I have nothing with this answer, Hamlet. These 94
words are not mine.   95

HAMLET   No, nor mine now. *[To Polonius.]* My lord, 96
you played once i' th' university, you say?

POLONIUS   That did I, my lord, and was accounted a
good actor.

HAMLET   What did you enact?

POLONIUS   I did enact Julius Caesar. I was killed i' the
Capitol; Brutus killed me.

HAMLET   It was a brute part of him to kill so capital a 103
calf there.—Be the players ready?   104

ROSENCRANTZ   Ay, my lord. They stay upon your patience.

QUEEN   Come hither, my dear Hamlet, sit by me.

HAMLET   No, good Mother, here's metal more attractive. 108

POLONIUS *[To the King]*   Oho, do you mark that?

HAMLET   Lady, shall I lie in your lap?
                         [Lying down at Ophelia's feet.]

OPHELIA   No, my lord.

HAMLET   I mean, my head upon your lap?

OPHELIA   Ay, my lord.

89 idle (1) unoccupied (2) mad   **91 cousin** i.e., close relative
92 chameleon's dish (Chameleons were supposed to feed on air. Hamlet
deliberately misinterprets the King's *fares* as "feeds." By his phrase *eat
the air* he also plays on the idea of feeding himself with the promise of
succession, of being the *heir*.)   **93 capons** roosters castrated and
crammed with feed to make them succulent   **94 have . . . with** make
nothing of, or gain nothing from   **95 are not mine** do not respond to
what I asked   **96 nor mine now** (Once spoken, words are proverbially
no longer the speaker's own—and hence should be uttered warily.)
103 brute (The Latin meaning of *brutus*, "stupid," was often used
punningly with the name Brutus.)   **part** (1) deed (2) role   **104 calf**
fool   **108 metal** substance that is *attractive*, i.e., magnetic, but with
suggestion also of *mettle*, disposition

HAMLET Do you think I meant country matters? 114
OPHELIA I think nothing, my lord.
HAMLET That's a fair thought to lie between maids' legs.
OPHELIA What is, my lord?
HAMLET Nothing. 119
OPHELIA You are merry, my lord.
HAMLET Who, I?
OPHELIA Ay, my lord.
HAMLET O God, your only jig maker. What should a 123 man do but be merry? For look you how cheerfully my mother looks, and my father died within 's two hours. 125
OPHELIA Nay, 'tis twice two months, my lord.
HAMLET So long? Nay then, let the devil wear black, for I'll have a suit of sables. O heavens! Die two months 128 ago, and not forgotten yet? Then there's hope a great man's memory may outlive his life half a year. But, by 'r Lady, 'a must build churches, then, or else shall 'a suffer not thinking on, with the hobbyhorse, whose 132 epitaph is "For O, for O, the hobbyhorse is forgot." 133

The trumpets sound. Dumb show follows.

Enter a King and a Queen [very lovingly]; the Queen embracing him, and he her. [She kneels, and makes show of protestation unto him.] He takes her up, and declines his head upon her neck. He lies him down upon a bank of flowers. She, seeing him asleep, leaves him. Anon comes in

114 country matters the coarse and bawdy things that country folk do (with a pun on the first syllable of *country*) **119 Nothing** the figure zero or naught, suggesting the female anatomy. (*Thing* not infrequently has a bawdy connotation of male or female anatomy, and the reference here could be male.) **123 only jig maker** very best composer of jigs (song and dance). (Hamlet replies sardonically to Ophelia's observation that he is merry by saying, "If you're looking for someone who is really merry, you've come to the right person.") **125 within 's** within this **128 suit of sables** garments trimmed with the fur of the sable, and hence suited for a wealthy person, not a mourner (but with a pun on *sable*, black, ironically suggesting mourning once again) **132 suffer . . . on** undergo oblivion **133 For . . . forgot** (Verse of a song occurring also in *Love's Labor's Lost*, 3.1.27–28. The hobbyhorse was a character made up to resemble a horse and rider, appearing in the morris dance and such May-game sports. This song laments the disappearance of such customs under pressure from the Puritans.)

another man, takes off his crown, kisses it, pours
poison in the sleeper's ears, and leaves him. The
Queen returns, finds the King dead, makes
passionate action. The Poisoner with some three or
four come in again, seem to condole with her. The
dead body is carried away. The Poisoner woos the
Queen with gifts; she seems harsh awhile, but in
the end accepts love.

                                         [Exeunt players.]

OPHELIA What means this, my lord?

HAMLET Marry, this' miching mallico; it means mis- 135
chief.

OPHELIA Belike this show imports the argument of the 137
play.

    Enter Prologue.

HAMLET We shall know by this fellow. The players cannot keep counsel; they'll tell all. 140

OPHELIA Will 'a tell us what this show meant?

HAMLET Ay, or any show that you will show him. Be 142
not you ashamed to show, he'll not shame to tell you 143
what it means.

OPHELIA You are naught, you are naught. I'll mark the 145
play.

PROLOGUE

    For us, and for our tragedy,

    Here stooping to your clemency, 148

    We beg your hearing patiently.   *[Exit.]*

HAMLET Is this a prologue, or the posy of a ring? 150

OPHELIA 'Tis brief, my lord.

HAMLET As woman's love.

    Enter [two Players as] King and Queen.

PLAYER KING

    Full thirty times hath Phoebus' cart gone round 153

135 **this' miching mallico** this is sneaking mischief   137 **Belike** probably. **argument** plot   140 **counsel** secret   142–143 **Be not you** if you are
not   145 **naught** indecent. (Ophelia is reacting to Hamlet's pointed
remarks about not being ashamed to show all.)   148 **stooping** bowing
150 **posy . . . ring** brief motto in verse inscribed in a ring   153 **Phoebus'**
cart the sun god's chariot, making its yearly cycle

Neptune's salt wash and Tellus' orbèd ground,   154
And thirty dozen moons with borrowed sheen   155
About the world have times twelve thirties been,
Since love our hearts and Hymen did our hands   157
Unite commutual in most sacred bands.   158

PLAYER QUEEN
So many journeys may the sun and moon
Make us again count o'er ere love be done!
But, woe is me, you are so sick of late,
So far from cheer and from your former state,
That I distrust you. Yet, though I distrust,   163
Discomfort you, my lord, it nothing must.   164
For women's fear and love hold quantity;   165
In neither aught, or in extremity.   166
Now, what my love is, proof hath made you know,   167
And as my love is sized, my fear is so.   168
Where love is great, the littlest doubts are fear;
Where little fears grow great, great love grows there.

PLAYER KING
Faith, I must leave thee, love, and shortly too;
My operant powers their functions leave to do.   172
And thou shalt live in this fair world behind,   173
Honored, beloved; and haply one as kind
For husband shalt thou—

PLAYER QUEEN   O, confound the rest!
Such love must needs be treason in my breast.
In second husband let me be accurst!
None wed the second but who killed the first.   178

HAMLET   Wormwood, wormwood.

PLAYER QUEEN
The instances that second marriage move   180
Are base respects of thrift, but none of love.   181

154 salt wash the sea. Tellus goddess of the earth, of the *orbèd
ground* 155 borrowed i.e., reflected 157 Hymen god of matrimony
158 commutual mutually. bands bonds 163 distrust am anxious
about 164 nothing not at all 165 hold quantity keep proportion with
one another 166 In . . . extremity i.e., women fear and love either too
little or too much, but the two, fear and love, are equal in either case
167 proof experience 168 sized in size 172 operant powers vital
functions. leave to do cease to perform 173 behind after I have
gone 178 None i.e., let no woman. but who except her who
180 instances motives. move motivate 181 base . . . thrift ignoble
considerations of material prosperity

A second time I kill my husband dead
When second husband kisses me in bed.

PLAYER KING

I do believe you think what now you speak,
But what we do determine oft we break.
Purpose is but the slave to memory,   186
Of violent birth, but poor validity,   187
Which now, like fruit unripe, sticks on the tree,   188
But fall unshaken when they mellow be.
Most necessary 'tis that we forget   190
To pay ourselves what to ourselves is debt.   191
What to ourselves in passion we propose,
The passion ending, doth the purpose lose.
The violence of either grief or joy
Their own enactures with themselves destroy.   195
Where joy most revels, grief doth most lament;   196
Grief joys, joy grieves, on slender accident.   197
This world is not for aye, nor 'tis not strange   198
That even our loves should with our fortunes change;
For 'tis a question left us yet to prove,
Whether love lead fortune, or else fortune love.
The great man down, you mark his favorite flies;   202
The poor advanced makes friends of enemies.   203
And hitherto doth love on fortune tend;   204
For who not needs shall never lack a friend,   205
And who in want a hollow friend doth try   206
Directly seasons him his enemy.   207
But, orderly to end where I begun,
Our wills and fates do so contrary run   209

186 **Purpose . . . memory** i.e., our good intentions are subject to forgetfulness   187 **validity** strength, durability   188 **Which** i.e., purpose
190–191 **Most . . . debt** i.e., it's inevitable that in time we forget the
obligations we have imposed on ourselves   195 **enactures** fulfillments
196–197 **Where . . . accident** i.e., the capacity for extreme joy and grief
go together, and often one extreme is instantly changed into its opposite
on the slightest provocation   198 **aye** ever   202 **down** fallen in fortune
203 **The poor . . . enemies** i.e., when one of humble station is promoted,
you see his enemies suddenly becoming his friends   204 **hitherto** up to
this point in the argument, or, to this extent.   **tend** attend   205 **who not
needs** he who is not in need (of wealth)   206 **who in want** he who, being
in need.   **try** test (his generosity)   207 **seasons him** ripens him into
209 **Our . . . run** what we want and what we get go so contrarily

That our devices still are overthrown;   210
Our thoughts are ours, their ends none of our own.   211
So think thou wilt no second husband wed,
But die thy thoughts when thy first lord is dead.

PLAYER QUEEN
Nor earth to me give food, nor heaven light,   214
Sport and repose lock from me day and night,   215
To desperation turn my trust and hope,
An anchor's cheer in prison be my scope!   217
Each opposite that blanks the face of joy   218
Meet what I would have well and it destroy!   219
Both here and hence pursue me lasting strife   220
If, once a widow, ever I be a wife!

HAMLET   If she should break it now!

PLAYER KING
'Tis deeply sworn. Sweet, leave me here awhile;
My spirits grow dull, and fain I would beguile   224
The tedious day with sleep.

PLAYER QUEEN   Sleep rock thy brain,
And never come mischance between us twain!
            [*He sleeps.*] *Exit* [*Player Queen*].

HAMLET   Madam, how like you this play?

QUEEN   The lady doth protest too much, methinks.   228

HAMLET   O, but she'll keep her word.

KING   Have you heard the argument? Is there no offense   230
in 't?

HAMLET   No, no, they do but jest, poison in jest. No of-   232
fense i' the world.   233

KING   What do you call the play?

HAMLET   *The Mousetrap.* Marry, how? Tropically.   235
This play is the image of a murder done in Vienna.

---

210 devices still intentions continually   **211 ends** results   **214 Nor** let
neither   **215 Sport . . . night** may day deny me its pastimes and night
its repose   **217 anchor's cheer** anchorite's or hermit's fare.   **my scope**
the extent of my happiness   **218–219 Each . . . destroy** may every
adverse thing that causes the face of joy to turn pale meet and destroy
everything that I desire to see prosper.   **blanks** causes to blanch or
grow pale   **220 hence** in the life hereafter   **224 spirits** vital spirits
228 doth . . . much makes too many promises and protestations
230 argument plot   **230–233 offense . . . offense** cause for objection . . .
crime   **232 jest** make believe   **235 Tropically** figuratively. (The first
quarto reading, *trapically,* suggests a pun on *trap* in *Mousetrap*.)

Gonzago is the Duke's name, his wife, Baptista. You 237
shall see anon. 'Tis a knavish piece of work, but what
of that? Your Majesty, and we that have free souls, it 239
touches us not. Let the galled jade wince, our withers 240
are unwrung.   241

Enter Lucianus.

This is one Lucianus, nephew to the King.

OPHELIA   You are as good as a chorus, my lord.   243

HAMLET   I could interpret between you and your love,
  if I could see the puppets dallying.   245

OPHELIA   You are keen, my lord, you are keen.   246

HAMLET   It would cost you a groaning to take off mine
edge.

OPHELIA   Still better, and worse.   249

HAMLET   So you mis-take your husbands.—Begin, mur-   250
derer; leave thy damnable faces and begin. Come, the
croaking raven doth bellow for revenge.

LUCIANUS
Thoughts black, hands apt, drugs fit, and time agreeing,
Confederate season, else no creature seeing,   254
Thou mixture rank, of midnight weeds collected,
With Hecate's ban thrice blasted, thrice infected,   256
Thy natural magic and dire property   257
On wholesome life usurp immediately.
    [*He pours the poison into the sleeper's ear.*]

---

237 Duke's i.e., King's. (A slip that may be due to Shakespeare's possible source, the actual murder of the Duke of Urbino by Luigi Gonzaga in 1538.)   **239 free** guiltless   **240 galled jade** horse whose hide is rubbed by saddle or harness.   **withers** the part between the horse's shoulder blades   **241 unwrung** not rubbed sore   **243 chorus** (In many Elizabethan plays the forthcoming action was explained by an actor known as the "chorus"; at a puppet show the actor who spoke the dialogue was known as an "interpreter," as indicated by the lines following.)   **245 puppets dallying** (With sexual suggestion, continued in *keen*, i.e., sexually aroused, *groaning*, i.e., moaning in pregnancy, and *edge*, i.e., sexual desire or impetuosity.)   **246 keen** sharp, bitter
249 Still . . . worse more keen, always *bettering* what other people say with witty wordplay, but at the same time more offensive   **250 So** even thus (in marriage).   **mis-take** take erringly, falseheartedly. (The marriage vows say, "for better, for worse.")   **254 Confederate season** the time and occasion conspiring (to assist the murderer).   **else** otherwise
256 Hecate's ban the curse of Hecate, the goddess of witchcraft
257 dire property baleful quality

HAMLET 'A poisons him i' the garden for his estate. His 259
name's Gonzago. The story is extant, and written in
very choice Italian. You shall see anon how the murderer gets the love of Gonzago's wife.

[Claudius rises.]

OPHELIA The King rises.

HAMLET What, frighted with false fire?   264

QUEEN How fares my lord?

POLONIUS Give o'er the play.

KING Give me some light. Away!

POLONIUS Lights, lights, lights!

Exeunt all but Hamlet and Horatio.

HAMLET
"Why, let the strucken deer go weep,   269
    The hart ungallèd play.   270
For some must watch, while some must sleep;   271
    Thus runs the world away."   272
Would not this, sir, and a forest of feathers—if the rest 273
of my fortunes turn Turk with me—with two Provin- 274
cial roses on my razed shoes, get me a fellowship in a 275
cry of players?   276

HORATIO Half a share.

HAMLET A whole one, I.
"For thou dost know, O Damon dear,   279
    This realm dismantled was   280
Of Jove himself, and now reigns here   281
    A very, very—pajock."   282

---

259 estate i.e., the kingship. **His** i.e., the King's **264 false fire**
the blank discharge of a gun loaded with powder but no shot
269–272 Why . . . away (Probably from an old ballad, with allusion to
the popular belief that a wounded deer retires to weep and die; cf. *As
You Like It*, 2.1.66.) **270 ungallèd** unafflicted **271 watch** remain
awake **272 Thus . . . away** thus the world goes **273 this** i.e., the play.
feathers (Allusion to the plumes that Elizabethan actors were fond of
wearing.) **274 turn Turk with** turn renegade against, go back on
274–275 Provincial roses rosettes of ribbon like the roses of a part of
France **275 razed** with ornamental slashing **275–276 fellowship
. . . players** partnership in a theatrical company. **cry** pack (of
hounds) **279 Damon** the friend of Pythias, as Horatio is friend of
Hamlet; or, a traditional pastoral name **280 dismantled** stripped,
divested **281 Of Jove** (Jove, like Hamlet's father, has been taken away,
leaving only a peacock or an ass.) **282 pajock** peacock, a bird with a
bad reputation. (Here substituted for the obvious rhyme-word "ass.")
Or possibly the word is *patchock*, savage, base person.

HORATIO You might have rhymed.

HAMLET O good Horatio, I'll take the ghost's word for
a thousand pound. Didst perceive?

HORATIO Very well, my lord.

HAMLET Upon the talk of the poisoning?

HORATIO I did very well note him.

Enter Rosencrantz and Guildenstern.

HAMLET Aha! Come, some music! Come, the record- 289
ers.   290

  "For if the King like not the comedy,
   Why then, belike, he likes it not, perdy."   292
Come, some music.

GUILDENSTERN Good my lord, vouchsafe me a word
with you.

HAMLET Sir, a whole history.

GUILDENSTERN The King, sir—

HAMLET Ay, sir, what of him?

GUILDENSTERN Is in his retirement marvelous dis- 299
tempered.   300

HAMLET With drink, sir?

GUILDENSTERN No, my lord, with choler.   302

HAMLET Your wisdom should show itself more richer
to signify this to the doctor, for for me to put him to
his purgation would perhaps plunge him into more 305
choler.

GUILDENSTERN Good my lord, put your discourse into
some frame and start not so wildly from my affair.   308

HAMLET I am tame, sir. Pronounce.

GUILDENSTERN The Queen, your mother, in most great
affliction of spirit, hath sent me to you.

HAMLET You are welcome.

289–290 recorders wind instruments of the flute kind   **292 perdy** (A
corruption of the French *par dieu,* "by God.")   **299 retirement** withdrawal to his chambers   **299–300 distempered** out of humor. (But
Hamlet deliberately plays on the wider application to any illness of
mind or body, as in ll. 335–336, especially to drunkenness.)   **302 choler**
i.e., anger. (But Hamlet takes the word in its more basic humors sense
of "bilious disorder.")   **305 purgation** (Hamlet hints at something going
beyond medical treatment to bloodletting and the extraction of confession.)   **308 frame** order.   **start** shy or jump away (like a horse; the
opposite of *tame* in l. 309)

GUILDENSTERN　Nay, good my lord, this courtesy is not
of the right breed. If it shall please you to make me a　314
wholesome answer, I will do your mother's commandment; if not, your pardon and my return shall be the　316
end of my business.

HAMLET　Sir, I cannot.

ROSENCRANTZ　What, my lord?

HAMLET　Make you a wholesome answer; my wit's diseased. But, sir, such answer as I can make, you shall
command, or rather, as you say, my mother. Therefore
no more, but to the matter. My mother, you say—

ROSENCRANTZ　Then thus she says: your behavior hath
struck her into amazement and admiration.　325

HAMLET　O wonderful son, that can so stonish a mother!
But is there no sequel at the heels of this mother's admiration? Impart.

ROSENCRANTZ　She desires to speak with you in her
closet ere you go to bed.　330

HAMLET　We shall obey, were she ten times our mother.
Have you any further trade with us?

ROSENCRANTZ　My lord, you once did love me.

HAMLET　And do still, by these pickers and stealers.　334

ROSENCRANTZ　Good my lord, what is your cause of distemper? You do surely bar the door upon your own
liberty if you deny your griefs to your friend.　337

HAMLET　Sir, I lack advancement.

ROSENCRANTZ　How can that be, when you have the
voice of the King himself for your succession in Denmark?

HAMLET　Ay, sir, but "While the grass grows"—the　342
proverb is something musty.　343

Enter the Players with recorders.

O, the recorders. Let me see one. [*He takes a recorder.*]

---

314 breed (1) kind (2) breeding, manners　**316 pardon** permission
to depart　**325 admiration** wonder　**330 closet** private chamber
334 pickers and stealers i.e., hands. (So called from the catechism, "to
keep my hands from picking and stealing.")　**337 deny** refuse to share
342 While . . . grows (The rest of the proverb is "the silly horse starves";
Hamlet may not live long enough to succeed to the kingdom.)
343 something somewhat　**s.d. Players** actors

To withdraw with you: why do you go about to recover 345
the wind of me, as if you would drive me into a toil? 346

GUILDENSTERN   O, my lord, if my duty be too bold, my 347
love is too unmannerly. 348

HAMLET   I do not well understand that. Will you play 349
upon this pipe?

GUILDENSTERN   My lord, I cannot.

HAMLET   I pray you.

GUILDENSTERN   Believe me, I cannot.

HAMLET   I do beseech you.

GUILDENSTERN   I know no touch of it, my lord.

HAMLET   It is as easy as lying. Govern these ventages 356
with your fingers and thumb, give it breath with your
mouth, and it will discourse most eloquent music.
Look you, these are the stops.

GUILDENSTERN   But these cannot I command to any
utterance of harmony. I have not the skill.

HAMLET   Why, look you now, how unworthy a thing
you make of me! You would play upon me, you would
seem to know my stops, you would pluck out the heart
of my mystery, you would sound me from my lowest 365
note to the top of my compass, and there is much 366
music, excellent voice, in this little organ, yet cannot 367
you make it speak. 'Sblood, do you think I am easier
to be played on than a pipe? Call me what instrument
you will, though you can fret me, you cannot play 370
upon me.

Enter Polonius.

God bless you, sir!

POLONIUS   My lord, the Queen would speak with you,
and presently. 374

HAMLET   Do you see yonder cloud that's almost in
shape of a camel?

---

345 withdraw speak privately   **345–346 recover the wind** get to the
windward side (thus driving the game into the toil, or net)   **346 toil**
snare   **347–348 if . . . unmannerly** if I am using an unmannerly boldness, it is my love that occasions it   **349 I . . . that** i.e., I don't understand how genuine love can be unmannerly   **356 ventages** stops of the
recorder   **365 sound** (1) fathom (2) produce sound in   **366 compass**
range (of voice)   **367 organ** musical instrument   **370 fret** irritate (with a
quibble on *fret* meaning the piece of wood, gut, or metal that regulates
the fingering on an instrument)   **374 presently** at once

POLONIUS　By the Mass and 'tis, like a camel indeed.
HAMLET　Methinks it is like a weasel.
POLONIUS　It is backed like a weasel.
HAMLET　Or like a whale?
POLONIUS　Very like a whale.
HAMLET　Then I will come to my mother by and by. 382
　[*Aside.*] They fool me to the top of my bent.—I will 383
　come by and by.
POLONIUS　I will say so.　　　　　　　　　　　　[*Exit.*]
HAMLET　"By and by" is easily said. Leave me, friends.
　　　　　　　　　　　　　　　　[*Exeunt all but Hamlet.*]
　'Tis now the very witching time of night,　　　　　387
　When churchyards yawn and hell itself breathes out
　Contagion to this world. Now could I drink hot blood 389
　And do such bitter business as the day
　Would quake to look on. Soft, now to my mother.
　O heart, lose not thy nature! Let not ever
　The soul of Nero enter this firm bosom.　　　　　393
　Let me be cruel, not unnatural;
　I will speak daggers to her, but use none.
　My tongue and soul in this be hypocrites:
　How in my words soever she be shent,　　　　　397
　To give them seals never my soul consent!　　*Exit.* 398

❖

3.3　*Enter King, Rosencrantz, and Guildenstern.*

KING
　I like him not, nor stands it safe with us　　　　1
　To let his madness range. Therefore prepare you.
　I your commission will forthwith dispatch,　　　　3
　And he to England shall along with you.

---

382 by and by quite soon　**383 fool me** make me play the fool.　**top of my bent** limit of my ability or endurance. (Literally, the extent to which a bow may be bent.)　**387 witching time** time when spells are cast and evil is abroad　**389 Now could I** i.e., now I might be tempted to　**393 Nero** murderer of his mother, Agrippina　**397 How . . . soever** however much by my words.　**shent** rebuked　**398 give them seals** i.e., confirm them with deeds

3.3. Location: The castle.
1 him i.e., his behavior　**3 dispatch** prepare, cause to be drawn up

The terms of our estate may not endure   5
Hazard so near 's as doth hourly grow
Out of his brows.
GUILDENSTERN   We will ourselves provide.   7
Most holy and religious fear it is   8
To keep those many many bodies safe
That live and feed upon Your Majesty.

ROSENCRANTZ
The single and peculiar life is bound   11
With all the strength and armor of the mind
To keep itself from noyance, but much more   13
That spirit upon whose weal depends and rests
The lives of many. The cess of majesty   15
Dies not alone, but like a gulf doth draw   16
What's near it with it; or it is a massy wheel   17
Fixed on the summit of the highest mount,
To whose huge spokes ten thousand lesser things
Are mortised and adjoined, which, when it falls,   20
Each small annexment, petty consequence,   21
Attends the boisterous ruin. Never alone   22
Did the King sigh, but with a general groan.

KING
Arm you, I pray you, to this speedy voyage,   24
For we will fetters put about this fear,
Which now goes too free-footed.
ROSENCRANTZ   We will haste us.
     Exeunt Gentlemen [*Rosencrantz and Guildenstern*].

     Enter Polonius.

POLONIUS
My lord, he's going to his mother's closet.
Behind the arras I'll convey myself   28

5 **terms** condition, circumstances.   **our estate** my royal position
7 **brows** i.e., effrontery, threatening frowns, or contrivances   8 **religious fear** sacred duty   11 **single and peculiar** individual and private
13 **noyance** harm   15 **cess** decease, cessation   16 **gulf** whirlpool
17 **massy** massive   20 **when it falls** i.e., when it descends, like the wheel of Fortune, bringing a king down with it   21 **Each . . . consequence** i.e., every hanger-on and unimportant person or thing connected with the King   22 **Attends** participates in   24 **Arm** prepare   28 **arras** screen of tapestry placed around the walls of household apartments. (On the Elizabethan stage, the arras was presumably over a door or discovery space in the tiring-house facade.)

To hear the process. I'll warrant she'll tax him home,   29
And, as you said—and wisely was it said—
'Tis meet that some more audience than a mother,   31
Since nature makes them partial, should o'erhear
The speech, of vantage. Fare you well, my liege.   33
I'll call upon you ere you go to bed
And tell you what I know.

KING   Thanks, dear my lord.

                        Exit [Polonius].

O, my offense is rank, it smells to heaven;
It hath the primal eldest curse upon 't,   37
A brother's murder. Pray can I not,
Though inclination be as sharp as will;   39
My stronger guilt defeats my strong intent,
And like a man to double business bound   41
I stand in pause where I shall first begin,
And both neglect. What if this cursèd hand
Were thicker than itself with brother's blood,
Is there not rain enough in the sweet heavens
To wash it white as snow? Whereto serves mercy   46
But to confront the visage of offense?   47
And what's in prayer but this twofold force,
To be forestallèd ere we come to fall,   49
Or pardoned being down? Then I'll look up.
My fault is past. But, O, what form of prayer
Can serve my turn? "Forgive me my foul murder"?
That cannot be, since I am still possessed
Of those effects for which I did the murder:
My crown, mine own ambition, and my queen.
May one be pardoned and retain th' offense?   56
In the corrupted currents of this world   57
Offense's gilded hand may shove by justice,   58

---

29 process proceedings.   **tax him home** reprove him severely   **31 meet**
fitting   **33 of vantage** from an advantageous place, or, in addition
37 the primal eldest curse the curse of Cain, the first murderer; he killed
his brother Abel   **39 Though . . . will** though my desire is as strong as
my determination   **41 bound** (1) destined (2) obliged. (The King wants to
repent and still enjoy what he has gained.)   **46–47 Whereto . . . offense**
i.e., for what function does mercy serve other than to undo the effects
of sin   **49 forestallèd** prevented (from sinning)   **56 th' offense** i.e., the
thing for which one offended   **57 currents** courses   **58 gilded hand**
hand offering gold as a bribe.   **shove by** thrust aside

And oft 'tis seen the wicked prize itself   59
Buys out the law. But 'tis not so above.
There is no shuffling, there the action lies   61
In his true nature, and we ourselves compelled,   62
Even to the teeth and forehead of our faults,   63
To give in evidence. What then? What rests?   64
Try what repentance can. What can it not?
Yet what can it, when one cannot repent?
O wretched state! O bosom black as death!
O limèd soul, that, struggling to be free,   68
Art more engaged! Help, angels! Make assay.   69
Bow, stubborn knees, and heart with strings of steel,
Be soft as sinews of the newborn babe!
All may be well.   [*He kneels.*]

        Enter Hamlet.

HAMLET
Now might I do it pat, now 'a is a-praying;   73
And now I'll do 't. [*He draws his sword.*] And so 'a
    goes to heaven,
And so am I revenged. That would be scanned: 75
A villain kills my father, and for that,
I, his sole son, do this same villain send
To heaven.
Why, this is hire and salary, not revenge.
'A took my father grossly, full of bread,   80
With all his crimes broad blown, as flush as May;   81
And how his audit stands who knows save heaven?   82
But in our circumstance and course of thought   83
'Tis heavy with him. And am I then revenged,
To take him in the purging of his soul,

59 wicked prize prize won by wickedness   **61 There** i.e., in heaven.
shuffling escape by trickery.   **the action lies** the accusation is made
manifest, comes up for consideration. (A legal metaphor.)   **62 his** its
63 to the teeth and forehead face to face, concealing nothing   **64 give in**
provide.   **rests** remains   **68 limèd** caught as with birdlime, a sticky
substance used to ensnare birds   **69 engaged** embedded.   **assay** trial.
(Said to himself.)   **73 pat** opportunely   **75 would be scanned** needs to
be looked into, or, would be interpreted as follows   **80 grossly** i.e., not
spiritually prepared.   **full of bread** i.e., enjoying his worldly pleasures.
(See Ezekiel 16:49.)   **81 crimes broad blown** sins in full bloom.   **flush**
lusty   **82 audit** account   **83 in . . . thought** as we see it from our mortal
perspective

When he is fit and seasoned for his passage?   86
No!
Up, sword, and know thou a more horrid hent.   88
                 [*He puts up his sword.*]
When he is drunk asleep, or in his rage,
Or in th' incestuous pleasure of his bed,
At game a-swearing, or about some act
That has no relish of salvation in 't—   92
Then trip him, that his heels may kick at heaven,
And that his soul may be as damned and black
As hell, whereto it goes. My mother stays.   95
This physic but prolongs thy sickly days.   *Exit.* 96

KING
My words fly up, my thoughts remain below.
Words without thoughts never to heaven go.   *Exit.*

✤

3.4   *Enter [Queen] Gertrude and Polonius.*

POLONIUS
'A will come straight. Look you lay home to him.   1
Tell him his pranks have been too broad to bear with,   2
And that Your Grace hath screened and stood between
Much heat and him. I'll shroud me even here.   4
Pray you, be round with him.   5
HAMLET (*Within*)   Mother, Mother, Mother!
QUEEN   I'll warrant you, fear me not.
Withdraw, I hear him coming.
            [*Polonius hides behind the arras.*]

    Enter Hamlet.

HAMLET   Now, Mother, what's the matter?

86 seasoned matured, readied   **88 know . . . hent** await to be grasped by me on a more horrid occasion   **92 relish** trace, savor   **95 stays** awaits (me)   **96 physic** purging (by prayer), or, Hamlet's postponement of the killing

3.4. Location: The Queen's private chamber.
1 lay thrust (i.e., reprove him soundly)   **2 broad** unrestrained   **4 Much heat** i.e., the King's anger.   **shroud** conceal (with ironic fitness to Polonius's imminent death. The word is only in the first quarto; the second quarto and the Folio read "silence.")   **5 round** blunt

QUEEN
  Hamlet, thou hast thy father much offended.   10
HAMLET
  Mother, you have my father much offended.
QUEEN
  Come, come, you answer with an idle tongue.   12
HAMLET
  Go, go, you question with a wicked tongue.
QUEEN
  Why, how now, Hamlet?
HAMLET   What's the matter now?
QUEEN
  Have you forgot me?
HAMLET   No, by the rood, not so: 15
  You are the Queen, your husband's brother's wife,
  And—would it were not so!—you are my mother.
QUEEN
  Nay, then, I'll set those to you that can speak.
HAMLET
  Come, come, and sit you down; you shall not budge.
  You go not till I set you up a glass
  Where you may see the inmost part of you.
QUEEN
  What wilt thou do? Thou wilt not murder me?
  Help, ho!
POLONIUS [Behind the arras]   What ho! Help!
HAMLET [Drawing]
  How now? A rat? Dead for a ducat, dead!   25
                    [He thrusts his rapier through the arras.]
POLONIUS [Behind the arras]
  O, I am slain!   [He falls and dies.]
QUEEN   O me, what hast thou done?
HAMLET   Nay, I know not. Is it the King?
QUEEN
  O, what a rash and bloody deed is this!
HAMLET
  A bloody deed—almost as bad, good Mother,
  As kill a king and marry with his brother.

10 thy father i.e., your stepfather, Claudius   12 idle foolish   15 forgot
me i.e., forgotten that I am your mother.   rood cross of Christ
25 Dead for a ducat i.e., I bet a ducat he's dead, whoever I killed; or, a
ducat is his life's fee

QUEEN
  As kill a king!
HAMLET   Ay, lady, it was my word.
        [*He parts the arras and discovers Polonius.*]
  Thou wretched, rash, intruding fool, farewell!
  I took thee for thy better. Take thy fortune.
  Thou find'st to be too busy is some danger.—   34
  Leave wringing of your hands. Peace, sit you down,
  And let me wring your heart, for so I shall,
  If it be made of penetrable stuff,
  If damnèd custom have not brazed it so   38
  That it be proof and bulwark against sense.   39
QUEEN
  What have I done, that thou dar'st wag thy tongue
  In noise so rude against me?
HAMLET   Such an act
  That blurs the grace and blush of modesty,
  Calls virtue hypocrite, takes off the rose
  From the fair forehead of an innocent love
  And sets a blister there, makes marriage vows   45
  As false as dicers' oaths. O, such a deed
  As from the body of contraction plucks   47
  The very soul, and sweet religion makes   48
  A rhapsody of words. Heaven's face does glow   49
  O'er this solidity and compound mass   50
  With tristful visage, as against the doom,   51
  Is thought-sick at the act.
QUEEN   Ay me, what act,   52
  That roars so loud and thunders in the index?   53
HAMLET [*Showing her two likenesses*]
  Look here upon this picture, and on this,
  The counterfeit presentment of two brothers.   55
  See what a grace was seated on this brow:

34 busy playing the busybody **38 damnèd custom** habitual wickedness. **brazed** brazened, hardened **39 proof** armor. **sense** feeling **45 sets a blister** i.e., brands as a harlot **47 contraction** the marriage contract **48 sweet religion makes** i.e., makes marriage vows **49 rhapsody** senseless string **49–52 Heaven's . . . act** heaven's face looks down upon this solid world, this compound mass, with sorrowful face as though the day of doom were near, and is thought-sick at the deed (i.e., Gertrude's marriage) **53 index** table of contents, prelude or preface **55 counterfeit presentment** portrayed representation

Hyperion's curls, the front of Jove himself,   57
An eye like Mars to threaten and command,
A station like the herald Mercury   59
New-lighted on a heaven-kissing hill—   60
A combination and a form indeed
Where every god did seem to set his seal   62
To give the world assurance of a man.
This was your husband. Look you now what follows:
Here is your husband, like a mildewed ear,   65
Blasting his wholesome brother. Have you eyes?   66
Could you on this fair mountain leave to feed
And batten on this moor? Ha, have you eyes?   68
You cannot call it love, for at your age
The heyday in the blood is tame, it's humble,   70
And waits upon the judgment, and what judgment
Would step from this to this? Sense, sure, you have,   72
Else could you not have motion, but sure that sense
Is apoplexed, for madness would not err,   74
Nor sense to ecstasy was ne'er so thralled,
But it reserved some quantity of choice   76
To serve in such a difference. What devil was 't   77
That thus hath cozened you at hoodman-blind?   78
Eyes without feeling, feeling without sight,
Ears without hands or eyes, smelling sans all,   80
Or but a sickly part of one true sense
Could not so mope. O shame, where is thy blush?   82
Rebellious hell,
If thou canst mutine in a matron's bones,   84

---

57 Hyperion's the sun god's. **front** brow **59 station** manner of standing. **Mercury** winged messenger of the gods **60 New-lighted** newly
alighted **62 set his seal** i.e., affix his approval **65 ear** i.e., of grain
66 Blasting blighting **68 batten** gorge. **moor** barren upland (suggesting also "dark-skinned") **70 heyday** state of excitement. **blood** passion **72 Sense** perception through the five senses (the functions of the
middle or sensible soul) **74 apoplexed** paralyzed. (Hamlet goes on to
explain that without such a paralysis of will, mere madness would not
so err, nor would the five senses so enthrall themselves to *ecstasy* or
lunacy; even such deranged states of mind would be able to make the
obvious choice between Hamlet Senior and Claudius.) **err** so err
76 But but that **77 To . . . difference** to help in making choice between
two such men **78 cozened** cheated. **hoodman-blind** blindman's buff.
(In this game, says Hamlet, the devil must have pushed Claudius toward
Gertrude while she was blindfolded.) **80 sans** without **82 mope** be
dazed, act aimlessly **84 mutine** incite mutiny

To flaming youth let virtue be as wax   85
And melt in her own fire. Proclaim no shame   86
When the compulsive ardor gives the charge,   87
Since frost itself as actively doth burn,   88
And reason panders will.   89

QUEEN   O Hamlet, speak no more!
Thou turn'st my eyes into my very soul,
And there I see such black and grainèd spots   92
As will not leave their tinct.

HAMLET   Nay, but to live   93
In the rank sweat of an enseamèd bed,   94
Stewed in corruption, honeying and making love   95
Over the nasty sty!

QUEEN   O, speak to me no more!
These words like daggers enter in my ears.
No more, sweet Hamlet!

HAMLET   A murderer and a villain,
A slave that is not twentieth part the tithe   100
Of your precedent lord, a vice of kings,   101
A cutpurse of the empire and the rule,
That from a shelf the precious diadem stole
And put it in his pocket!

QUEEN   No more!

Enter Ghost [in his nightgown].

HAMLET   A king of shreds and patches—   106
Save me, and hover o'er me with your wings,
You heavenly guards! What would your gracious figure?

QUEEN   Alas, he's mad!

HAMLET
Do you not come your tardy son to chide,

85–86 be as wax . . . fire i.e., melt like a candle or stick of sealing wax
held over its own flame   **86–89 Proclaim . . . will** call it no shameful
business when the compelling ardor of youth delivers the attack, i.e.,
commits lechery, since the frost of advanced age burns with as active a
fire of lust and reason perverts itself by fomenting lust rather than
restraining it   **92 grainèd** dyed in grain, indelible   **93 leave their tinct**
surrender their color   **94 enseamèd** saturated in the grease and filth of
passionate lovemaking   **95 Stewed** soaked, bathed (with a suggestion of
stew, brothel)   **100 tithe** tenth part   **101 precedent** former (i.e., the
elder Hamlet).   **vice** buffoon. (A reference to the Vice of the morality
plays.)   **106 shreds and patches** i.e., motley, the traditional costume of
the clown or fool

That, lapsed in time and passion, lets go by   111
Th' important acting of your dread command?   112
O, say!

GHOST
  Do not forget. This visitation
  Is but to whet thy almost blunted purpose.
  But look, amazement on thy mother sits.
  O, step between her and her fighting soul!   116
  Conceit in weakest bodies strongest works.   118
  Speak to her, Hamlet.

HAMLET   How is it with you, lady?

QUEEN   Alas, how is 't with you,
  That you do bend your eye on vacancy,
  And with th' incorporal air do hold discourse?   122
  Forth at your eyes your spirits wildly peep,
  And, as the sleeping soldiers in th' alarm,   124
  Your bedded hair, like life in excrements,   125
  Start up and stand on end. O gentle son,
  Upon the heat and flame of thy distemper
  Sprinkle cool patience. Whereon do you look?

HAMLET
  On him, on him! Look you how pale he glares!
  His form and cause conjoined, preaching to stones, 130
  Would make them capable.—Do not look upon me,   131
  Lest with this piteous action you convert   132
  My stern effects. Then what I have to do   133
  Will want true color—tears perchance for blood.   134

QUEEN   To whom do you speak this?

HAMLET   Do you see nothing there?

111 **lapsed in time and passion** having allowed time to lapse and passion to cool, or, having lost momentum through excessive indulgence in
passion 112 **important** importunate, urgent 116 **amazement** distraction 118 **Conceit** imagination 122 **incorporal** immaterial 124 **as . . .
alarm** like soldiers called out of sleep by an alarum 125 **bedded** laid in
smooth layers. **like life in excrements** i.e., as though hair, an out-
growth of the body, had a life of its own. (Hair was thought to be lifeless
because it lacks sensation, and so its standing on end would be unnatural and ominous.) 130 **His . . . conjoined** his appearance joined to his
cause for speaking 131 **capable** receptive 132–133 **convert . . . effects**
divert me from my stern duty 134 **want . . . blood** lack plausibility so
that (with a play on the normal sense of *color*) I shall shed colorless
tears instead of blood

QUEEN
  Nothing at all, yet all that is I see.
HAMLET   Nor did you nothing hear?
QUEEN   No, nothing but ourselves.
HAMLET
  Why, look you there, look how it steals away!
  My father, in his habit as he lived!   141
  Look where he goes even now out at the portal!
                                            Exit Ghost.

QUEEN
  This is the very coinage of your brain.   143
  This bodiless creation ecstasy   144
  Is very cunning in.   145
HAMLET   Ecstasy?
  My pulse as yours doth temperately keep time,
  And makes as healthful music. It is not madness
  That I have uttered. Bring me to the test,
  And I the matter will reword, which madness   150
  Would gambol from. Mother, for love of grace,   151
  Lay not that flattering unction to your soul   152
  That not your trespass but my madness speaks.
  It will but skin and film the ulcerous place,   154
  Whiles rank corruption, mining all within,   155
  Infects unseen. Confess yourself to heaven,
  Repent what's past, avoid what is to come,
  And do not spread the compost on the weeds   158
  To make them ranker. Forgive me this my virtue;   159
  For in the fatness of these pursy times   160
  Virtue itself of vice must pardon beg,
  Yea, curb and woo for leave to do him good.   162
QUEEN
  O Hamlet, thou hast cleft my heart in twain.
HAMLET
  O, throw away the worser part of it,

141 **habit** dress. **as** as when   143 **very** mere   144–145 **This . . . in**
madness is skillful in creating this kind of hallucination   150 **reword**
repeat word for word   151 **gambol** skip away   152 **unction** ointment
154 **skin** grow a skin for   155 **mining** working under the surface
158 **compost** manure   159 **this my virtue** my virtuous talk in reproving
you   160 **fatness** grossness. **pursy** flabby, out of shape   162 **curb** bow,
bend the knee. **leave** permission

And live the purer with the other half.
Good night. But go not to my uncle's bed;
Assume a virtue, if you have it not.
That monster, custom, who all sense doth eat,   168
Of habits devil, is angel yet in this,   169
That to the use of actions fair and good
He likewise gives a frock or livery   171
That aptly is put on. Refrain tonight,   172
And that shall lend a kind of easiness
To the next abstinence; the next more easy;
For use almost can change the stamp of nature,   175
And either . . . the devil, or throw him out   176
With wondrous potency. Once more, good night;
And when you are desirous to be blest,   178
I'll blessing beg of you. For this same lord,   179
                              [*Pointing to Polonius*]
I do repent; but heaven hath pleased it so
To punish me with this, and this with me,
That I must be their scourge and minister.   182
I will bestow him, and will answer well   183
The death I gave him. So, again, good night.
I must be cruel only to be kind.
This bad begins, and worse remains behind.   186
One word more, good lady.
QUEEN   What shall I do?
HAMLET
Not this by no means that I bid you do:
Let the bloat king tempt you again to bed,   189
Pinch wanton on your cheek, call you his mouse,   190

168 who . . . eat which consumes all proper or natural feeling, all
sensibility   169 Of habits devil devil-like in prompting evil habits
171 livery an outer appearance, a customary garb (and hence a predis-
position easily assumed in time of stress)   172 aptly readily   175 use
habit.   the stamp of nature our inborn traits   176 And either (A defective line usually emended by inserting the word *master* after *either*,
following the fourth quarto and early editors.)   178–179 when . . . you
i.e., when you are ready to be penitent and seek God's blessing, I will
ask your blessing as a dutiful son should (on the occasion of departure)
182 their scourge and minister i.e., agent of heavenly retribution. (By
scourge, Hamlet also suggests that he himself will eventually suffer
punishment in the process of fulfilling heaven's will.)   183 bestow stow,
dispose of.   answer account for   186 This i.e., the killing of Polonius.
behind to come   189 bloat bloated   190 Pinch wanton i.e., leave his
love pinches on your cheeks, branding you as wanton

And let him, for a pair of reechy kisses, 191
Or paddling in your neck with his damned fingers, 192
Make you to ravel all this matter out 193
That I essentially am not in madness,
But mad in craft. 'Twere good you let him know, 195
For who that's but a queen, fair, sober, wise,
Would from a paddock, from a bat, a gib, 197
Such dear concernings hide? Who would do so? 198
No, in despite of sense and secrecy,
Unpeg the basket on the house's top, 200
Let the birds fly, and like the famous ape, 201
To try conclusions, in the basket creep 202
And break your own neck down. 203

QUEEN
Be thou assured, if words be made of breath,
And breath of life, I have no life to breathe
What thou hast said to me.

HAMLET
I must to England. You know that?

QUEEN   Alack,
I had forgot. 'Tis so concluded on.

HAMLET
There's letters sealed, and my two schoolfellows,
Whom I will trust as I will adders fanged,
They bear the mandate; they must sweep my way 211
And marshal me to knavery. Let it work. 212
For 'tis the sport to have the enginer 213
Hoist with his own petard, and 't shall go hard 214
But I will delve one yard below their mines 215

191 **reechy** dirty, filthy   192 **paddling** fingering amorously   193 **ravel
. . . out** unravel, disclose   195 **in craft** by cunning.   **good** (Said sarcasti-
cally; also the following 8 lines.)   197 **paddock** toad.   **gib** tomcat
198 **dear concernings** important affairs   200 **Unpeg the basket** open the
cage, i.e., let out the secret   201 **famous ape** (in a story now lost)
202 **conclusions** experiments (in which the ape apparently enters a cage
from which birds have been released and then tries to fly out of the
cage as they have done, falling to his death)   203 **down** in the fall;
utterly   211–212 **sweep . . . knavery** sweep a path before me and conduct me to some *knavery* or treachery prepared for me   212 **work**
proceed   213 **enginer** maker of military contrivances   214 **Hoist with**
blown up by.   **petard** an explosive used to blow in a door or make a
breach   214–215 **'t shall . . . will** unless luck is against me, I will
215 **mines** tunnels used in warfare to undermine the enemy's emplace-
ments; Hamlet will countermine by going under their mines

And blow them at the moon. O, 'tis most sweet
When in one line two crafts directly meet.   217
This man shall set me packing.   218
I'll lug the guts into the neighbor room.
Mother, good night indeed. This counselor
Is now most still, most secret, and most grave,
Who was in life a foolish prating knave.—
Come, sir, to draw toward an end with you.—   223
Good night, Mother.

> *Exeunt [separately, Hamlet*
> *dragging in Polonius].*

✦

217 in one line i.e., mines and countermines on a collision course, or
the countermines directly below the mines.   **crafts** acts of guile, plots
218 set me packing set me to making schemes, and set me to lugging
(him), and, also, send me off in a hurry   **223 draw . . . end** finish up
(with a pun on *draw*, pull)

4.1 *Enter King and Queen, with Rosencrantz and Guildenstern.*

KING
There's matter in these sighs, these profound heaves. 1
You must translate; 'tis fit we understand them.
Where is your son?
QUEEN
Bestow this place on us a little while.
             [Exeunt Rosencrantz and Guildenstern.]
Ah, mine own lord, what have I seen tonight!
KING
What, Gertrude? How does Hamlet?
QUEEN
Mad as the sea and wind when both contend
Which is the mightier. In his lawless fit,
Behind the arras hearing something stir,
Whips out his rapier, cries, "A rat, a rat!"
And in this brainish apprehension kills 11
The unseen good old man.
KING   O heavy deed! 12
It had been so with us, had we been there. 13
His liberty is full of threats to all—
To you yourself, to us, to everyone.
Alas, how shall this bloody deed be answered? 16
It will be laid to us, whose providence 17
Should have kept short, restrained, and out of haunt 18
This mad young man. But so much was our love,
We would not understand what was most fit,
But, like the owner of a foul disease,
To keep it from divulging, let it feed 22
Even on the pith of life. Where is he gone?

4.1. Location: The castle.
s.d. Enter . . . Queen (Some editors argue that Gertrude never exits in
3.4 and that the scene is continuous here, but the second quarto marks
an entrance for her and at l. 35 Claudius speaks of Gertrude's *closet* as
though it were elsewhere. A short time has elapsed during which the
King has become aware of her highly wrought emotional state.)
1 matter significance **11 brainish apprehension** headstrong conception **12 heavy** grievous **13 us** i.e., me. (The royal "we"; also in l. 15.)
16 answered explained **17 providence** foresight **18 short** i.e., on a
short tether. **out of haunt** secluded **22 divulging** becoming evident

QUEEN
  To draw apart the body he hath killed,
  O'er whom his very madness, like some ore   25
  Among a mineral of metals base,   26
  Shows itself pure: 'a weeps for what is done.
KING   O Gertrude, come away!
  The sun no sooner shall the mountains touch
  But we will ship him hence, and this vile deed
  We must with all our majesty and skill
  Both countenance and excuse.—Ho, Guildenstern!

        Enter Rosencrantz and Guildenstern.

  Friends both, go join you with some further aid.
  Hamlet in madness hath Polonius slain,
  And from his mother's closet hath he dragged him.
  Go seek him out, speak fair, and bring the body
  Into the chapel. I pray you, haste in this.
              [*Exeunt Rosencrantz and Guildenstern.*]
  Come, Gertrude, we'll call up our wisest friends
  And let them know both what we mean to do
  And what's untimely done.   40
  Whose whisper o'er the world's diameter,   41
  As level as the cannon to his blank,   42
  Transports his poisoned shot, may miss our name
  And hit the woundless air. O, come away!   44
  My soul is full of discord and dismay.   *Exeunt.*

                    ❖

4.2   *Enter Hamlet.*

HAMLET   Safely stowed.
ROSENCRANTZ, GUILDENSTERN (*Within*) Hamlet! Lord
  Hamlet!

---

25 ore vein of gold   **26 mineral** mine   **40 And . . . done** (A defective line;
conjectures as to the missing words include *So, haply, slander* [Capell
and others]; *For, haply, slander* [Theobald and others]; and *So envious
slander* [Jenkins].)   **41 diameter** extent from side to side   **42 As level**
with as direct aim.   **his blank** its target at point-blank range
44 woundless invulnerable

4.2. Location: The castle.

HAMLET But soft, what noise? Who calls on Hamlet? O, here they come.

Enter Rosencrantz and Guildenstern.

ROSENCRANTZ
What have you done, my lord, with the dead body?
HAMLET
Compounded it with dust, whereto 'tis kin.
ROSENCRANTZ
Tell us where 'tis, that we may take it thence
And bear it to the chapel.
HAMLET Do not believe it.
ROSENCRANTZ Believe what?
HAMLET That I can keep your counsel and not mine 12
own. Besides, to be demanded of a sponge, what rep- 13
lication should be made by the son of a king? 14
ROSENCRANTZ Take you me for a sponge, my lord?
HAMLET Ay, sir, that soaks up the King's countenance, 16
his rewards, his authorities. But such officers do the
King best service in the end. He keeps them, like an
ape, in the corner of his jaw, first mouthed to be last
swallowed. When he needs what you have gleaned, it
is but squeezing you, and, sponge, you shall be dry
again.
ROSENCRANTZ I understand you not, my lord.
HAMLET I am glad of it. A knavish speech sleeps in a 24
foolish ear.
ROSENCRANTZ My lord, you must tell us where the
body is and go with us to the King.
HAMLET The body is with the King, but the King is not 28
with the body. The King is a thing— 29
GUILDENSTERN A thing, my lord?

12–13 That . . . own (Perhaps Hamlet is suggesting that they have their
secrets and he has his.) **13 demanded of** questioned by **13–14 rep-
lication** reply **16 countenance** favor **24 sleeps in** has no meaning to
28–29 The . . . body (Perhaps alludes to the legal commonplace of "the
king's two bodies," which drew a distinction between the sacred office
of kingship and the particular mortal who possessed it at any given
time. Hence, although Claudius's body is necessarily a part of him, true
kingship is not contained in it. Similarly, Claudius will have Polonius's
body when it is found, but there is no kingship in this business either.)

HAMLET Of nothing. Bring me to him. Hide fox, and ³¹
  all after!   *Exeunt.* ³²

❖

4.3   *Enter King, and two or three.*

KING
  I have sent to seek him, and to find the body.
  How dangerous is it that this man goes loose!
  Yet must not we put the strong law on him.
  He's loved of the distracted multitude,   4
  Who like not in their judgment, but their eyes,   5
  And where 'tis so, th' offender's scourge is weighed, 6
  But never the offense. To bear all smooth and even,   7
  This sudden sending him away must seem
  Deliberate pause. Diseases desperate grown   9
  By desperate appliance are relieved,   10
  Or not at all.

      *Enter Rosencrantz, [Guildenstern,] and all the
      rest.*

              How now, what hath befall'n?
ROSENCRANTZ
  Where the dead body is bestowed, my lord,
  We cannot get from him.
KING   But where is he?
ROSENCRANTZ
  Without, my lord; guarded, to know your pleasure.
KING
  Bring him before us.
ROSENCRANTZ   Ho! Bring in the lord.

      They enter [with Hamlet].

31 Of nothing (1) of no account (2) lacking the essence of kingship, as
in ll. 28–29 and note   **31–32 Hide . . . after** (An old signal cry in the game
of hide-and-seek, suggesting that Hamlet now runs away from them.)

4.3. Location: The castle.
4 distracted fickle, unstable   **5 Who . . . eyes** who choose not by judgment but by appearance   **6 scourge** punishment.   **weighed** sympatheti-
cally considered   **7 To . . . even** to manage the business in an unprovoc-
ative way   **9 Deliberate pause** carefully considered action   **10 appliance** remedy, treatment

KING Now, Hamlet, where's Polonius?

HAMLET At supper.

KING At supper? Where?

HAMLET Not where he eats, but where 'a is eaten. A
certain convocation of politic worms are e'en at him. 20
Your worm is your only emperor for diet. We fat all 21
creatures else to fat us, and we fat ourselves for maggots. Your fat king and your lean beggar is but
variable service—two dishes, but to one table. That's 24
the end.

KING Alas, alas!

HAMLET A man may fish with the worm that hath eat 27
of a king, and eat of the fish that hath fed of that
worm.

KING What dost thou mean by this?

HAMLET Nothing but to show you how a king may go
a progress through the guts of a beggar.   32

KING Where is Polonius?

HAMLET In heaven. Send thither to see. If your messenger find him not there, seek him i' th' other place yourself. But if indeed you find him not within this month,
you shall nose him as you go up the stairs into the
lobby.

KING [*To some attendants*] Go seek him there.

HAMLET 'A will stay till you come. [*Exeunt attendants.*]

KING
Hamlet, this deed, for thine especial safety—
Which we do tender, as we dearly grieve   42
For that which thou hast done—must send thee hence
With fiery quickness. Therefore prepare thyself.
The bark is ready, and the wind at help,   45
Th' associates tend, and everything is bent   46
For England.

HAMLET For England!

KING Ay, Hamlet.

20 politic worms crafty worms (suited to a master spy like Polonius).
e'en even now   **21 Your worm** your average worm. (On *your*, compare
your fat king and your lean beggar in l. 23.)   **diet** food, eating (with a
punning reference to the Diet of Worms, a famous *convocation* held in
1521)   **24 variable service** different courses of a single meal   **27 eat**
eaten. (Pronounced *et.*)   **32 progress** royal journey of state   **42 tender**
regard, hold dear.   **dearly** intensely   **45 bark** sailing vessel   **46 tend**
wait.   **bent** in readiness

HAMLET Good.

KING
So is it, if thou knew'st our purposes.

HAMLET I see a cherub that sees them. But come, for 52
England! Farewell, dear Mother.

KING Thy loving father, Hamlet.

HAMLET My mother. Father and mother is man and
wife, man and wife is one flesh, and so, my mother.
Come, for England!   *Exit.*

KING
Follow him at foot; tempt him with speed aboard.   58
Delay it not. I'll have him hence tonight.
Away! For everything is sealed and done
That else leans on th' affair. Pray you, make haste.   61
                    [*Exeunt all but the King.*]
And, England, if my love thou hold'st at aught—   62
As my great power thereof may give thee sense,   63
Since yet thy cicatrice looks raw and red   64
After the Danish sword, and thy free awe   65
Pays homage to us—thou mayst not coldly set   66
Our sovereign process, which imports at full,   67
By letters congruing to that effect,   68
The present death of Hamlet. Do it, England,   69
For like the hectic in my blood he rages,   70
And thou must cure me. Till I know 'tis done,
Howe'er my haps, my joys were ne'er begun.   *Exit.* 72

✜

4.4   *Enter Fortinbras with his army over the stage.*

FORTINBRAS
Go, Captain, from me greet the Danish king.

52 **cherub** (Cherubim are angels of knowledge. Hamlet hints that both
he and heaven are onto Claudius's tricks.) 58 **at foot** close behind, at
heel 61 **leans on** bears upon, is related to 62 **England** i.e., King of
England. **at aught** at any value 63 **As . . . sense** for so my great power
may give you a just appreciation of the importance of valuing my love
64 **cicatrice** scar 65 **free awe** voluntary show of respect 66 **coldly set**
regard with indifference 67 **process** command. **imports at full** conveys specific directions for 68 **congruing** agreeing 69 **present** immediate 70 **hectic** persistent fever 72 **haps** fortunes

4.4. **Location:** The coast of Denmark.

Tell him that by his license Fortinbras   2
Craves the conveyance of a promised march   3
Over his kingdom. You know the rendezvous.
If that His Majesty would aught with us,
We shall express our duty in his eye;   6
And let him know so.

CAPTAIN   I will do 't, my lord.

FORTINBRAS   Go softly on.   [*Exeunt all but the Captain.*]   9

Enter Hamlet, Rosencrantz, [Guildenstern,] etc.

HAMLET   Good sir, whose powers are these?   10
CAPTAIN   They are of Norway, sir.
HAMLET   How purposed, sir, I pray you?
CAPTAIN   Against some part of Poland.
HAMLET   Who commands them, sir?
CAPTAIN
The nephew to old Norway, Fortinbras.
HAMLET
Goes it against the main of Poland, sir,   16
Or for some frontier?
CAPTAIN
Truly to speak, and with no addition,   18
We go to gain a little patch of ground
That hath in it no profit but the name.
To pay five ducats, five, I would not farm it;   21
Nor will it yield to Norway or the Pole
A ranker rate, should it be sold in fee.   23
HAMLET
Why, then the Polack never will defend it.
CAPTAIN
Yes, it is already garrisoned.
HAMLET
Two thousand souls and twenty thousand ducats
Will not debate the question of this straw.   27
This is th' impostume of much wealth and peace,   28

2 **license** permission   3 **the conveyance of** escort during   6 **duty** respect.   **eye** presence   9 **softly** slowly, circumspectly   10 **powers**
forces   16 **main** main part   18 **addition** exaggeration   21 **To pay** i.e.,
for a yearly rental of.   **farm it** take a lease of it   23 **ranker** higher.   **in
fee** fee simple, outright   27 **debate . . . straw** settle this trifling matter
28 **impostume** abscess

That inward breaks, and shows no cause without
Why the man dies. I humbly thank you, sir.

CAPTAIN
God b' wi' you, sir.   [*Exit.*]

ROSENCRANTZ   Will 't please you go, my lord?

HAMLET
I'll be with you straight. Go a little before.
                              [*Exeunt all except Hamlet.*]
How all occasions do inform against me   33
And spur my dull revenge! What is a man,
If his chief good and market of his time   35
Be but to sleep and feed? A beast, no more.
Sure he that made us with such large discourse,   37
Looking before and after, gave us not
That capability and godlike reason
To fust in us unused. Now, whether it be   40
Bestial oblivion, or some craven scruple   41
Of thinking too precisely on th' event—   42
A thought which, quartered, hath but one part wisdom
And ever three parts coward—I do not know
Why yet I live to say "This thing's to do,"
Sith I have cause, and will, and strength, and means   46
To do 't. Examples gross as earth exhort me: 47
Witness this army of such mass and charge,   48
Led by a delicate and tender prince,   49
Whose spirit with divine ambition puffed
Makes mouths at the invisible event,   51
Exposing what is mortal and unsure
To all that fortune, death, and danger dare,
Even for an eggshell. Rightly to be great
Is not to stir without great argument,
But greatly to find quarrel in a straw
When honor's at the stake. How stand I then,   57
That have a father killed, a mother stained,
Excitements of my reason and my blood,   59

33 inform against denounce, betray; take shape against   **35 market of**
profit of, compensation for   **37 discourse** power of reasoning   **40 fust**
grow moldy   **41 oblivion** forgetfulness   **42 precisely** scrupulously.
event outcome   **46 Sith** since   **47 gross** obvious   **48 charge** expense
49 delicate and tender of fine and youthful qualities   **51 Makes mouths**
makes scornful faces.   **invisible event** unforeseeable outcome   **57 at
the stake** at risk (in gambling)   **59 Excitements of** promptings by

And let all sleep, while to my shame I see
The imminent death of twenty thousand men
That for a fantasy and trick of fame   62
Go to their graves like beds, fight for a plot   63
Whereon the numbers cannot try the cause,   64
Which is not tomb enough and continent   65
To hide the slain? O, from this time forth
My thoughts be bloody or be nothing worth!   *Exit.*

✤

4.5   *Enter Horatio, [Queen] Gertrude, and a*
          Gentleman.

QUEEN
  I will not speak with her.
GENTLEMAN   She is importunate,
  Indeed distract. Her mood will needs be pitied.   2
QUEEN What would she have?
GENTLEMAN
  She speaks much of her father, says she hears
  There's tricks i' the world, and hems, and beats her
    heart,   5
  Spurns enviously at straws, speaks things in doubt   6
  That carry but half sense. Her speech is nothing,
  Yet the unshapèd use of it doth move   8
  The hearers to collection; they yawn at it,   9
  And botch the words up fit to their own thoughts,   10
  Which, as her winks and nods and gestures yield them, 11
  Indeed would make one think there might be thought,   12
  Though nothing sure, yet much unhappily.   13

62 fantasy fanciful caprice, illusion. **trick** trifle, deceit **63 plot** i.e., of
ground **64 Whereon . . . cause** i.e., on which there is insufficient room
for the soldiers needed to engage in a military contest **65 continent**
receptacle, container

4.5. Location: The castle.
2 distract distracted **5 tricks** deceptions. **heart** i.e., breast **6 Spurns
. . . straws** kicks spitefully, takes offense at trifles. **in doubt** obscurely
8 unshapèd use distracted manner **9 collection** inference, a guess at
some sort of meaning. **yawn** gape, wonder; grasp. (The Folio reading,
aim, is possible.) **10 botch** patch **11 Which** i.e., the words. **yield**
deliver, represent **12 thought** conjectured **13 much unhappily** very
unskillfully, clumsily

HORATIO
  'Twere good she were spoken with, for she may strew
  Dangerous conjectures in ill-breeding minds.   15
QUEEN   Let her come in.   *[Exit Gentleman.]*
  [Aside.] To my sick soul, as sin's true nature is,
  Each toy seems prologue to some great amiss.   18
  So full of artless jealousy is guilt,   19
  It spills itself in fearing to be spilt.   20

     Enter Ophelia [distracted].

OPHELIA
  Where is the beauteous majesty of Denmark?
QUEEN   How now, Ophelia?
OPHELIA *(She sings)*
     "How should I your true love know
      From another one?
     By his cockle hat and staff,   25
      And his sandal shoon."   26
QUEEN
  Alas, sweet lady, what imports this song?
OPHELIA   Say you? Nay, pray you, mark.
     "He is dead and gone, lady,   *(Song.)*
      He is dead and gone;
    At his head a grass-green turf,
      At his heels a stone."
  Oho!
QUEEN   Nay, but Ophelia—
OPHELIA   Pray you, mark.
  [Sings.] "White his shroud as the mountain snow"—

     Enter King.

QUEEN   Alas, look here, my lord.
OPHELIA
     "Larded with sweet flowers;   *(Song.)* 38

---

15 ill-breeding prone to suspect the worst and to make mischief **18 toy** trifle. **amiss** calamity **19–20 So . . . spilt** guilt is so full of suspicion that it unskillfully betrays itself in fearing betrayal **20 s.d. Enter Ophelia** (In the first quarto, Ophelia enters "playing on a lute, and her hair down, singing.") **25 cockle hat** hat with cockleshell stuck in it as a sign that the wearer had been a pilgrim to the shrine of Saint James of Compostella in Spain **26 shoon** shoes **38 Larded** decorated

Which bewept to the ground did not go
   With true-love showers." 40

KING   How do you, pretty lady?

OPHELIA   Well, God 'ild you! They say the owl was a 42
baker's daughter. Lord, we know what we are, but
know not what we may be. God be at your table!

KING   Conceit upon her father. 45

OPHELIA   Pray let's have no words of this; but when
they ask you what it means, say you this:
      "Tomorrow is Saint Valentine's day,   (Song.) 48
         All in the morning betime, 49
      And I a maid at your window,
         To be your Valentine.
      Then up he rose, and donned his clothes,
         And dupped the chamber door, 53
      Let in the maid, that out a maid
         Never departed more."

KING   Pretty Ophelia—

OPHELIA   Indeed, la, without an oath, I'll make an end
on 't:

[Sings.] "By Gis and by Saint Charity, 59
         Alack, and fie for shame!
      Young men will do 't, if they come to 't;
         By Cock, they are to blame. 62
      Quoth she, 'Before you tumbled me,
         You promised me to wed.'"

He answers:
      " 'So would I ha' done, by yonder sun,
         An thou hadst not come to my bed.'" 67

KING   How long hath she been thus?

OPHELIA   I hope all will be well. We must be patient,
but I cannot choose but weep to think they would lay
him i' the cold ground. My brother shall know of it.
And so I thank you for your good counsel. Come, my
coach! Good night, ladies, good night, sweet ladies,
good night, good night.   [Exit.]

---

40 showers i.e., tears   **42 God 'ild** God yield or reward.   **owl** (Refers to a legend about a baker's daughter who was turned into an owl for refusing Jesus bread.)   **45 Conceit** brooding   **48 Valentine's** (This song alludes to the belief that the first girl seen by a man on the morning of this day was his valentine or truelove.)   **49 betime** early   **53 dupped** opened   **59 Gis** Jesus   **62 Cock** (A perversion of "God" in oaths.)   **67 An** if

KING [*To Horatio*]
    Follow her close. Give her good watch, I pray you.
                                  [*Exit Horatio.*]
    O, this is the poison of deep grief; it springs
    All from her father's death—and now behold!
    O Gertrude, Gertrude,
    When sorrows come, they come not single spies,   79
    But in battalions. First, her father slain;
    Next, your son gone, and he most violent author
    Of his own just remove; the people muddied,   82
    Thick and unwholesome in their thoughts and whispers
    For good Polonius' death—and we have done but
       greenly   84
    In hugger-mugger to inter him; poor Ophelia   85
    Divided from herself and her fair judgment,
    Without the which we are pictures or mere beasts;
    Last, and as much containing as all these,   88
    Her brother is in secret come from France,
    Feeds on his wonder, keeps himself in clouds,   90
    And wants not buzzers to infect his ear   91
    With pestilent speeches of his father's death,
    Wherein necessity, of matter beggared,   93
    Will nothing stick our person to arraign   94
    In ear and ear. O my dear Gertrude, this,   95
    Like to a murdering piece, in many places   96
    Gives me superfluous death.   *A noise within.*   97
QUEEN   Alack, what noise is this?
KING   Attend!   99
    Where are my Switzers? Let them guard the door.   100

    Enter a Messenger.

    What is the matter?
MESSENGER   Save yourself, my lord!

79 spies scouts sent in advance of the main force   **82 muddied** stirred
up, confused   **84 greenly** imprudently, foolishly   **85 hugger-mugger**
secret haste   **88 as much containing** i.e., as full of serious matter
90 in clouds i.e., of suspicion and rumor   **91 wants** lacks. **buzzers**
gossipers, informers   **93 necessity** i.e., the need to invent some plausible explanation. **of matter beggared** unprovided with facts
94–95 Will . . . ear will not hesitate to accuse my (royal) person in
everybody's ears   **96 murdering piece** cannon loaded so as to scatter its
shot   **97 Gives . . . death** kills me over and over   **99 Attend** i.e., guard
me   **100 Switzers** Swiss guards, mercenaries

The ocean, overpeering of his list,   102
Eats not the flats with more impetuous haste   103
Than young Laertes, in a riotous head,   104
O'erbears your officers. The rabble call him lord,
And, as the world were now but to begin,   106
Antiquity forgot, custom not known,
The ratifiers and props of every word,   108
They cry, "Choose we! Laertes shall be king!"
Caps, hands, and tongues applaud it to the clouds,   110
"Laertes shall be king, Laertes king!"   *A noise within.*

QUEEN
How cheerfully on the false trail they cry!
O, this is counter, you false Danish dogs!   113

        Enter Laertes with others.

KING   The doors are broke.
LAERTES
Where is this King?—Sirs, stand you all without.
ALL   No, let's come in.
LAERTES   I pray you, give me leave.
ALL   We will, we will.
LAERTES
I thank you. Keep the door. [*Exeunt followers.*] O thou
   vile king,
Give me my father!
QUEEN [*Holding him*]Calmly, good Laertes.
LAERTES
That drop of blood that's calm proclaims me bastard,
Cries cuckold to my father, brands the harlot
Even here, between the chaste unsmirchèd brow   123
Of my true mother.
KING   What is the cause, Laertes,
That thy rebellion looks so giantlike?
Let him go, Gertrude. Do not fear our person.   126

---

102 overpeering of his list overflowing its shore, boundary   **103 flats**
i.e., flatlands near shore.   **impetuous** violent (also with the meaning of
impiteous [*impitious*, Q2], pitiless)   **104 head** armed force   **106 as** as if
108 The ratifiers . . . word i.e., *antiquity* (or tradition) and *custom* ought
to confirm (*ratify*) and underprop our every word or promise   **110 Caps**
(The caps are thrown in the air.)   **113 counter** (A hunting term meaning
to follow the trail in a direction opposite to that which the game has
taken.)   **123 between** in the middle of   **126 fear our** fear for my

There's such divinity doth hedge a king   127
That treason can but peep to what it would,   128
Acts little of his will. Tell me, Laertes,   129
Why thou art thus incensed. Let him go, Gertrude.
Speak, man.

LAERTES   Where is my father?

KING   Dead.

QUEEN
But not by him.

KING   Let him demand his fill.

LAERTES
How came he dead? I'll not be juggled with.   133
To hell, allegiance! Vows, to the blackest devil!
Conscience and grace, to the profoundest pit!
I dare damnation. To this point I stand,
That both the worlds I give to negligence,   137
Let come what comes, only I'll be revenged
Most throughly for my father.   139

KING   Who shall stay you?

LAERTES   My will, not all the world's.   141
And for my means, I'll husband them so well
They shall go far with little.

KING   Good Laertes,
If you desire to know the certainty
Of your dear father, is 't writ in your revenge
That, swoopstake, you will draw both friend and foe,   146
Winner and loser?

LAERTES   None but his enemies.

KING   Will you know them, then?

LAERTES
To his good friends thus wide I'll ope my arms,
And like the kind life-rendering pelican   151

---

127 hedge protect as with a surrounding barrier   **128 can . . . would**
can only glance, as from afar off or through a barrier, at what it would
intend   **129 Acts . . . will** (but) performs little of what it intends
133 juggled with cheated, deceived   **137 both . . . negligence** i.e., both
this world and the next are of no consequence to me   **139 throughly**
thoroughly   **141 My will . . . world's** i.e., I'll stop (*stay*) when my will is
accomplished, not for anyone else's   **146 swoopstake** (Literally, taking
all stakes on the gambling table at once, i.e., indiscriminately; *draw* is
also a gambling term.)   **151 pelican** (Refers to the belief that the female
pelican fed its young with its own blood.)

Repast them with my blood.

KING   Why, now you speak   152
Like a good child and a true gentleman.
That I am guiltless of your father's death,
And am most sensibly in grief for it,   155
It shall as level to your judgment 'pear   156
As day does to your eye.   *A noise within.*

LAERTES
How now, what noise is that?

     Enter Ophelia.

KING   Let her come in.

LAERTES
O heat, dry up my brains! Tears seven times salt
Burn out the sense and virtue of mine eye!   160
By heaven, thy madness shall be paid with weight   161
Till our scale turn the beam. O rose of May!   162
Dear maid, kind sister, sweet Ophelia!
O heavens, is 't possible a young maid's wits
Should be as mortal as an old man's life?
Nature is fine in love, and where 'tis fine   166
It sends some precious instance of itself   167
After the thing it loves.   168

OPHELIA
   "They bore him barefaced on the bier,   (*Song.*)
     Hey non nonny, nonny, hey nonny,
     And in his grave rained many a tear—"
Fare you well, my dove!

LAERTES
Hadst thou thy wits and didst persuade revenge,   173
It could not move thus.

OPHELIA   You must sing "A-down a-down," and you   175
"call him a-down-a." O, how the wheel becomes it!   176
It is the false steward that stole his master's daughter.   177

---

152 **Repast** feed   155 **sensibly** feelingly   156 **level** plain   160 **virtue**
faculty, power   161 **paid with weight** repaid, avenged equally or more
162 **beam** crossbar of a balance   166 **fine in** refined by   167 **instance**
token   168 **After . . . loves** i.e., into the grave, along with Polonius
173 **persuade** argue cogently for   175–176 **You . . . a-down-a** (Ophelia
assigns the singing of refrains, like her own "Hey non nonny," to various imaginary singers.)   176 **wheel** spinning wheel as accompaniment
to the song, or refrain   177 **false steward** (The story is unknown.)

LAERTES This nothing's more than matter.   178

OPHELIA There's rosemary, that's for remembrance;   179
pray you, love, remember. And there is pansies; that's   180
for thoughts.

LAERTES A document in madness, thoughts and re-   182
membrance fitted.

OPHELIA There's fennel for you, and columbines.   184
There's rue for you, and here's some for me; we may   185
call it herb of grace o' Sundays. You must wear your
rue with a difference. There's a daisy. I would give   187
you some violets, but they withered all when my father   188
died. They say 'a made a good end—
[*Sings.*] "For bonny sweet Robin is all my joy."

LAERTES
Thought and affliction, passion, hell itself,   191
She turns to favor and to prettiness.   192

OPHELIA
         "And will 'a not come again?   (*Song.*)
          And will 'a not come again?
             No, no, he is dead.
             Go to thy deathbed,
          He never will come again.

         "His beard was as white as snow,
          All flaxen was his poll.   199
             He is gone, he is gone.
             And we cast away moan.
          God ha' mercy on his soul!"
And of all Christian souls, I pray God. God b' wi' you.
                                              [*Exit.*]

LAERTES Do you see this, O God?

---

178 This . . . matter this seeming nonsense is more eloquent than sane
utterance   **179 rosemary** (Used as a symbol of remembrance both at
weddings and at funerals.)   **180 pansies** (Emblems of love and court-
ship; perhaps from French *pensées*, thoughts.)   **182 document** instruction, lesson   **184 fennel** (Emblem of flattery.)   **columbines** (Emblems of
unchastity or ingratitude.)   **185 rue** (Emblem of repentance; when
mingled with holy water, it was known as *herb of grace*.)   **187 with a
difference** (A device used in heraldry to distinguish one family from
another on the coat of arms, here suggesting that Ophelia and the
Queen have different causes of sorrow and repentance; perhaps with a
play on *rue* in the sense of ruth, pity.)   **daisy** (Emblem of dissembling,
faithlessness.)   **188 violets** (Emblems of faithfulness.)   **191 Thought**
melancholy   **192 favor** grace, beauty   **199 poll** head

KING
  Laertes, I must commune with your grief,
  Or you deny me right. Go but apart,
  Make choice of whom your wisest friends you will,   207
  And they shall hear and judge twixt you and me.
  If by direct or by collateral hand   209
  They find us touched, we will our kingdom give,   210
  Our crown, our life, and all that we call ours
  To you in satisfaction; but if not,
  Be you content to lend your patience to us,
  And we shall jointly labor with your soul
  To give it due content.

LAERTES   Let this be so.
  His means of death, his obscure funeral—
  No trophy, sword, nor hatchment o'er his bones,   217
  No noble rite, nor formal ostentation—   218
  Cry to be heard, as 'twere from heaven to earth,
  That I must call 't in question.

KING   So you shall,   220
  And where th' offense is, let the great ax fall.
  I pray you, go with me.   *Exeunt.*

❖

4.6   *Enter Horatio and others.*

HORATIO
  What are they that would speak with me?
GENTLEMAN   Seafaring men, sir. They say they have let-
  ters for you.
HORATIO   Let them come in.   *[Exit Gentleman.]*
  I do not know from what part of the world
  I should be greeted, if not from Lord Hamlet.

    Enter Sailors.

FIRST SAILOR   God bless you, sir.
HORATIO   Let him bless thee too.

207 whom whichever of **209 collateral** indirect **210 us touched** me
implicated **217 trophy** memorial. **hatchment** tablet displaying the
armorial bearings of a deceased person **218 ostentation** ceremony
220 That so that. **call 't in question** demand an explanation

4.6. Location: The castle.

FIRST SAILOR 'A shall, sir, an please him. There's a   9
letter for you, sir—it came from th' ambassador that   10
was bound for England—if your name be Horatio, as
I am let to know it is.   [*He gives a letter.*]

HORATIO [*Reads*] "Horatio, when thou shalt have over-   13
looked this, give these fellows some means to the King;   14
they have letters for him. Ere we were two days old at
sea, a pirate of very warlike appointment gave us   16
chase. Finding ourselves too slow of sail, we put on a
compelled valor, and in the grapple I boarded them.
On the instant they got clear of our ship, so I alone
became their prisoner. They have dealt with me like
thieves of mercy, but they knew what they did: I am to   21
do a good turn for them. Let the King have the letters
I have sent, and repair thou to me with as much speed   23
as thou wouldest fly death. I have words to speak in
thine ear will make thee dumb, yet are they much too
light for the bore of the matter. These good fellows will   26
bring thee where I am. Rosencrantz and Guildenstern
hold their course for England. Of them I have much to
tell thee. Farewell.

> He that thou knowest thine, Hamlet."

Come, I will give you way for these your letters,   31
And do 't the speedier that you may direct me
To him from whom you brought them.   *Exeunt.*

❖

4.7   *Enter King and Laertes.*

KING

Now must your conscience my acquittance seal,   1
And you must put me in your heart for friend,
Sith you have heard, and with a knowing ear,   3

---

9 an if it   **10 th' ambassador** (Evidently Hamlet. The sailor is being cir-
cumspect.)   **13–14 overlooked** looked over   **14 means** means of access
16 appointment equipage   **21 thieves of mercy** merciful thieves   **23 repair** come   **26 bore** caliber, i.e., importance   **31 way** means of access

4.7. Location: The castle.
1 my acquittance seal confirm or acknowledge my innocence   **3 Sith**
since

That he which hath your noble father slain
Pursued my life.

LAERTES　　　　　　　It well appears. But tell me
Why you proceeded not against these feats　　　　6
So crimeful and so capital in nature,　　　　7
As by your safety, greatness, wisdom, all things else,
You mainly were stirred up.

KING　O, for two special reasons,
Which may to you perhaps seem much unsinewed,　　11
But yet to me they're strong. The Queen his mother
Lives almost by his looks, and for myself—
My virtue or my plague, be it either which—
She is so conjunctive to my life and soul　　　　15
That, as the star moves not but in his sphere,　　16
I could not but by her. The other motive
Why to a public count I might not go　　　　18
Is the great love the general gender bear him,　　19
Who, dipping all his faults in their affection,
Work like the spring that turneth wood to stone,　　21
Convert his gyves to graces, so that my arrows,　　22
Too slightly timbered for so loud a wind,　　　23
Would have reverted to my bow again　　　　24
But not where I had aimed them.

LAERTES
And so have I a noble father lost,
A sister driven into desperate terms,　　　　27
Whose worth, if praises may go back again,　　28
Stood challenger on mount of all the age　　　29
For her perfections. But my revenge will come.

KING
Break not your sleeps for that. You must not think
That we are made of stuff so flat and dull

6 **feats** acts　7 **capital** punishable by death　9 **mainly** greatly
11 **unsinewed** weak　15 **conjunctive** closely united　16 **his** its.　**sphere**
one of the hollow spheres in which, according to Ptolemaic astronomy,
the planets were supposed to move　18 **count** account, reckoning, indict-
ment　19 **general gender** common people　21 **Work** operate, act.
spring i.e., a spring with such a concentration of lime that it coats a
piece of wood with limestone, in effect gilding it　22 **gyves** fetters
(which, gilded by the people's praise, would look like badges of honor)
23 **slightly timbered** light.　**loud** strong　24 **reverted** returned
27 **terms** state, condition　28 **go back** i.e., recall what she was　29 **on
mount** set up on high

That we can let our beard be shook with danger
And think it pastime. You shortly shall hear more.
I loved your father, and we love ourself;
And that, I hope, will teach you to imagine—

   Enter a Messenger with letters.

How now? What news?

MESSENGER   Letters, my lord, from Hamlet:
This to Your Majesty, this to the Queen.
                                        [He gives letters.]

KING   From Hamlet? Who brought them?

MESSENGER
Sailors, my lord, they say. I saw them not.
They were given me by Claudio. He received them
Of him that brought them.

KING   Laertes, you shall hear them.—
Leave us.   *[Exit Messenger.]*
[Reads.] "High and mighty, you shall know I am set
naked on your kingdom. Tomorrow shall I beg leave   45
to see your kingly eyes, when I shall, first asking your
pardon, thereunto recount the occasion of my sudden   47
and more strange return.   Hamlet."
What should this mean? Are all the rest come back?
Or is it some abuse, and no such thing?   50

LAERTES
Know you the hand?

KING   'Tis Hamlet's character. "Naked!"   51
And in a postscript here he says "alone."
Can you devise me?   53

LAERTES
I am lost in it, my lord. But let him come.
It warms the very sickness in my heart
That I shall live and tell him to his teeth,
"Thus didst thou."

KING   If it be so, Laertes—   57
As how should it be so? How otherwise?—   57
Will you be ruled by me?

---

45 naked destitute, unarmed, without following   **47 pardon** permission   **50 abuse** deceit.   **no such thing** no such thing has occurred
51 character handwriting   **53 devise** explain to   **57 Thus didst thou** i.e., here's for what you did to my father   **58 As . . . otherwise** how can this (Hamlet's return) be true? Yet how otherwise than true (since we have the evidence of his letter)

LAERTES   Ay, my lord,
  So you will not o'errule me to a peace.   60
KING
  To thine own peace. If he be now returned,
  As checking at his voyage, and that he means   62
  No more to undertake it, I will work him
  To an exploit, now ripĕ in my device,   64
  Under the which he shall not choose but fall;
  And for his death no wind of blame shall breathe,
  But even his mother shall uncharge the practice   67
  And call it accident.
LAERTES   My lord, I will be ruled,
  The rather if you could devise it so
  That I might be the organ.
KING   It falls right.   70
  You have been talked of since your travel much,
  And that in Hamlet's hearing, for a quality
  Wherein they say you shine. Your sum of parts   73
  Did not together pluck such envy from him
  As did that one, and that, in my regard,
  Of the unworthiest siege.   76
LAERTES   What part is that, my lord?
KING
  A very ribbon in the cap of youth,
  Yet needful too, for youth no less becomes   79
  The light and careless livery that it wears
  Than settled age his sables and his weeds   81
  Importing health and graveness. Two months since   82
  Here was a gentleman of Normandy.
  I have seen myself, and served against, the French,
  And they can well on horseback, but this gallant   85
  Had witchcraft in 't; he grew unto his seat,
  And to such wondrous doing brought his horse

---

60 So provided that   **62 checking at** i.e., turning aside from (like a
falcon leaving the quarry to fly at a chance bird).   **that** if   **64 device**
devising, invention   **67 uncharge the practice** acquit the stratagem of
being a plot   **70 organ** agent, instrument   **73 Your . . . parts** i.e., all
your other virtues   **76 unworthiest siege** least important rank   **79 no
less becomes** is no less suited by   **81 sables** rich robes furred with
sable.   **weeds** garments   **82 Importing health** signifying a concern for
health and dignified prosperity; also, giving an impression of comfort-
able prosperity   **85 can well** are skilled

As had he been incorpsed and demi-natured   88
With the brave beast. So far he topped my thought 89
That I in forgery of shapes and tricks   90
Come short of what he did.

LAERTES   A Norman was 't?

KING   A Norman.

LAERTES
Upon my life, Lamord.

KING   The very same.

LAERTES
I know him well. He is the brooch indeed   94
And gem of all the nation.

KING   He made confession of you,   96
And gave you such a masterly report
For art and exercise in your defense,   98
And for your rapier most especial,
That he cried out 'twould be a sight indeed
If one could match you. Th' escrimers of their nation, 101
He swore, had neither motion, guard, nor eye
If you opposed them. Sir, this report of his
Did Hamlet so envenom with his envy
That he could nothing do but wish and beg
Your sudden coming o'er, to play with you.   106
Now, out of this—

LAERTES   What out of this, my lord?

KING
Laertes, was your father dear to you?
Or are you like the painting of a sorrow,
A face without a heart?

LAERTES   Why ask you this?

KING
Not that I think you did not love your father,
But that I know love is begun by time,   112
And that I see, in passages of proof,   113
Time qualifies the spark and fire of it.   114

---

88 incorpsed and demi-natured of one body and nearly of one nature (like
the centaur)   **89 topped** surpassed   **90 forgery** imagining   **94 brooch** ornament   **96 confession** testimonial, admission of superiority   **98 For . . .
defense** in respect to your skill and practice with your weapon
101 escrimers fencers   **106 play** fence   **112 begun by time** i.e., created
by the right circumstance and hence subject to change   **113 passages
of proof** actual instances   **114 qualifies** weakens, moderates

There lives within the very flame of love
A kind of wick or snuff that will abate it,   116
And nothing is at a like goodness still,   117
For goodness, growing to a pleurisy,   118
Dies in his own too much. That we would do,   119
We should do when we would; for this "would" changes
And hath abatements and delays as many   121
As there are tongues, are hands, are accidents,   122
And then this "should" is like a spendthrift sigh,   123
That hurts by easing. But, to the quick o' th' ulcer: 124
Hamlet comes back. What would you undertake
To show yourself in deed your father's son
More than in words?

LAERTES   To cut his throat i' the church.

KING
No place, indeed, should murder sanctuarize;   128
Revenge should have no bounds. But good Laertes,
Will you do this, keep close within your chamber.   130
Hamlet returned shall know you are come home.
We'll put on those shall praise your excellence   132
And set a double varnish on the fame
The Frenchman gave you, bring you in fine together,   134
And wager on your heads. He, being remiss,   135
Most generous, and free from all contriving,   136
Will not peruse the foils, so that with ease,
Or with a little shuffling, you may choose
A sword unbated, and in a pass of practice   139
Requite him for your father.

LAERTES   I will do 't,
And for that purpose I'll anoint my sword.

---

116 snuff the charred part of a candlewick   **117 nothing . . . still** nothing
remains at a constant level of perfection   **118 pleurisy** excess, plethora.
(Literally, a chest inflammation.)   **119 in . . . much** of its own excess.
That that which   **121 abatements** diminutions   **122 accidents** occur-
rences, incidents   **123 spendthrift sigh** (An allusion to the belief that
sighs draw blood from the heart.)   **124 hurts by easing** i.e., costs the
heart blood even while it affords emotional relief.   **quick o' th' ulcer**
heart of the matter   **128 sanctuarize** protect from punishment. (Alludes
to the right of sanctuary with which certain religious places were
invested.)   **130 Will you do this** if you wish to do this   **132 put on those
shall** arrange for some to   **134 in fine** finally   **135 remiss** negligently
unsuspicious   **136 generous** noble-minded   **139 unbated** not blunted,
having no button.   **pass of practice** treacherous thrust

I bought an unction of a mountebank   142
So mortal that, but dip a knife in it,
Where it draws blood no cataplasm so rare,   144
Collected from all simples that have virtue   145
Under the moon, can save the thing from death   146
That is but scratched withal. I'll touch my point
With this contagion, that if I gall him slightly,   148
It may be death.
KING   Let's further think of this,
Weigh what convenience both of time and means
May fit us to our shape. If this should fail,   151
And that our drift look through our bad performance,   152
'Twere better not assayed. Therefore this project
Should have a back or second, that might hold
If this did blast in proof. Soft, let me see.   155
We'll make a solemn wager on your cunnings—   156
I ha 't!
When in your motion you are hot and dry—
As make your bouts more violent to that end—   159
And that he calls for drink, I'll have prepared him
A chalice for the nonce, whereon but sipping,   161
If he by chance escape your venomed stuck,   162
Our purpose may hold there. [*A cry within.*] But stay,
    what noise?

    Enter Queen.

QUEEN
One woe doth tread upon another's heel,
So fast they follow. Your sister's drowned, Laertes.
LAERTES   Drowned! O, where?
QUEEN
There is a willow grows askant the brook,   167
That shows his hoar leaves in the glassy stream;   168
Therewith fantastic garlands did she make

---

142 **unction** ointment. **mountebank** quack doctor 144 **cataplasm**
plaster or poultice 145 **simples** herbs 146 **Under the moon** i.e.,
anywhere 148 **gall** graze, wound 151 **shape** part we propose to act
152 **drift . . . performance** i.e., intention should be made visible by our
bungling 155 **blast in proof** burst in the test (like a cannon)
156 **cunnings** respective skills 159 **As** i.e., and you should 161 **nonce**
occasion 162 **stuck** thrust. (From *stoccado*, a fencing term.)
167 **askant** aslant 168 **hoar** white or gray

Of crowflowers, nettles, daisies, and long purples,   170
That liberal shepherds give a grosser name,   171
But our cold maids do dead men's fingers call them.   172
There on the pendent boughs her crownet weeds   173
Clamb'ring to hang, an envious sliver broke,   174
When down her weedy trophies and herself   175
Fell in the weeping brook. Her clothes spread wide,
And mermaidlike awhile they bore her up,
Which time she chanted snatches of old lauds,   178
As one incapable of her own distress,   179
Or like a creature native and endued   180
Unto that element. But long it could not be
Till that her garments, heavy with their drink,
Pulled the poor wretch from her melodious lay
To muddy death.
LAERTES   Alas, then she is drowned?
QUEEN   Drowned, drowned.
LAERTES
Too much of water hast thou, poor Ophelia,
And therefore I forbid my tears. But yet
It is our trick; nature her custom holds,   188
Let shame say what it will. [*He weeps.*] When these are
   gone,   189
The woman will be out. Adieu, my lord.   190
I have a speech of fire that fain would blaze,
But that this folly douts it.   *Exit.*
KING   Let's follow, Gertrude.   192
How much I had to do to calm his rage!
Now fear I this will give it start again;
Therefore let's follow.   *Exeunt.*

❖

170 **long purples** early purple orchids   171 **liberal** free-spoken.   **a
grosser name** (The testicle-resembling tubers of the orchid, also in some
cases resembling *dead men's fingers*, have earned various slang names
like dogstones and cullions.)   172 **cold** chaste   173 **crownet** made into a
chaplet or coronet   174 **envious sliver** malicious branch   175 **weedy**
i.e., of plants   178 **lauds** hymns   179 **incapable** lacking capacity to
apprehend   180 **endued** adapted by nature   188 **It is our trick** i.e.,
weeping is our natural way (when sad)   189–190 **When . . . out** when
my tears are all shed, the woman in me will be expended, satisfied
192 **douts** extinguishes. (The second quarto reads "drowns.")

5.1 *Enter two Clowns [with spades and mattocks].*

FIRST CLOWN Is she to be buried in Christian burial,
when she willfully seeks her own salvation?   2

SECOND CLOWN I tell thee she is; therefore make her
grave straight. The crowner hath sat on her, and finds   4
it Christian burial.   5

FIRST CLOWN How can that be, unless she drowned herself in her own defense?

SECOND CLOWN Why, 'tis found so.   8

FIRST CLOWN It must be *se offendendo*, it cannot be   9
else. For here lies the point: if I drown myself wittingly,
it argues an act, and an act hath three branches—it is
to act, to do, and to perform. Argal, she drowned her- 12
self wittingly.

SECOND CLOWN Nay, but hear you, goodman delver—   14

FIRST CLOWN Give me leave. Here lies the water; good.
Here stands the man; good. If the man go to this water and drown himself, it is, will he, nill he, he goes, 17
mark you that. But if the water come to him and
drown him, he drowns not himself. Argal, he that is
not guilty of his own death shortens not his own life.

SECOND CLOWN But is this law?

FIRST CLOWN Ay, marry, is 't—crowner's quest law.   22

SECOND CLOWN Will you ha' the truth on 't? If this had
not been a gentlewoman, she should have been buried out o' Christian burial.

FIRST CLOWN Why, there thou sayst. And the more   26
pity that great folk should have countenance in this   27
world to drown or hang themselves more than their

5.1. Location: A churchyard.
s.d. Clowns rustics **2 salvation** (A blunder for "damnation," or perhaps a suggestion that Ophelia was taking her own shortcut to
heaven.) **4 straight** straightway, immediately. (But with a pun on *strait*,
narrow.) **crowner** coroner. **sat on her** conducted a session on her
case **4–5 finds it** gives his official verdict that her means of death was
consistent with **8 found so** determined so in the coroner's verdict
9 se offendendo (A comic mistake for *se defendendo*, term used in
verdicts of justifiable homicide.) **12 Argal** (Corruption of *ergo*, therefore.) **14 goodman** (An honorific title often used with the name of a
profession or craft.) **17 will he, nill he** whether he will or no, willy-
nilly **22 quest** inquest **26 there thou sayst** i.e., that's right
27 countenance privilege

even-Christian. Come, my spade. There is no ancient 29
gentlemen but gardeners, ditchers, and grave makers.
They hold up Adam's profession. 31

SECOND CLOWN Was he a gentleman?

FIRST CLOWN 'A was the first that ever bore arms. 33

SECOND CLOWN Why, he had none.

FIRST CLOWN What, art a heathen? How dost thou understand the Scripture? The Scripture says Adam
digged. Could he dig without arms? I'll put another 37
question to thee. If thou answerest me not to the purpose, confess thyself— 39

SECOND CLOWN Go to.

FIRST CLOWN What is he that builds stronger than either the mason, the shipwright, or the carpenter?

SECOND CLOWN The gallows maker, for that frame out- 43
lives a thousand tenants.

FIRST CLOWN I like thy wit well, in good faith. The gallows does well. But how does it well? It does well to 46
those that do ill. Now thou dost ill to say the gallows
is built stronger than the church. Argal, the gallows
may do well to thee. To 't again, come.

SECOND CLOWN "Who builds stronger than a mason, a
shipwright, or a carpenter?"

FIRST CLOWN Ay, tell me that, and unyoke. 52

SECOND CLOWN Marry, now I can tell.

FIRST CLOWN To 't.

SECOND CLOWN Mass, I cannot tell. 55

Enter Hamlet and Horatio [at a distance].

FIRST CLOWN Cudgel thy brains no more about it, for
your dull ass will not mend his pace with beating;
and when you are asked this question next, say "a
grave maker." The houses he makes lasts till dooms-

---

29 even-Christian fellow Christians. **ancient** going back to ancient
times **31 hold up** maintain **33 bore arms** (To be entitled to bear a coat
of arms would make Adam a gentleman, but as one who bore a spade
our common ancestor was an ordinary delver in the earth.) **37 arms**
i.e., the arms of the body **39 confess thyself** (The saying continues,
"and be hanged.") **43 frame** (1) gallows (2) structure **46 does well**
(1) is an apt answer (2) does a good turn **52 unyoke** i.e., after this great
effort you may unharness the team of your wits **55 Mass** by the Mass

day. Go get thee in and fetch me a stoup of liquor. 60
    [*Exit Second Clown. First Clown digs.*]
            Song.

  "In youth, when I did love, did love,   61
   Methought it was very sweet,
  To contract—O—the time for—a—my behove, 63
   O, methought there—a—was nothing—a—meet." 64

HAMLET Has this fellow no feeling of his business, 'a 65
sings in grave-making?

HORATIO Custom hath made it in him a property of 67
easiness. 68

HAMLET 'Tis e'en so. The hand of little employment
hath the daintier sense. 70

FIRST CLOWN   *Song.*

  "But age with his stealing steps
   Hath clawed me in his clutch,
  And hath shipped me into the land,   73
   As if I had never been such."

        [*He throws up a skull.*]

HAMLET That skull had a tongue in it and could sing
once. How the knave jowls it to the ground, as if 76
'twere Cain's jawbone, that did the first murder! This
might be the pate of a politician, which this ass now 78
o'erreaches, one that would circumvent God, might 79
it not?

HORATIO It might, my lord.

HAMLET Or of a courtier, which could say, "Good mor-
row, sweet lord! How dost thou, sweet lord?" This
might be my Lord Such-a-one, that praised my Lord
Such-a-one's horse when 'a meant to beg it, might
it not?

HORATIO Ay, my lord.

---

60 stoup two-quart measure **61 In . . . love** (This and the two following
stanzas, with nonsensical variations, are from a poem attributed to Lord
Vaux and printed in *Tottel's Miscellany*, 1557. The *O* and *a* [for "ah"]
seemingly are the grunts of the digger.) **63 To contract . . . behove** i.e.,
to shorten the time for my own advantage. (Perhaps he means to
prolong it.) **64 meet** suitable, i.e., more suitable **65 'a** that he
67–68 property of easiness i.e., something he can do easily and indifferently **70 daintier sense** more delicate sense of feeling **73 into the land**
i.e., toward my grave (?) (But note the lack of rhyme in *steps, land*.)
76 jowls dashes **78 politician** schemer, plotter **79 o'erreaches** circum-
vents, gets the better of (with a quibble on the literal sense)

HAMLET Why, e'en so, and now my Lady Worm's,
chapless, and knocked about the mazard with a sex- 89
ton's spade. Here's fine revolution, an we had the trick 90
to see 't. Did these bones cost no more the breeding 91
but to play at loggets with them? Mine ache to think 92
on 't.

FIRST CLOWN   *Song.*
     "A pickax and a spade, a spade,
          For and a shrouding sheet;
     O, a pit of clay for to be made   95
          For such a guest is meet."

                         [*He throws up another skull.*]

HAMLET There's another. Why may not that be the skull
of a lawyer? Where be his quiddities now, his quilli- 99
ties, his cases, his tenures, and his tricks? Why does 100
he suffer this mad knave now to knock him about the
sconce with a dirty shovel, and will not tell him of his 102
action of battery? Hum, this fellow might be in 's time 103
a great buyer of land, with his statutes, his recogni- 104
zances, his fines, his double vouchers, his recoveries. 105
Is this the fine of his fines and the recovery of his 106
recoveries, to have his fine pate full of fine dirt? Will 107
his vouchers vouch him no more of his purchases, and
double ones too, than the length and breadth of a
pair of indentures? The very conveyances of his lands 110

---

89 chapless having no lower jaw. **mazard** i.e., head. (Literally, a drinking vessel.) **90 revolution** turn of Fortune's wheel, change. **an** if
90–91 trick to see knack of seeing **91–92 cost . . . but** involve so little
expense and care in upbringing that we may **92 loggets** a game in
which pieces of hard wood shaped like Indian clubs or bowling pins are
thrown to lie as near as possible to a stake **95 For and** and moreover
99 quiddities subtleties, quibbles. (From Latin *quid*, a thing.)
99–100 quillities verbal niceties, subtle distinctions. (Variation of *quiddities*.) **100 tenures** the holding of a piece of property or office, or the
conditions or period of such holding **102 sconce** head **103 action of
battery** lawsuit about physical assault **104–105 statutes, recognizances**
legal documents guaranteeing a debt by attaching land and property
105 fines, recoveries ways of converting entailed estates into "fee simple" or freehold. **double** signed by two signatories. **vouchers** guaran-
tees of the legality of a title to real estate **106–107 fine of his fines . . .
fine pate . . . fine dirt** end of his legal maneuvers . . . elegant head . . .
minutely sifted dirt **110 pair of indentures** legal document drawn up
in duplicate on a single sheet and then cut apart on a zigzag line so that
each pair was uniquely matched. (Hamlet may refer to two rows of
teeth, or dentures.) **conveyances** deeds

will scarcely lie in this box, and must th' inheritor 111
himself have no more, ha?

HORATIO   Not a jot more, my lord.

HAMLET   Is not parchment made of sheepskins?

HORATIO   Ay, my lord, and of calves' skins too.

HAMLET   They are sheep and calves which seek out as- 116
surance in that. I will speak to this fellow.—Whose 117
grave's this, sirrah?   118

FIRST CLOWN   Mine, sir.
   [*Sings.*] "O, a pit of clay for to be made
            For such a guest is meet."

HAMLET   I think it be thine, indeed, for thou liest in 't.

FIRST CLOWN   You lie out on 't, sir, and therefore 'tis not
yours. For my part, I do not lie in 't, yet it is mine.

HAMLET   Thou dost lie in 't, to be in 't and say it is
thine. 'Tis for the dead, not for the quick; therefore 126
thou liest.

FIRST CLOWN   'Tis a quick lie, sir; 'twill away again from
me to you.

HAMLET   What man dost thou dig it for?

FIRST CLOWN   For no man, sir.

HAMLET   What woman, then?

FIRST CLOWN   For none, neither.

HAMLET   Who is to be buried in 't?

FIRST CLOWN   One that was a woman, sir, but, rest her
soul, she's dead.

HAMLET   How absolute the knave is! We must speak by 137
the card, or equivocation will undo us. By the Lord, 138
Horatio, this three years I have took note of it: the age 139
is grown so picked that the toe of the peasant comes so 140
near the heel of the courtier, he galls his kibe.—How 141
long hast thou been grave maker?

FIRST CLOWN   Of all the days i' the year, I came to 't that
day that our last king Hamlet overcame Fortinbras.

---

111 box (1) deed box (2) coffin. ("Skull" has been suggested.)   **inheritor**
possessor, owner   **116–117 assurance in that** safety in legal parch-
ments   **118 sirrah** (A term of address to inferiors.)   **126 quick** living
137 absolute strict, precise   **137–138 by the card** by the mariner's card
or chart on which the points of the compass were marked, i.e., with
precision   **138 equivocation** ambiguity in the use of terms   **139 took**
taken   **140 picked** refined, fastidious   **141 galls his kibe** chafes the
courtier's chilblain

HAMLET How long is that since?

FIRST CLOWN Cannot you tell that? Every fool can tell that. It was that very day that young Hamlet was born—he that is mad and sent into England.

HAMLET Ay, marry, why was he sent into England?

FIRST CLOWN Why, because 'a was mad. 'A shall recover his wits there, or if 'a do not, 'tis no great matter there.

HAMLET Why?

FIRST CLOWN 'Twill not be seen in him there. There the men are as mad as he.

HAMLET How came he mad?

FIRST CLOWN Very strangely, they say.

HAMLET How strangely?

FIRST CLOWN Faith, e'en with losing his wits.

HAMLET Upon what ground?   160

FIRST CLOWN Why, here in Denmark. I have been sexton here, man and boy, thirty years.

HAMLET How long will a man lie i' th' earth ere he rot?

FIRST CLOWN Faith, if 'a be not rotten before 'a die—as we have many pocky corpses nowadays that will   165
scarce hold the laying in—'a will last you some eight   166
year or nine year. A tanner will last you nine year.

HAMLET Why he more than another?

FIRST CLOWN Why, sir, his hide is so tanned with his trade that 'a will keep out water a great while, and your water is a sore decayer of your whoreson dead   171
body. [He picks up a skull.] Here's a skull now hath lien you i' th' earth three-and-twenty years.   173

HAMLET Whose was it?

FIRST CLOWN A whoreson mad fellow's it was. Whose do you think it was?

HAMLET Nay, I know not.

FIRST CLOWN A pestilence on him for a mad rogue! 'A poured a flagon of Rhenish on my head once. This   179
same skull, sir, was, sir, Yorick's skull, the King's jester.

---

160 ground cause. (But in the next line the gravedigger takes the word in the sense of "land," "country.") **165 pocky** rotten, diseased. (Literally, with the pox, or syphilis.) **166 hold the laying in** hold together long enough to be interred **171 sore** i.e., terrible, great. **whoreson** i.e., vile, scurvy **173 lien you** lain. (*You* is used colloquially.) **179 Rhenish** Rhine wine

HAMLET   This?

FIRST CLOWN   E'en that.

HAMLET   Let me see. [*He takes the skull.*] Alas, poor Yorick! I knew him, Horatio, a fellow of infinite jest, of
most excellent fancy. He hath bore me on his back a   185
thousand times, and now how abhorred in my imagination it is! My gorge rises at it. Here hung those lips   187
that I have kissed I know not how oft. Where be your
gibes now? Your gambols, your songs, your flashes of
merriment that were wont to set the table on a roar?
Not one now, to mock your own grinning? Quite   191
chopfallen? Now get you to my lady's chamber and   192
tell her, let her paint an inch thick, to this favor she   193
must come. Make her laugh at that. Prithee, Horatio,
tell me one thing.

HORATIO   What's that, my lord?

HAMLET   Dost thou think Alexander looked o' this fashion i' th' earth?

HORATIO   E'en so.

HAMLET   And smelt so? Pah!   [*He puts down the skull.*]

HORATIO   E'en so, my lord.

HAMLET   To what base uses we may return, Horatio!
Why may not imagination trace the noble dust of Alexander till 'a find it stopping a bunghole?   204

HORATIO   'Twere to consider too curiously to consider   205
so.

HAMLET   No, faith, not a jot, but to follow him thither
with modesty enough, and likelihood to lead it. As   208
thus: Alexander died, Alexander was buried, Alexander returneth to dust, the dust is earth, of earth we
make loam, and why of that loam whereto he was   211
converted might they not stop a beer barrel?

Imperious Caesar, dead and turned to clay,   213
Might stop a hole to keep the wind away.
O, that that earth which kept the world in awe
Should patch a wall t' expel the winter's flaw!   216

---

185 bore borne   **187 My gorge rises** i.e., I feel nauseated   **191 mock your own grinning** i.e., laugh at the faces you make   **192 chopfallen** (1) lacking the lower jaw (2) dejected   **193 favor** aspect, appearance   **204 bunghole** hole for filling or emptying a cask   **205 curiously** minutely   **208 modesty** moderation   **211 loam** mortar consisting chiefly of moistened clay and straw   **213 Imperious** imperial   **216 flaw** gust of wind

Enter King, Queen, Laertes, and the corpse [of
Ophelia, in procession, with Priest, lords, etc.].

But soft, but soft awhile! Here comes the King,   217
The Queen, the courtiers. Who is this they follow?
And with such maimèd rites? This doth betoken   219
The corpse they follow did with desperate hand
Fordo its own life. 'Twas of some estate.   221
Couch we awhile and mark.   222
                    [*He and Horatio conceal themselves.*
                    Ophelia's body is taken to the grave.]

LAERTES   What ceremony else?
HAMLET [*To Horatio*]
   That is Laertes, a very noble youth. Mark.
LAERTES   What ceremony else?
PRIEST
   Her obsequies have been as far enlarged
   As we have warranty. Her death was doubtful,   227
   And but that great command o'ersways the order   228
   She should in ground unsanctified been lodged   229
   Till the last trumpet. For charitable prayers,   230
   Shards, flints, and pebbles should be thrown on her.   231
   Yet here she is allowed her virgin crants,   232
   Her maiden strewments, and the bringing home   233
   Of bell and burial.   234
LAERTES
   Must there no more be done?
PRIEST   No more be done.
   We should profane the service of the dead
   To sing a requiem and such rest to her   237
   As to peace-parted souls.
LAERTES   Lay her i' th' earth,   238
   And from her fair and unpolluted flesh

---

217 soft i.e., wait, be careful   **219 maimèd** mutilated, incomplete
221 Fordo destroy.   **estate** rank   **222 Couch we** let's hide, lurk
227 warranty i.e., ecclesiastical authority   **228 great . . . order** orders
from on high overrule the prescribed procedures   **229 She should . . .
lodged** i.e., she should have been buried in unsanctified ground   **230 For**
in place of   **231 Shards** broken bits of pottery   **232 crants** garlands
betokening maidenhood   **233 strewments** flowers strewn on a coffin
233–234 bringing . . . burial laying to rest of the body in consecrated
ground, to the sound of the bell   **237 such rest** i.e., to pray for such
rest   **238 peace-parted souls** those who have died at peace with God

May violets spring! I tell thee, churlish priest,   240
A ministering angel shall my sister be
When thou liest howling.

HAMLET [*To Horatio*]   What, the fair Ophelia!   242

QUEEN [*Scattering flowers*]   Sweets to the sweet! Farewell.
I hoped thou shouldst have been my Hamlet's wife.
I thought thy bride-bed to have decked, sweet maid,
And not have strewed thy grave.

LAERTES   O, treble woe
Fall ten times treble on that cursèd head
Whose wicked deed thy most ingenious sense   248
Deprived thee of!—Hold off the earth awhile,
Till I have caught her once more in mine arms.   250
     [*He leaps into the grave and embraces Ophelia.*]
Now pile your dust upon the quick and dead,
Till of this flat a mountain you have made
T' o'ertop old Pelion or the skyish head   253
Of blue Olympus.

HAMLET [*Coming forward*]   What is he whose grief   254
Bears such an emphasis, whose phrase of sorrow   255
Conjures the wandering stars and makes them stand   256
Like wonder-wounded hearers? This is I,   257
Hamlet the Dane.   258

LAERTES [*Grappling with him*]   The devil take thy soul!   259

HAMLET   Thou pray'st not well.
I prithee, take thy fingers from my throat,
For though I am not splenitive and rash,   262
Yet have I in me something dangerous,
Which let thy wisdom fear. Hold off thy hand.

KING   Pluck them asunder.

QUEEN   Hamlet, Hamlet!

ALL   Gentlemen!

---

240 violets (See 4.5.188 and note.)   **242 howling** i.e., in hell
248 ingenious sense a mind that is quick, alert, of fine qualities
250 Till . . . arms (Implies an open coffin.)   **253–254 Pelion, Olympus**
mountains in the north of Thessaly; see also *Ossa*, below, at l. 286
255 emphasis i.e., rhetorical and florid emphasis. (*Phrase* has a similar
rhetorical connotation.)   **256 wandering stars** planets   **257 wonder-
wounded** struck with amazement   **258 the Dane** (This title normally
signifies the King; see 1.1.17 and note.)   **259 s.d. Grappling with him**
(Most editors think, despite the testimony of the first quarto that *"Hamlet leaps in after Laertes,"* that Laertes jumps out of the grave to attack
Hamlet.)   **262 splenitive** quick-tempered

HORATIO   Good my lord, be quiet.
                    [*Hamlet and Laertes are parted.*]
HAMLET
  Why, I will fight with him upon this theme
  Until my eyelids will no longer wag.   270
QUEEN   O my son, what theme?
HAMLET
  I loved Ophelia. Forty thousand brothers
  Could not with all their quantity of love
  Make up my sum. What wilt thou do for her?
KING   O, he is mad, Laertes.
QUEEN   For love of God, forbear him.   276
HAMLET
  'Swounds, show me what thou'lt do.   277
  Woo't weep? Woo't fight? Woo't fast? Woo't tear
    thyself?   278
  Woo't drink up eisel? Eat a crocodile?   279
  I'll do 't. Dost come here to whine?
  To outface me with leaping in her grave?
  Be buried quick with her, and so will I.   282
  And if thou prate of mountains, let them throw
  Millions of acres on us, till our ground,
  Singeing his pate against the burning zone,   285
  Make Ossa like a wart! Nay, an thou'lt mouth,   286
  I'll rant as well as thou.
QUEEN   This is mere madness,   287
  And thus awhile the fit will work on him;
  Anon, as patient as the female dove
  When that her golden couplets are disclosed,   290
  His silence will sit drooping.
HAMLET   Hear you, sir.
  What is the reason that you use me thus?

270 wag move. (A fluttering eyelid is a conventional sign that life has
not yet gone.)   **276 forbear him** leave him alone   **277 'Swounds** by His
(Christ's) wounds   **278 Woo't** wilt thou   **279 drink up** drink deeply.
eisel vinegar.   **crocodile** (Crocodiles were supposed to shed hypocritical
tears.)   **282 quick** alive   **285 his pate** its head, i.e., top.   **burning zone**
zone in the celestial sphere containing the sun's orbit, between the
tropics of Cancer and Capricorn   **286 Ossa** another mountain in Thessaly. (In their war against the Olympian gods, the giants attempted to
heap Ossa, Pelion, and Olympus on one another to scale heaven.)   **an**
if.   **mouth** i.e., rant   **287 mere** utter   **290 golden couplets** two baby
pigeons, covered with yellow down.   **disclosed** hatched

I loved you ever. But it is no matter.
Let Hercules himself do what he may,   294
The cat will mew, and dog will have his day.   295

KING
I pray thee, good Horatio, wait upon him.
                    Exit Hamlet and Horatio.
[*To Laertes.*] Strengthen your patience in our last night's
    speech;   297
We'll put the matter to the present push.—   298
Good Gertrude, set some watch over your son.—
This grave shall have a living monument.   300
An hour of quiet shortly shall we see;   301
Till then, in patience our proceeding be.   *Exeunt.*

❖

5.2   *Enter Hamlet and Horatio.*

HAMLET
So much for this, sir; now shall you see the other.   1
You do remember all the circumstance?
HORATIO   Remember it, my lord!
HAMLET
Sir, in my heart there was a kind of fighting
That would not let me sleep. Methought I lay
Worse than the mutines in the bilboes. Rashly,   6
And praised be rashness for it—let us know   7
Our indiscretion sometimes serves us well   8
When our deep plots do pall, and that should learn us   9
There's a divinity that shapes our ends,
Rough-hew them how we will—
HORATIO   That is most certain.   11

294–295 Let . . . day i.e., (1) even Hercules couldn't stop Laertes's theatrical rant (2) I too will have my turn; i.e., despite any blustering attempts at interference, every person will sooner or later do what he
must do   **297 in** i.e., by recalling   **298 present push** immediate test
300 living lasting; also refers (for Laertes's benefit) to the plot against
Hamlet   **301 hour of quiet** time free of conflict

5.2. Location: The castle.
1 see the other i.e., hear the other news   **6 mutines** mutineers.   **bilboes**
shackles.   **Rashly** on impulse. (This adverb goes with ll. 12ff.)   **7 know**
acknowledge   **8 indiscretion** lack of foresight and judgment (not an
indiscreet act)   **9 pall** fail, falter, go stale.   **learn** teach   **11 Rough-hew**
shape roughly, botch

HAMLET   Up from my cabin,
My sea-gown scarfed about me, in the dark   13
Groped I to find out them, had my desire,
Fingered their packet, and in fine withdrew   15
To mine own room again, making so bold,
My fears forgetting manners, to unseal
Their grand commission; where I found, Horatio—
Ah, royal knavery!—an exact command,
Larded with many several sorts of reasons   20
Importing Denmark's health and England's too,   21
With, ho! such bugs and goblins in my life,   22
That on the supervise, no leisure bated,   23
No, not to stay the grinding of the ax,   24
My head should be struck off.
HORATIO   Is 't possible?
HAMLET [*Giving a document*]
Here's the commission. Read it at more leisure.
But wilt thou hear now how I did proceed?
HORATIO   I beseech you.
HAMLET
Being thus benetted round with villainies—
Ere I could make a prologue to my brains,   30
They had begun the play—I sat me down,   31
Devised a new commission, wrote it fair.   32
I once did hold it, as our statists do,   33
A baseness to write fair, and labored much   34
How to forget that learning, but, sir, now
It did me yeoman's service. Wilt thou know   36
Th' effect of what I wrote?
HORATIO   Ay, good my lord.   37
HAMLET
An earnest conjuration from the King,   38
As England was his faithful tributary,

---

13 sea-gown seaman's coat. **scarfed** loosely wrapped **15 Fingered**
pilfered, pinched. **in fine** finally, in conclusion **20 Larded** garnished,
decorated **21 Importing** relating to **22 bugs** bugbears, hobgoblins.
in my life i.e., to be feared if I were allowed to live **23 supervise** reading. **leisure bated** delay allowed **24 stay** await **30–31 Ere ... play**
i.e., before I could consciously turn my brain to the matter, it had
started working on a plan **32 fair** in a clear hand **33 statists** states-
men **34 baseness** i.e., lower-class trait **36 yeoman's** i.e., substantial,
faithful, loyal. (In the British navy, the ship's yeoman is usually a scribe
or clerk.) **37 effect** purport **38 conjuration** entreaty

As love between them like the palm might flourish,
As peace should still her wheaten garland wear   41
And stand a comma 'tween their amities,   42
And many suchlike "as"es of great charge,   43
That on the view and knowing of these contents,
Without debatement further more or less,
He should those bearers put to sudden death,
Not shriving time allowed.

HORATIO   How was this sealed?   47

HAMLET

Why, even in that was heaven ordinant.   48
I had my father's signet in my purse,   49
Which was the model of that Danish seal;   50
Folded the writ up in the form of th' other,   51
Subscribed it, gave 't th' impression, placed it safely,   52
The changeling never known. Now, the next day   53
Was our sea fight, and what to this was sequent
Thou knowest already.

HORATIO

So Guildenstern and Rosencrantz go to 't.

HAMLET

Why, man, they did make love to this employment.
They are not near my conscience. Their defeat   58
Does by their own insinuation grow.   59
'Tis dangerous when the baser nature comes   60
Between the pass and fell incensèd points   61
Of mighty opposites.

HORATIO   Why, what a king is this!   62

HAMLET

Does it not, think thee, stand me now upon—   63
He that hath killed my king and whored my mother,

---

41 still always. **wheaten garland** (Symbolic of fruitful agriculture, of peace and plenty.) **42 comma** (Indicating continuity, link.) **43 "as"es** (1) the "whereases" of a formal document (2) asses. **charge** (1) import (2) burden (appropriate to asses) **47 shriving time** time for confession and absolution **48 ordinant** directing **49 signet** small seal **50 model** replica **51 writ** writing **52 Subscribed** signed (with forged signature). **impression** i.e., with a wax seal **53 changeling** i.e., the substituted letter. (Literally, a fairy child substituted for a human one.) **58 defeat** destruction **59 insinuation** intrusive intervention, sticking their noses in my business **60 baser** of lower social station **61 pass** thrust. **fell** fierce **62 opposites** antagonists **63 stand me now upon—** become incumbent on me now

Popped in between th' election and my hopes,   65
Thrown out his angle for my proper life,   66
And with such cozenage—is 't not perfect conscience 67
To quit him with this arm? And is 't not to be damned 68
To let this canker of our nature come   69
In further evil?   70

HORATIO
It must be shortly known to him from England
What is the issue of the business there.

HAMLET
It will be short. The interim is mine,
And a man's life's no more than to say "one."   74
But I am very sorry, good Horatio,
That to Laertes I forgot myself,
For by the image of my cause I see
The portraiture of his. I'll court his favors.
But, sure, the bravery of his grief did put me   79
Into a tow'ring passion.

HORATIO   Peace, who comes here?

Enter a Courtier [Osric].

OSRIC   Your lordship is right welcome back to Denmark.

HAMLET   I humbly thank you, sir. [*To Horatio.*] Dost
know this water fly?

HORATIO   No, my good lord.

HAMLET   Thy state is the more gracious, for 'tis a vice to
know him. He hath much land, and fertile. Let a beast 86
be lord of beasts, and his crib shall stand at the King's 87
mess. 'Tis a chuff, but, as I say, spacious in the pos- 88
session of dirt.

OSRIC   Sweet lord, if your lordship were at leisure, I
should impart a thing to you from His Majesty.

HAMLET   I will receive it, sir, with all diligence of spirit.

---

65 election (The Danish monarch was "elected" by a small number of
high-ranking electors.)   **66 angle** fishing line.   **proper** very
67 cozenage trickery   **68 quit** requite, pay back   **69 canker** ulcer
69–70 come In grow into   **74 a man's . . . one** i.e., one's whole life
occupies such a short time, only as long as it takes to count to one
79 bravery bravado   **86–88 Let . . . mess** i.e., if a man, no matter how
beastlike, is as rich in possessions as Osric, he may eat at the King's
table   **88 chuff** boor, churl. (The second quarto spelling, *chough*, is a vari-
ant spelling that also suggests the meaning here of "chattering jackdaw.")

Put your bonnet to his right use; 'tis for the head.   93
OSRIC   I thank your lordship, it is very hot.
HAMLET   No, believe me, 'tis very cold. The wind is
   northerly.
OSRIC   It is indifferent cold, my lord, indeed.   97
HAMLET   But yet methinks it is very sultry and hot for
   my complexion.   99
OSRIC   Exceedingly, my lord. It is very sultry, as
   'twere—I cannot tell how. My lord, His Majesty bade
   me signify to you that 'a has laid a great wager on your
   head. Sir, this is the matter—
HAMLET   I beseech you, remember.
      [*Hamlet moves him to put on his hat.*]
OSRIC   Nay, good my lord; for my ease, in good faith.   105
   Sir, here is newly come to court Laertes—believe me,
   an absolute gentleman, full of most excellent differ-   107
   ences, of very soft society and great showing. Indeed,   108
   to speak feelingly of him, he is the card or calendar of   109
   gentry, for you shall find in him the continent of what   110
   part a gentleman would see.   111
HAMLET   Sir, his definement suffers no perdition in   112
   you, though I know to divide him inventorially   113
   would dozy th' arithmetic of memory, and yet but yaw   114
   neither in respect of his quick sail. But, in the verity of   115
   extolment, I take him to be a soul of great article and   116
   his infusion of such dearth and rareness as, to make   117
   true diction of him, his semblable is his mirror and   118

93 bonnet any kind of cap or hat.   **his** its   **97 indifferent** somewhat
99 complexion temperament   **105 for my ease** (A conventional reply
declining the invitation to put his hat back on.)   **107 absolute** perfect
107–108 differences special qualities   **108 soft society** agreeable manners.   **great showing** distinguished appearance   **109 feelingly** with just
perception.   **card** chart, map.   **calendar** guide   **110 gentry** good breeding   **110–111 the continent . . . part** one who contains in him all the
qualities. (A *continent* is that which contains.)   **what part** whatever
part, any part which   **112 definement** definition. (Hamlet proceeds to
mock Osric by using his lofty diction back at him.)   **perdition** loss,
diminution   **113 divide him inventorially** i.e., enumerate his graces
114 dozy dizzy.   **yaw** swing unsteadily off course. (Said of a ship.)
115 neither for all that.   **in respect of** in comparison with   **115–116 in
. . . extolment** in true praise (of him)   **116 of great article** one with
many articles in his inventory   **117 infusion** essence, character infused
into him by nature.   **dearth and rareness** rarity   **117–118 make true
diction** speak truly   **118 semblable** only true likeness

who else would trace him his umbrage, nothing 119
more.

OSRIC   Your lordship speaks most infallibly of him.

HAMLET   The concernancy, sir? Why do we wrap the 122
gentleman in our more rawer breath? 123

OSRIC   Sir?

HORATIO   Is 't not possible to understand in another 125
tongue? You will do 't, sir, really. 126

HAMLET   What imports the nomination of this gen- 127
tleman?

OSRIC   Of Laertes?

HORATIO   [*To Hamlet*] His purse is empty already; all 's
golden words are spent.

HAMLET   Of him, sir.

OSRIC   I know you are not ignorant—

HAMLET   I would you did, sir. Yet in faith if you did,
it would not much approve me. Well, sir? 135

OSRIC   You are not ignorant of what excellence Laertes
is—

HAMLET   I dare not confess that, lest I should compare 138
with him in excellence. But to know a man well were 139
to know himself. 140

OSRIC   I mean, sir, for his weapon; but in the imputa- 141
tion laid on him by them in his meed, he's unfellowed. 142

HAMLET   What's his weapon?

OSRIC   Rapier and dagger.

HAMLET   That's two of his weapons—but well. 145

OSRIC   The King, sir, hath wagered with him six Barbary

---

119 who . . . trace any other person who would wish to follow. **umbrage** shadow   **122 concernancy** import, relevance   **123 rawer breath**
i.e., speech which can only come short in praising him   **125–126 to
understand . . . tongue** i.e., for you, Osric, to understand when someone
else speaks your language. (Horatio twits Osric for not being able to
understand the kind of flowery speech he himself uses, when Hamlet
speaks in such a vein. Alternatively, all this could be said to Hamlet.)
126 You will do 't i.e., you can if you try   **127 nomination** naming
135 approve commend   **138–140 I dare . . . himself** i.e., I dare not
boast of knowing Laertes's excellence lest I seem to compare his with
my own, since to appreciate excellence in another one must possess
it oneself; by the same token, it is presumptuous to claim the self-
knowledge necessary to know another person well   **141 for** i.e., with
141–142 imputation . . . them reputation given him by others   **142 meed**
merit.   **unfellowed** unmatched   **145 but well** but never mind

horses, against the which he has impawned, as I take 147
it, six French rapiers and poniards, with their assigns, 148
as girdle, hangers, and so. Three of the carriages, in 149
faith, are very dear to fancy, very responsive to the 150
hilts, most delicate carriages, and of very liberal con- 151
ceit. 152

HAMLET   What call you the carriages?

HORATIO [*To Hamlet*]   I knew you must be edified by
the margent ere you had done. 155

OSRIC   The carriages, sir, are the hangers.

HAMLET   The phrase would be more germane to the
matter if we could carry a cannon by our sides; I would
it might be hangers till then. But, on: six Barbary horses
against six French swords, their assigns, and three lib-
eral-conceited carriages; that's the French bet against
the Danish. Why is this impawned, as you call it?

OSRIC   The King, sir, hath laid, sir, that in a dozen 163
passes between yourself and him, he shall not exceed 164
you three hits. He hath laid on twelve for nine, and it
would come to immediate trial, if your lordship would
vouchsafe the answer. 167

HAMLET   How if I answer no?

OSRIC   I mean, my lord, the opposition of your person
in trial.

HAMLET   Sir, I will walk here in the hall. If it please His
Majesty, it is the breathing time of day with me. Let 172
the foils be brought, the gentleman willing, and the
King hold his purpose, I will win for him an I can; if
not, I will gain nothing but my shame and the odd
hits.

---

147 he i.e., Laertes.   **impawned** staked, wagered   **148 poniards** daggers.
assigns appurtenances   **149 hangers** straps on the sword belt (*girdle*) from
which the sword hung.   **and so** and so on.   **carriages** (An affected way of
saying *hangers*; literally, gun carriages.)   **150 dear to fancy** fancifully
designed, tasteful.   **responsive** corresponding closely, matching or well
adjusted   **151 delicate** (i.e., in workmanship)   **151–152 liberal conceit**
elaborate design   **155 margent** margin of a book, place for explanatory
notes   **163 laid** wagered   **164 passes** bouts. (The odds of the betting are
hard to explain. Possibly the King bets that Hamlet will win at least five out
of twelve, at which point Laertes raises the odds against himself by betting
he will win nine.)   **167 vouchsafe the answer** be so good as to accept the
challenge. (Hamlet deliberately takes the phrase in its literal sense.)
172 breathing time exercise period.   **Let** i.e., if

OSRIC Shall I deliver you so? 177

HAMLET To this effect, sir—after what flourish your nature will.

OSRIC I commend my duty to your lordship. 180

HAMLET Yours, yours. [*Exit Osric.*] 'A does well to commend it himself; there are no tongues else for 's 182
turn. 183

HORATIO This lapwing runs away with the shell on his 184
head.

HAMLET 'A did comply with his dug before 'a sucked 186
it. Thus has he—and many more of the same breed
that I know the drossy age dotes on—only got the 188
tune of the time and, out of an habit of encounter, a 189
kind of yeasty collection, which carries them through 190
and through the most fanned and winnowed opinions; 191
and do but blow them to their trial, the bubbles are 192
out. 193

    Enter a Lord.

LORD My lord, His Majesty commended him to you by
young Osric, who brings back to him that you attend
him in the hall. He sends to know if your pleasure
hold to play with Laertes, or that you will take longer 197
time.

HAMLET I am constant to my purposes; they follow the
King's pleasure. If his fitness speaks, mine is ready; 200
now or whensoever, provided I be so able as now.

LORD The King and Queen and all are coming down.

---

177 **deliver** report what you say 180 **commend** commit to your favor.
(A conventional salutation; but Hamlet wryly uses a more literal meaning, "recommend," in l. 182.) 182–183 **for 's turn** for his purposes, i.e.,
to do it for him 184 **lapwing** (A proverbial type of youthful forwardness. Also, a bird that draws intruders away from its nest and was
thought to run about when newly hatched with its head in the shell; a
seeming reference to Osric's hat.) 186 **comply . . . dug** observe ceremonious formality toward his nurse's or mother's teat 188 **drossy** laden
with scum and impurities, frivolous 189 **tune** temper, mood, manner
of speech. **habit of encounter** demeanor of social intercourse
190 **yeasty** frothy. **collection** i.e., of current phrases 191 **fanned and
winnowed** select and refined. (Literally, like grain separated from its
chaff. Osric is both the chaff and the bubbly froth on the surface of the
liquor that is soon blown away.) 192–193 **blow . . . out** i.e., put them to
the test, and their ignorance is exposed 197 **that** if 200 **If . . . ready** if
he declares his readiness, my convenience waits on his

HAMLET   In happy time.   203
LORD   The Queen desires you to use some gentle enter-   204
tainment to Laertes before you fall to play.   205
HAMLET   She well instructs me.   [*Exit Lord.*]
HORATIO   You will lose, my lord.
HAMLET   I do not think so. Since he went into France, I
have been in continual practice; I shall win at the
odds. But thou wouldst not think how ill all's here
about my heart; but it is no matter.
HORATIO   Nay, good my lord—
HAMLET   It is but foolery, but it is such a kind of gain-   213
giving as would perhaps trouble a woman.   214
HORATIO   If your mind dislike anything, obey it. I will
forestall their repair hither and say you are not fit.   216
HAMLET   Not a whit, we defy augury. There is special
providence in the fall of a sparrow. If it be now, 'tis
not to come; if it be not to come, it will be now; if it
be not now, yet it will come. The readiness is all. Since 220
no man of aught he leaves knows, what is 't to leave   221
betimes? Let be.   222

A table prepared. [Enter] trumpets, drums, and
officers with cushions; King, Queen, [Osric,] and
all the state; foils, daggers, [and wine borne in,]
and Laertes.

KING
Come, Hamlet, come and take this hand from me.
          [*The King puts Laertes's hand into Hamlet's.*]
HAMLET
Give me your pardon, sir. I have done you wrong,
But pardon 't as you are a gentleman.
This presence knows,   226
And you must needs have heard, how I am punished
With a sore distraction. What I have done
That might your nature, honor, and exception   229

203 **In happy time** (A phrase of courtesy indicating acceptance.)
204–205 **entertainment** greeting   213–214 **gaingiving** misgiving
216 **repair** coming   220–222 **Since . . . Let be** since no one has knowledge of what he is leaving behind, what does an early death matter after
all? Enough; don't struggle against it.   226 **presence** royal assembly
229 **exception** disapproval

Roughly awake, I here proclaim was madness.
Was 't Hamlet wronged Laertes? Never Hamlet.
If Hamlet from himself be ta'en away,
And when he's not himself does wrong Laertes,
Then Hamlet does it not, Hamlet denies it.
Who does it, then? His madness. If 't be so,
Hamlet is of the faction that is wronged;   236
His madness is poor Hamlet's enemy.
Sir, in this audience,
Let my disclaiming from a purposed evil
Free me so far in your most generous thoughts
That I have shot my arrow o'er the house   241
And hurt my brother.

LAERTES   I am satisfied in nature,   242
Whose motive in this case should stir me most   243
To my revenge. But in my terms of honor
I stand aloof, and will no reconcilement
Till by some elder masters of known honor
I have a voice and precedent of peace   247
To keep my name ungored. But till that time,   248
I do receive your offered love like love,
And will not wrong it.

HAMLET   I embrace it freely,
And will this brothers' wager frankly play.—   251
Give us the foils. Come on.

LAERTES   Come, one for me.

HAMLET
I'll be your foil, Laertes. In mine ignorance   253
Your skill shall, like a star i' the darkest night,
Stick fiery off indeed.

LAERTES   You mock me, sir.   255

HAMLET   No, by this hand.

KING
Give them the foils, young Osric. Cousin Hamlet,
You know the wager?

---

236 faction party   **241 That I have** as if I had   **242 in nature** i.e., as to my
personal feelings   **243 motive** prompting   **247 voice** authoritative pro-
nouncement.   **of peace** for reconciliation   **248 name ungored** reputation
unwounded   **251 frankly** without ill feeling or the burden of rancor
253 foil thin metal background which sets a jewel off (with pun on the
blunted rapier for fencing)   **255 Stick fiery off** stand out brilliantly

HAMLET   Very well, my lord.
  Your Grace has laid the odds o' the weaker side.   259
KING
  I do not fear it; I have seen you both.
  But since he is bettered, we have therefore odds.   261
LAERTES
  This is too heavy. Let me see another.
                [He exchanges his foil for another.]
HAMLET
  This likes me well. These foils have all a length?   263
                      [They prepare to play.]
OSRIC   Ay, my good lord.
KING
  Set me the stoups of wine upon that table.
  If Hamlet give the first or second hit,
  Or quit in answer of the third exchange,   267
  Let all the battlements their ordnance fire.
  The King shall drink to Hamlet's better breath,   269
  And in the cup an union shall he throw   270
  Richer than that which four successive kings
  In Denmark's crown have worn. Give me the cups,
  And let the kettle to the trumpet speak,   273
  The trumpet to the cannoneer without,
  The cannons to the heavens, the heaven to earth,
  "Now the King drinks to Hamlet." Come, begin.
                      Trumpets the while.
  And you, the judges, bear a wary eye.
HAMLET   Come on, sir.
LAERTES   Come, my lord. *[They play. Hamlet scores a hit.]*
HAMLET   One.
LAERTES   No.
HAMLET   Judgment.
OSRIC   A hit, a very palpable hit.
           Drum, trumpets, and shot. Flourish.
                   A piece goes off.

259 laid the odds o' bet on, backed   **261 is bettered** has improved; is the
odds-on favorite. (Laertes's handicap is the "three hits" specified in
l. 165.)   **263 likes me** pleases me   **267 Or . . . exchange** i.e., or requites
Laertes in the third bout for having won the first two   **269 better
breath** improved vigor   **270 union** pearl. (So called, according to Pliny's
Natural History, 9, because pearls are *unique*, never identical.)
273 kettle kettledrum

LAERTES Well, again.

KING

Stay, give me drink. Hamlet, this pearl is thine.

> [*He throws a pearl in Hamlet's cup,
>   and drinks.*]

Here's to thy health. Give him the cup.

HAMLET

I'll play this bout first. Set it by awhile.

Come. [*They play.*] Another hit; what say you?

LAERTES A touch, a touch, I do confess 't.

KING

Our son shall win.

QUEEN   He's fat and scant of breath.   289

Here, Hamlet, take my napkin, rub thy brows.   290

The Queen carouses to thy fortune, Hamlet.   291

HAMLET Good madam!

KING Gertrude, do not drink.

QUEEN

I will, my lord, I pray you pardon me.   [*She drinks.*]

KING [*Aside*]

It is the poisoned cup. It is too late.

HAMLET

I dare not drink yet, madam; by and by.

QUEEN Come, let me wipe thy face.

LAERTES [*To the King*]

My lord, I'll hit him now.

KING   I do not think 't.

LAERTES [*Aside*]

And yet it is almost against my conscience.

HAMLET

Come, for the third, Laertes. You do but dally.

I pray you, pass with your best violence;   301

I am afeard you make a wanton of me.   302

LAERTES Say you so? Come on.   [*They play.*]

OSRIC Nothing neither way.

LAERTES

Have at you now!

---

289 fat not physically fit, out of training   **290 napkin** handkerchief
291 carouses drinks a toast   **301 pass** thrust   **302 make . . . me** i.e.,
treat me like a spoiled child, holding back to give me an advantage

[*Laertes wounds Hamlet; then, in scuffling,*
they change rapiers, and Hamlet wounds Laertes.]

KING   Part them! They are incensed.   305

HAMLET
  Nay, come, again.   [*The Queen falls.*]

OSRIC   Look to the Queen there, ho!

HORATIO
  They bleed on both sides. How is it, my lord?

OSRIC   How is 't, Laertes?

LAERTES
  Why, as a woodcock to mine own springe, Osric;   309
  I am justly killed with mine own treachery.

HAMLET
  How does the Queen?

KING   She swoons to see them bleed.

QUEEN
  No, no, the drink, the drink—O my dear Hamlet—
  The drink, the drink! I am poisoned.   [*She dies.*]

HAMLET
  O villainy! Ho, let the door be locked!
  Treachery! Seek it out.   [*Laertes falls. Exit Osric.*]

LAERTES
  It is here, Hamlet. Hamlet, thou art slain.
  No med'cine in the world can do thee good;
  In thee there is not half an hour's life.
  The treacherous instrument is in thy hand,
  Unbated and envenomed. The foul practice   320
  Hath turned itself on me. Lo, here I lie,
  Never to rise again. Thy mother's poisoned.
  I can no more. The King, the King's to blame.

HAMLET
  The point envenomed too? Then, venom, to thy work.
                    [*He stabs the King.*]

ALL   Treason! Treason!

KING
  O, yet defend me, friends! I am but hurt.

---

305 s.d. in scuffling, they change rapiers (This stage direction occurs in
the Folio. According to a widespread stage tradition, Hamlet receives a
scratch, realizes that Laertes's sword is unbated, and accordingly forces
an exchange.)   **309 woodcock** a bird, a type of stupidity or as a decoy.
springe trap, snare   **320 Unbated** not blunted with a button.   **practice**
plot

HAMLET [*Forcing the King to drink*]
   Here, thou incestuous, murderous, damnèd Dane,
   Drink off this potion. Is thy union here?   328
   Follow my mother.   [*The King dies.*]
LAERTES   He is justly served.
   It is a poison tempered by himself.   330
   Exchange forgiveness with me, noble Hamlet.
   Mine and my father's death come not upon thee,
   Nor thine on me!   [*He dies.*]
HAMLET
   Heaven make thee free of it! I follow thee.
   I am dead, Horatio. Wretched Queen, adieu!
   You that look pale and tremble at this chance,   336
   That are but mutes or audience to this act,   337
   Had I but time—as this fell sergeant, Death,   338
   Is strict in his arrest—O, I could tell you—   339
   But let it be. Horatio, I am dead;
   Thou livest. Report me and my cause aright
   To the unsatisfied.
HORATIO   Never believe it.
   I am more an antique Roman than a Dane.   343
   Here's yet some liquor left.
          [*He attempts to drink from the poisoned cup.
                         Hamlet prevents him.*]
HAMLET   As thou'rt a man,
   Give me the cup! Let go! By heaven, I'll ha''t.
   O God, Horatio, what a wounded name,
   Things standing thus unknown, shall I leave behind me!
   If thou didst ever hold me in thy heart,
   Absent thee from felicity awhile,
   And in this harsh world draw thy breath in pain
   To tell my story. (*A march afar off* [*and a volley within*].)
      What warlike noise is this?

      Enter Osric.

OSRIC
   Young Fortinbras, with conquest come from Poland,

---

328 union pearl. (See l. 270; with grim puns on the word's other meanings: marriage, shared death.) **330 tempered** mixed **336 chance** mischance **337 mutes** silent observers **338 fell** cruel. **sergeant** sheriff's officer **339 strict** (1) severely just (2) unavoidable. **arrest** (1) taking into custody (2) stopping my speech **343 Roman** (It was the Roman custom to follow masters in death.)

To th' ambassadors of England gives
This warlike volley.

HAMLET   O, I die, Horatio!
The potent poison quite o'ercrows my spirit.   355
I cannot live to hear the news from England,
But I do prophesy th' election lights
On Fortinbras. He has my dying voice.   358
So tell him, with th' occurrents more and less   359
Which have solicited—the rest is silence.   [*He dies.*] 360

HORATIO
Now cracks a noble heart. Good night, sweet prince,
And flights of angels sing thee to thy rest!

                                        [*March within.*]
Why does the drum come hither?

*Enter Fortinbras, with the [English] Ambassadors
[with drum, colors, and attendants].*

FORTINBRAS
Where is this sight?

HORATIO   What is it you would see?
If aught of woe or wonder, cease your search.

FORTINBRAS
This quarry cries on havoc. O proud Death,   366
What feast is toward in thine eternal cell,   367
That thou so many princes at a shot
So bloodily hast struck?

FIRST AMBASSADOR   The sight is dismal,
And our affairs from England come too late.
The ears are senseless that should give us hearing,
To tell him his commandment is fulfilled,
That Rosencrantz and Guildenstern are dead.
Where should we have our thanks?

HORATIO   Not from his mouth,   374
Had it th' ability of life to thank you.

---

355 o'ercrows triumphs over (like the winner in a cockfight)   **358 voice**
vote   **359 occurrents** events, incidents   **360 solicited** moved, urged.
(Hamlet doesn't finish saying what the events have prompted; presumably his acts of vengeance, or his reporting those events to Fortinbras.)   **366 quarry** heap of dead.   **cries on havoc** proclaims a general
slaughter   **367 feast** i.e., Death feasting on those who have fallen.
toward in preparation   **374 his** i.e., Claudius's

He never gave commandment for their death.
But since, so jump upon this bloody question,   377
You from the Polack wars, and you from England,
Are here arrived, give order that these bodies
High on a stage be placèd to the view,   380
And let me speak to th' yet unknowing world
How these things came about. So shall you hear
Of carnal, bloody, and unnatural acts,
Of accidental judgments, casual slaughters,   384
Of deaths put on by cunning and forced cause,   385
And, in this upshot, purposes mistook
Fall'n on th' inventors' heads. All this can I
Truly deliver.
FORTINBRAS   Let us haste to hear it,
And call the noblest to the audience.
For me, with sorrow I embrace my fortune.
I have some rights of memory in this kingdom,   391
Which now to claim my vantage doth invite me.   392
HORATIO
Of that I shall have also cause to speak,
And from his mouth whose voice will draw on more.   394
But let this same be presently performed,   395
Even while men's minds are wild, lest more mischance
On plots and errors happen.
FORTINBRAS   Let four captains   397
Bear Hamlet, like a soldier, to the stage,
For he was likely, had he been put on,   399
To have proved most royal; and for his passage,   400
The soldiers' music and the rite of war
Speak loudly for him.
Take up the bodies. Such a sight as this
Becomes the field, but here shows much amiss.   404
Go bid the soldiers shoot.
        Exeunt [marching, bearing off the dead bodies;
            a peal of ordnance is shot off].

377 **jump** precisely, immediately.   **question** dispute   380 **stage** platform
384 **judgments** retributions.   **casual** occurring by chance   385 **put on**
instigated   391 **of memory** traditional, remembered, unforgotten
392 **vantage** i.e., presence at this opportune moment   394 **voice . . .
more** vote will influence still others   395 **presently** immediately
397 **On** on the basis of, on top of   399 **put on** i.e., invested in royal
office, and so put to the test   400 **passage** death   404 **field** i.e., of battle

Date and Text

Like everything else about *Hamlet,* the textual problem is complicated. On July 26, 1602, James Roberts entered in the Stationers' Register, the official record book of the London Company of Stationers (booksellers and printers), "A booke called the Revenge of Hamlett Prince Denmarke as yt was latelie Acted by the Lord Chamberleyn his servantes." For some reason, however, Roberts did not print his copy of *Hamlet* until 1604, by which time had appeared the following unauthorized edition:

> THE Tragicall Historie of HAMLET *Prince of Denmarke*[.] By William Shake-speare. As it hath beene diuerse times acted by his Highnesse seruants in the Cittie of London: as also in the two Vniuersities of Cambridge and Oxford, and elsewhere At London printed for N. L. [Nicholas Ling] and Iohn Trundell. 1603.

This edition, the bad quarto of *Hamlet,* seems to have been memorially reconstructed by actors who toured the provinces (note the references to Cambridge, Oxford, etc.), with some recollection of an earlier *Hamlet* play (the *Ur-Hamlet*) written before 1589 and acted during the 1590s. The piratical actors had no recourse to an authoritative manuscript. One may have played Marcellus and possibly Lucianus and Voltimand. Their version seems to have been based on an adaptation of the company's original promptbook, which itself stood at one remove from Shakespeare's foul papers by way of an intermediate manuscript. The resulting text is very corrupt, and yet it seems to have affected the more authentic text because the compositors of the second quarto made use of it, especially when they typeset the first act.

The authorized quarto of *Hamlet* appeared in 1604. Roberts, the printer, seems to have reached some agreement with Ling, one of the publishers of the bad quarto, for their initials are now paired on the title page:

> THE Tragicall Historie of HAMLET, *Prince of Denmarke.* By William Shakespeare. Newly imprinted and enlarged to almost as much againe as it was, according to the true and perfect Coppie. AT LONDON, Printed by I. R. [James Roberts]

for N. L. [Nicholas Ling] and are to be sold at his shoppe
vnder Saint Dunstons Church in Fleetstreet. 1604.

Some copies of this edition are dated 1605. This text was
based seemingly on Shakespeare's own papers with the
bookkeeper's annotations, but is marred by printing errors
and is at times contaminated by the bad quarto—presumably when the printers found Shakespeare's manuscript
unreadable. This second quarto served as copy for a third
quarto in 1611, Ling having meanwhile transferred his
rights in the play to John Smethwick. A fourth quarto, un-
dated but before 1623, was based on the third.

The First Folio text of 1623 omits more than two hundred
lines found in the second quarto. Yet it supplies some
clearly authentic passages. It seems to derive from a transcript of Shakespeare's draft in which cuts made by the
author were observed—cuts made by Shakespeare quite
possibly because he knew the draft to be too long for performance, and which had either not been marked in the second
quarto copy or had been ignored there by the compositors.
The Folio also incorporates other alterations seemingly
made for clarity or in anticipation of performance. To this
theatrically motivated transcript Shakespeare apparently
contributed some revisions. Subsequently, this version evidently was copied again by a careless scribe who took many
liberties with the text. Typesetting from this inferior manuscript, the Folio compositors occasionally consulted the
second quarto, but not often enough. Thus, even though the
Folio supplies some genuine readings, as does the first
quarto when both the Folio and the second quarto are
wrong, the second quarto remains the most authentic version of the text.

Since the text of the second quarto is too long to be ac-
commodated in the two hours' traffic of the stage and it
becomes even longer when the words found only in the Folio are added, Shakespeare must have known it would have to
be cut for performance and probably marked at least some
omissions himself. Since he may have consented to such
cuts primarily because of the constraints of time, however,
this present edition holds to the view that the passages in
question should not be excised from the text we read. The
Hamlet presented here is doubtless longer than any version

ever acted in Shakespeare's day, and thus does not represent a script for any actual performance, but it may well represent the play as Shakespeare wrote it and then somewhat expanded it; it also includes passages that he may reluctantly have consented to cut for performance. It is also possible that some cuts were artistically intended, but, in the face of real uncertainty in this matter, an editorial policy of inclusion gives to the reader those passages that would otherwise have to be excised or put in an appendix on questionable grounds of authorial "intent."

Hamlet must have been produced before the Stationers' Register entry of July 26, 1602. Francis Meres does not mention the play in 1598 in his *Palladis Tamia: Wit's Treasury* (a slender volume on contemporary literature and art; valuable because it lists most of the plays of Shakespeare that existed at that time). Gabriel Harvey attributes the "tragedy of Hamlet, Prince of Denmark" to Shakespeare in a marginal note in Harvey's copy of Speght's Chaucer; Harvey acquired the book in 1598, but could have written the note any time between then and 1601 or even 1603. More helpful in dating is Hamlet's clear reference to the so-called "War of the Theaters," the rivalry between the adult actors and the boy actors whose companies had newly revived in 1598–1599 after nearly a decade of inactivity. The Children of the Chapel Royal began acting at Blackfriars in 1598 and provided such keen competition in 1599–1601 that the adult actors were at times forced to tour the provinces (see *Hamlet*, 2.2.332–362). Revenge tragedy was also in fashion during these years: John Marston's *Antonio's Revenge*, for example, dates from 1599–1601, and *The Malcontent* is from about the same time or slightly later.

Textual Notes

These textual notes are not a historical collation, either of the early quartos and the early folios or of more recent editions; they are simply a record of departures in this edition from the copy text. The reading adopted in this edition appears in boldface, followed by the rejected reading from the copy text, i.e., the second quarto of 1604. Only major alterations in punctuation are noted. Changes in lineation are not indicated, nor are some minor and obvious typographical errors.

Abbreviations used:
F the First Folio
Q quarto
s.d. stage direction
s.p. speech prefix

Copy text: the second quarto of 1604–1605 [Q2]. The First Folio text also represents an independently authoritative text; although seemingly not the correct choice for copy text, the Folio text is considerably less marred by typographical errors than is Q2. The adopted readings in these notes are from F unless otherwise indicated; [eds.] means that the adopted reading was first proposed by some editor since the time of F. Some readings are also supplied from the pirated first quarto of 1603 [Q1].

1.1. 1 Who's Whose   **19 soldier** [F, Q1] souldiers   **44 off** [Q1] of   **48 harrows** horrowes   **67 sledded Polacks** [eds.] sleaded pollax   **77 why** [F, Q1] with   **cast** cost   **91 heraldry** [F, Q1] heraldy   **92 those** [F, Q1] these   **95 returned** returne   **97 covenant** comart   **98 designed** [eds.] desseigne   **112 e'en so** [eds.] enso   **119 tenantless** tennatlesse   **125 feared** [eds.] feare   **142 you** [F, Q1] your   **144 at it** it   **181 conveniently** [F, Q1] conuenient

1.2. s.d. Gertrude Gertradt (and elsewhere; also Gertrad)   **1 s.p. King** Claud   **67 so** so much   **77 good** coold   **82 shapes** [Q3] chapes   **83 denote** deuote   **96 a** or   **105 corpse** [eds.] course   **112 you. For** you for   **129 sullied** [eds.] sallied [Q2] solid [F]   **132 self** seale   **133 weary** wary   **137 to this** thus   **140 satyr** [F4] satire   **143 would** [F, Q1] should   **149 even she** [F; not in Q2]   **175 to drink deep** [F, Q1] for to drinke   **178 to see** [F, Q1] to   **199 waste** [F2] wast [Q2, F]   **210 Where, as** [Q5] Whereas   **225 Indeed, indeed** [F, Q1] Indeede   **241 Very like, very like** [F, Q1] Very like   **242 hundred** hundreth   **243 s.p. Marcellus, Bernardo** [eds.] Both   **247 tonight** to nigh   **256 fare** farre   **257 eleven** a leaven   **259 Exeunt** [at l. 258 in Q2]   **262 Foul** [F, Q1] fonde

1.3. 3 convoy is conuay, in   **12 bulk** bulkes   **18** [F; not in Q2]   **29 weigh** way   **49 like a** a   **74 Are** Or   **75 be** boy   **76 loan** loue   **77 dulls the** dulleth   **110 Running** [eds.] Wrong [Q2] Roaming [F]   **116 springes** springs   **126 tether** tider   **130 implorators** imploratotors   **131 bawds** [eds.] bonds   **132 beguile** beguile

1.4. 2 is a is   **6 s.d. go off** [eds.] goes of   **17 revel** [Q3] reueale   **36 evil** [eds.] eale [Q2] ease [Q3]   **37 often dout** [eds.] of a doubt   **49 inurned** interr'd [Q2, Q1]   **61, 79 wafts** waues   **80 off** of   **82 artery** arture   **86 s.d. Exeunt** Exit   **87 imagination** [F, Q1] imagion

1.5. 1 Whither [eds.] Whether   **21 fretful** [F, Q1] fearfull   **44 wit** [eds.] wits
48 what a what   **56 lust** [F, Q1] but   **57 sate** [F] sort   **59 scent** [eds.] sent
68 alleys [eds.] allies   **69 posset** possesse   **96 stiffly** swiftly   **119 bird** and
128 s.p. Horatio, Marcellus Booth [also at l. 151]   **heaven, my lord**
heauen   **138 Look you, I'll** I will   **179 soe'er** so mere   **185 Well** well, well
[Q1, Q2]

2.1. s.d. man [eds.] man or two   **29 Faith, no** Fayth   **41 warrant** wit
42 sullies sallies   **43 wi' the** with   **60 o'ertook** or tooke   **64 takes** take
76 s.d. Exit Reynaldo [at l. 75 in Q2]   **107 passion** passions

2.2. 57 o'erhasty hastie   **73 three** [F, Q1] threescore   **90 since brevity**
breuitie   **125 This** [Q2 has a speech prefix: *Pol.* This]   **126 above** about
137 winking working   **143 his** her   **148 watch** wath   **149 to a** to   **151 'tis**
[F, Q1; not in Q2]   **170 s.d. Exeunt** [eds.] Exit   **210 sanity** sanctity
212–213 and suddenly . . . him [F; not in Q2]   **213 honorable lord** lord
214 most humbly take take   **215 cannot, sir** cannot   **216 more** not more
224 excellent extent   **228–229 overhappy. On** euer happy on   **229 cap** lap
240–270 Let . . . attended [F; not in Q2]   **267 s.p. Rosencrantz, Guildenstern**
Both [F]   **273 even** euer   **288 could** can   **292 off** of   **304 What a** What
306–307 admirable, in action how . . . angel, in [F, subst.] admirable in action,
how . . . Angell in   **310 no, nor** nor   **314 you** yet   **321 of** on   **324–325 the**
clown . . . sear [F; not in Q2]   **tickle** [eds.] tickled [F]   **326 blank** black
337–362 How . . . too [F; not in Q2]   **342 berattle** [eds.] be-ratled [F]
349 most like [eds.] like most [F]   **373 lest my** let me   **381 too** to
398–399 tragical-historical, tragical-comical-historical-pastoral [F; not in Q2]
400–401 light . . . these [eds.] light for the lawe of writ, and the liberty: these
425 By 'r by   **429 e'en to 't** ento 't   **French falconers** friendly Fankners
433 s.p. [and elsewhere] First Player Player   **443 affectation** affection
446 tale [F, Q1] talke   **454 the th'** talke   **456 heraldry** [F, Q1] heraudy   **dismal.**
Head dismall head   **474 Then senseless Ilium** [F; not in Q2]   **481 And, like**
Like   **495 fellies** [F4] follies [Q2] Fallies [F]   **504 "Mobled queen" is good**
[F; not in Q2; F reads "Inobled"]   **506 bisson** Bison   **514 husband's** [F, Q1]
husband   **541 or** [F, Q1] lines, or   **547 till** tell   **548 s.d. Exeunt** [F; Q2 has
"Exeunt Pol. and Players" at l. 547]   **554 his** the   **556 and** an   **559 to Hec-**
uba [F, Q1] to her   **561 the cue** that   **582 O, vengeance** [F; not in Q2]
584 father [Q1, Q3, Q4; not in Q2, F]   **588 scullion** [F] stallyon [Q2] scalion
[Q1]   **600 the devil a** deale   **the devil** the deale

3.1. 1 And An   **28 too** two   **32 lawful espials** [F; not in Q2]   **33 Will** Wee'le
46 loneliness lowlines   **56 Let's withdraw** withdraw   **56 s.d. Enter Hamlet**
[at l. 55 in Q2]   **65 wished. To** wisht to   **73 disprized** despiz'd   **84 of us all**
[F, Q1; not in Q2]   **86 sicklied** sickled   **93 well, well, well** well   **100 the**
these   **108 your honesty** you   **119 inoculate** euocutat   **122 to a** a
130 knaves al knaues   **144 paintings too** [Q1] paintings   **146 jig, you amble**
gig & amble   **147 lisp** list   **148 your ignorance** [F, Q1] ignorance   **155 Th'**
expectancy Th' expectation   **159 music** musickt   **160 that** what   **161 tune**
time   **162 feature** stature   **164** [Q2 has "Exit" at the end of this line]
191 unwatched vnmatcht

3.2. 10 tatters totters   **split** [F, Q1] spleet   **27 of the** of   **29 praise** praysd
37 sir [F; not in Q2]   **45 s.d. Enter . . . Rosencrantz** [at l. 47 in Q2]
88 detecting detected   **107 s.p.** [and elsewhere] Queen Ger   **112–113** [F; not
in Q2]   **127 devil** deule [Q2] Diuel [F]   **133 s.d. sound** [eds.] sounds   **Anon**

comes Anon come   **135 miching** [F, Q1] munching   **140 keep counsel** [F, Q1] keepe   **153 s.p. [and throughout scene] Player King** King   **154 orbèd** orb'd the   **159 s.p. [and throughout scene] Player Queen** Quee   **162 your** our **164** [Q2 follows here with an extraneous unrhymed line: "For women feare too much, euen as they loue"]   **165 For** And   **166 In** Eyther none in **167 love** Lord   **179 Wormwood, wormwood** That's wormwood   **180 s.p. Player Queen** [not in Q2]   **188 like** the   **197 joys** ioy   **217 An** And   **221 a widow** [F, Q1] I be a widow   **be** be a   **226 s.d. Exit** [F, Q1] Exeunt **240 wince** [Q1] winch [Q2, F]   **241 s.d.** [at l. 242 in Q2]   **254 Confederate** [F, Q1] Considerat   **256 infected** [F, Q1, Q4] inuected   **258 usurp** vsurps **264** [F; not in Q2]   **274 with two** with   **288 s.d.** [F; at l. 293 in Q2]   **308 start** stare   **317 of my** of   **343 s.d.** [at l. 341 in Q2]   **357 thumb** the vmber **366 to the top of** to   **370 can fret me** [F] fret me not [Q2] can fret me, yet [Q1]   **371 s.d.** [at l. 372 in Q2]   **385 s.p. Polonius** [F; not in Q2]   **386 Leave me, friends** [so F; Q2 places before "I will say so," and assigns both to Hamlet]   **388 breathes** breakes   **390 bitter ... day** busines as the bitter day **395 daggers** [F, Q1] dagger

3.3. 19 huge hough   **22 ruin** raine   **23 but with** but   **50 pardoned** pardon **58 Offense's** [eds.] Offences   **shove** showe   **73 pat ... a-praying** but now a is a praying   **75 revenged** reuendge   **79 hire and salary** base and silly

3.4. 4 shroud [Q1] [eds.] silence [Q2, F]   **5–6 with him ... Mother** [F; not in Q2]   **7 warrant** wait   **8 s.d. Enter Hamlet** [at l. 5 in Q2]   **21 inmost** most **43 off** of   **51 tristful** heated   **53** [assigned in Q2 to Hamlet]   **60 heaven-kissing** heaue, a kissing   **89 panders** pardons   **91 my ... soul** [eds.] my very eyes into my soule [Q2] mine eyes into my very soul [F]   **92 grainèd** greeued **93 not leave** leaue there   **100 tithe** kyth   **146 Ecstasy** [F; not in Q2]   **150 I the** the   **165 live** leaue   **172 Refrain tonight** to refraine night   **193 ravel** rouell   **205 to breathe** [eds.] to breath   **222 a** [F, Q1] a most   **224 s.d. Exeunt** [eds.] Exit

4.2. s.d. [Q2: "Enter Hamlet, Rosencraus, and others."]   **2** [F; not in Q2] **3 s.p. Hamlet** [not in Q2]   **4 s.d.** [F; not in Q2]   **7 Compounded** Compound **19 ape** apple   **31–32 Hide ... after** [F; not in Q2]

4.3. 44 With fiery quickness [F; not in Q2]   **56 and so** so   **72 were** will **begun** begin

4.4. 20–21 name. To name To

4.5. 16 Let ... in [assigned in Q2 to Horatio]   **20 s.d.** [at l. 16 in Q2]   **38 with** all with   **57 Indeed, la** Indeede   **83 in their** in   **90 his** this   **98** [F; not in Q2]   **100 are** is   **100 s.d.** [at l. 97 in Q2]   **103 impetuous** [Q3, F2] impitious [Q2] impittious [F]   **109 They** The   **146 swoopstake** [eds.] soopstake [Q1 reads "Swoop-stake-like"]   **158 Let her come in** [assigned in Q2 to Laertes and placed before "How now, what noyse is that?"]   **s.d. Enter Ophelia** [after l. 157 in Q2]   **162 Till** Tell   **165 an old** [F, Q1] a poore   **166–168, 170** [F; not in Q2]   **186 must** [F, Q1] may   **191 affliction** [F, Q1] afflictions   **199 All flaxen** Flaxen   **203 Christian** [F] Christians   **souls, I pray God** [F, Q1] souls **204 you see** you   **217 trophy, sword** trophe sword

4.6. 7, 9 s.p. First Sailor Say   **22 good turn** turn   **26 bore** bord   **30 He** So **31 will give** will

4.7. 6 proceeded proceede   **7 crimeful** criminall   **15 conjunctive** concliue

22 gyves Giues   **23 loud a wind** loued   Arm'd   **25 had** haue   **37 How . . . Hamlet** [F; not in Q2]   **38 This** These   **46–47 your pardon** you pardon   **48 and more strange** [F; not in Q2]   **Hamlet** [F; not in Q2]   **56 shall live** [F, Q1] liue   **62 checking** the King   **78 ribbon** [eds.] ribaud   **89 my** me   **116 wick** [eds.] weeke   **123 spendthrift** [Q5] spend thirfts   **126 yourself in deed** indeede your fathers sonne   **135 on** ore   **139 pass** pace   **141 for that** for   **157 ha 't** hate   **160 prepared** prefard   **168 hoar** horry   **172 cold** cull-cold   **192 douts** [F "doubts"] drownes

5.1. 1 s.p [and throughout] **First Clown** Clowne   **3 s.p.** [and throughout] **Second Clown** Other   **9 se offendendo** so offended   **12 and to** to   **Argal** or all   **34–37 Why . . . arms** [F; not in Q2]   **55 s.d.** [at l. 65 in Q2]   **60 stoup** soope   **85 meant** [F, Q1, Q3] went   **89 mazard** massene   **106–107 Is . . . recoveries** [F; not in Q2]   **107–108 Will his** will   **109 double ones too** doubles   **120 O** or   **121** [F; not in Q2]   **143 Of all** Of   **165 nowadays** [F; not in Q2]   **183 Let me see** [F; not in Q]   **192 chamber** [F, Q1] table   **208–209 As thus** [F; not in Q2]   **216 winter's** waters   **226, 235 s.p. Priest** Doct   **231 Shards, flints** Flints   **247 treble** double   **262 and rash** rash   **288 thus** this   **301 shortly** thereby   **302 Till** Tell

5.2. 5 Methought my thought   **6 bilboes** bilbo   **9 pall** fall   **17 unseal** vnfold   **19 Ah** [eds.] A   **29 villainies** villaines   **30 Ere** Or   **43 "as"es** as sir   **52 Subscribed** Subscribe   **57, 68–80** [F; not in Q2]   **73 interim is** [eds.] interim's [F]   **78 court** [eds.] count [F]   **81 s.p.** [and throughout] **Osric** Cour   **82 humbly** humble   **93 Put your** your   **98 sultry** sully   **for** or   **107 gentleman** [eds.] gentlemen   **109 feelingly** [Q4] fellingly   **114 dozy** [eds.] dazzie   **yaw** [eds.] raw   **141 his** [eds.] this   **149 hangers** hanger   **156 carriages** carriage   **159 might be** be might   **162 impawned, as** [eds.] all [Q2] impon'd, as [F]   **181 Yours, yours. 'A does** Yours doo's   **186 comply** so   **190 yeasty** histy   **191 fanned** [eds.] prophane [Q2] fond [F]   **winnowed** trennowed   **210 But thou** thou   **218 be now be**   **220 will come** well come   **238** [F; not in Q2]   **248 To keep** To   **till all**   **252 foils. Come on** foils   **255 off** of   **261 bettered** better   **270 union** Vnice ["Onixe" in some copies]   **288 A touch, a touch, I** I I   **302 afeard** sure   **316 Hamlet. Hamlet** Hamlet   **319 thy** [F, Q1] my   **327 murderous** [F; not in Q2]   **328 off** of   **thy union** [F, Q1] the Onixe   **345 ha 't** hate [Q2] have 't [F]   **366 proud** prou'd   **369 s.p. First Ambassador** Embas   **373** [and some other places] **Rosencrantz** Rosencraus   **381 th'** yet yet   **385 forced** for no   **394 on** no

Passages contained only in F and omitted from Q2 are noted in the textual notes above. It might be useful here to list the more important instances in which Q2 contains words, lines, and passages omitted in F.

1.1. 112–129 BERNARDO I think . . . countrymen

1.2. 58–60 wrung . . . consent

1.3. 9 perfume and

1.4. 17–38 This heavy-headed . . . scandal   **75–78** The very . . . beneath

2.1. 122 Come

2.2. 17 Whether . . . thus   **217** except my life   **363** very   **366** 'Sblood (and some other profanity passim)   **371** then   **444–445** as wholesome . . . fine   **521–522** of this   **589** Hum

3.2. 169–170 Where . . . there   **216–217** To . . . scope

3.4. 72–77 Sense . . . difference   **79–82** Eyes . . . mope   **168–172** That monster . . . put on
174–177 the next . . . potency   **187** One word . . . lady   **209–217** There's . . . meet

4.1. 4 Bestow . . . while   **41–44** Whose . . . air

4.2. 4 But soft

4.3. 26–29 KING Alas . . . worm

4.4. 9–67 *Enter Hamlet* . . . worth

4.5. 33 Oho

4.7. 68–82 LAERTES My lord . . . graveness   **101–103** Th' escrimers . . . them
115–124 There . . . ulcer

5.1. 154 There

5.2. 106–142 here is . . . unfellowed (replaced in F by "you are not ignorant of what
excellence Laertes is at his weapon")   **154–155** HORATIO [*To Hamlet*] I knew . . . done
193–207 *Enter a Lord* . . . lose, my lord (replaced in F by "You will lose this wager, my
lord")   **222** Let be

Shakespeare's Sources

The ultimate source of the *Hamlet* story is Saxo Grammaticus's *Historia Danica* (1180–1208), the saga of one Amlothi or (as Saxo calls him) Amlethus. The outline of the story is essentially that of Shakespeare's play, even though the emphasis of the Danish saga is overwhelmingly on cunning, brutality, and bloody revenge. Amlethus' father is Horwendil, a Governor of Jutland, who bravely kills the King of Norway in single combat and thereby wins the hand in marriage of Gerutha, daughter of the King of Denmark. This good fortune goads the envious Feng into slaying his brother Horwendil and marrying Gerutha, "capping unnatural murder with incest." Though the deed is known to everyone, Feng invents excuses and soon wins the approbation of the fawning courtiers. Young Amlethus vows revenge, but, perceiving his uncle's cunning, he feigns madness. His mingled words of craft and candor awaken suspicions that he may be playing a game of deception.

Two attempts are made to lure Amlethus into revealing that he is actually sane. The first plan is to tempt him into lechery, on the theory that one who lusts for women cannot be truly insane. Feng causes an attractive woman to be placed in a forest where Amlethus will meet her as though by chance; but Amlethus, secretly warned of the trap by a kindly foster brother, spirits the young lady off to a hideaway where they can make love unobserved by Feng's agents. She confesses the plot to Amlethus. In a second stratagem, a courtier who is reported to be "gifted with more assurance than judgment" hides himself under some straw in the Queen's chamber in order to overhear her private conversations with Amlethus. The hero, suspecting just such a trap, feigns madness and begins crowing like a noisy rooster, bouncing up and down on the straw until he finds the eavesdropper. Amlethus stabs the man to death, drags him forth, cuts the body into morsels, boils them, and flings the bits "through the mouth of an open sewer for the swine to eat." Thereupon he returns to his mother to accuse her of being an infamous harlot. He wins her over to repentant virtue and even cooperation. When Feng, returning from a journey, looks around for his counselor, Amlethus jestingly (but in part truly) suggests that the man went to the sewer and fell in.

Feng now sends Amlethus to the King of Britain with secret orders for his execution. However, Amlethus finds the letter to the British King in the coffers of the two unnamed retainers accompanying him on the journey, and substitutes a new letter ordering their execution instead. The new letter, purportedly written and signed by Feng, goes on to urge that the King of Britain marry his daughter to a young Dane being sent from the Danish court. By this means Amlethus gains an English wife and rids himself of the escorts. A year later Amlethus returns to Jutland, gets the entire court drunk, flings a tapestry (knitted for him by his mother) over the prostrate courtiers, secures the tapestry with stakes, and then sets fire to the palace. Feng escapes this holocaust, but Amlethus cuts him down with the King's own sword. (Amlethus exchanges swords because his own has been nailed fast into its scabbard by his enemies.) Subsequently, Amlethus convinces the people of the justice of his cause and is chosen King of Jutland. After ruling for several years, he returns to Britain, bigamously marries a Scottish queen, fights a battle with his first father-in-law, is betrayed by his second wife, and is finally killed in battle.

In Saxo's account we thus find the prototypes of Hamlet, Claudius, Gertrude, Polonius, Ophelia, Rosencrantz, and Guildenstern. Several episodes are close in narrative detail to Shakespeare's play: the original murder and incestuous marriage, the feigned madness, the woman used as a decoy, the eavesdropping counselor, and especially the trip to England. A translation of Saxo into French by François de Belleforest, in *Histoires Tragiques* (1576 edition), adds a few details, such as Gertrude's adultery before the murder and Hamlet's melancholy. Belleforest's version is longer than Saxo's, with more psychological and moral observation and more dialogue. Shakespeare probably consulted it.

Shakespeare need not have depended extensively on these older versions of his story, however. His main source was almost certainly an old play of *Hamlet*. Much evidence testifies to the existence of such a play. The *Diary* of Philip

Henslowe, a theater owner and manager, records a performance, not marked as "new," of a *Hamlet* at Newington Butts on June 11, 1594, by "my Lord Admiral's men" or "my Lord Chamberlain's men," probably the latter. Thomas Lodge's pamphlet *Wit's Misery and the World's Madness* (1596) refers to "the vizard of the ghost which cried so miserably at the theater, like an oyster wife, 'Hamlet, revenge!' " And Thomas Nashe, in his *Epistle* prefixed to Robert Greene's romance *Menaphon* (1589), offers the following observation:

> It is a common practice nowadays amongst a sort of shifting companions, that run through every art and thrive by none, to leave the trade of noverint, whereto they were born, and busy themselves with the endeavors of art, that could scarcely Latinize their neck verse if they should have need; yet English Seneca read by candlelight yields many good sentences, as "Blood is a beggar" and so forth; and if you entreat him fair in a frosty morning, he will afford you whole *Hamlets*, I should say handfuls, of tragical speeches. But O grief! *Tempus edax rerum*, what's that will last always? The sea exhaled by drops will in continuance be dry, and Seneca, let blood line by line and page by page, at length must needs die to our stage; which makes his famished followers to imitate the Kid in Aesop, who, enamored with the Fox's newfangles, forsook all hopes of life to leap into a new occupation; and these men, renouncing all possibilities of credit or estimation, to intermeddle with Italian translations . . .

Nashe's testimonial describes a *Hamlet* play, written in the Senecan style by some person born to the trade of "noverint," or scrivener, who has turned to hack writing and translation. The description has often been fitted to Thomas Kyd, though this identification is not certain. (Nashe could be punning on Kyd's name when he refers to "the Kid in Aesop.") Certainly Thomas Kyd's *The Spanish Tragedy* (c. 1587) shows many affinities with Shakespeare's play, and provides many Senecan ingredients missing from Saxo and Belleforest: the ghost, the difficulty in ascertaining whether the ghost's words are believable, the resulting need for delay and a feigning of madness, the moral perplexities afflicting a sensitive man called upon to revenge, the play within the play, the clever reversals and ironically

caused deaths in the catastrophe, the rhetoric of tragical
passion. Whether or not Kyd in fact wrote the *Ur-Hamlet*,
his extant play enables us to see more clearly what that lost
play must have contained. The pirated first quarto of
Hamlet (1603) also offers a few seemingly authentic details
that are not found in the authoritative second quarto but
are found in the earlier sources and may have been a part of
the *Ur-Hamlet*. For example, after Hamlet has killed Coram-
bis (corresponding to Polonius), the Queen vows to assist
Hamlet in his strategies against the King; and later, when
Hamlet has returned to England, the Queen sends him a
message by Horatio warning him to be careful.

One last document sheds light on the *Ur-Hamlet*. A German play, *Der bestrafte Brudermord* (*Fratricide Punished*),
from a now-lost manuscript dated 1710, seems to have been
based on a text used by English actors traveling in Germany
in 1586 and afterward. Though changed by translation and
manuscript transmission, and too entirely different from
Shakespeare's play to have been based on it, this German
version may well have been based on Shakespeare's source-
play. Polonius's name in this text, Corambus, is the Coram-
bis of the first quarto of 1603. (The name may mean
"cabbage cooked twice," for *coramble-bis*, a proverbially
dull dish.)

Der bestrafte Brudermord begins with a prologue in the
Senecan manner, followed by the appearance of the ghost to
Francisco, Horatio, and sentinels of the watch. Within the
palace, meanwhile, the King carouses. Hamlet joins the
watch, confiding to Horatio that he is "sick at heart" over
his father's death and mother's hasty remarriage. The
ghost appears to Hamlet, tells him how the juice of hebona
was poured into his ear, and urges revenge. When Hamlet
swears Horatio and Francisco to silence, the ghost (now invisible) says several times "We swear," his voice following
the men as they move from place to place. Hamlet reveals to
Horatio the entire circumstance of the murder. Later, in a
formal session of the court, the new King speaks hypocriti-
cally of his brother's death and explains the reasons for his
marriage to the Queen. Hamlet is forbidden to return to
Wittenberg, though Corambus's son Leonhardus has already set out for France.

Some time afterward, Corambus reports the news of Hamlet's madness to the King and Queen, and presumes on the basis of his own youthful passions to diagnose Hamlet's malady as lovesickness. Concealed, he and the King overhear Hamlet tell Ophelia to "go to a nunnery." When players arrive from Germany, Hamlet instructs them in the natural style of acting, and then requests them to perform a play before the King about the murder of King Pyrrus by his brother. (Death is again inflicted by hebona poured in the ear.) After the King's guilty reaction to the play, Hamlet finds him alone at prayers but postpones the killing lest the King's soul be sent to heaven. Hamlet kills Corambus behind the tapestry in the Queen's chamber, and is visited again by the ghost (who says nothing, however). Ophelia, her mind deranged, thinks herself in love with a court butterfly named Phantasmo. (This creature is also involved in a comic action to help the clown Jens with a tax problem.)

The King sends Hamlet to England with two unnamed courtiers who are instructed to kill Hamlet after their arrival. A contrary wind takes them instead to an island near Dover, where Hamlet foils his two enemies by kneeling between them and asking them to shoot him on signal; at the proper moment, he ducks and they shoot each other. He finishes them off with their own swords, and discovers letters on their persons ordering Hamlet's execution by the English King if the original plot should fail. When Hamlet returns to Denmark, the King arranges a duel between him and Corambus's son Leonhardus. If Leonhardus's poisoned dagger misses its mark, a beaker of wine containing finely ground oriental diamond dust is to do the rest. Hamlet is informed of the impending duel by Phantasmo (compare Osric), whom Hamlet taunts condescendingly and calls "Signora Phantasmo." Shortly before the duel takes place, Ophelia is reported to have thrown herself off a hill to her death. The other deaths occur much as in Shakespeare's play. The dying Hamlet bids that the crown be conveyed to his cousin, Duke Fortempras of Norway, of whom we have not heard earlier.

From the extensive similarities between *Hamlet* and this German play, we can see that Shakespeare inherited his narrative material almost intact, though in a jumble and so

pitifully mangled that the modern reader can only laugh at
the contrast. No source study in Shakespeare reveals so
clearly the extent of Shakespeare's wholesale borrowing of
plot, and the incredible transformation he achieved in re-
ordering his materials.

  The following excerpt is from the English *The History of
Hamlet*, 1608, an unacknowledged translation of Belleforest
that in one or two places seems to have been influenced by
Shakespeare's play—as when Hamlet beats his arms on the
hangings of the Queen's apartment instead of jumping on
the quilt or bed, as in Belleforest, and cries, "A rat! a rat!"
It is otherwise a close translation and, although too late for
Shakespeare to have used, provides an Elizabethan version
of the account Shakespeare most likely used.

The History of Hamlet
Prince of Denmark

CHAPTER 1

*How Horvendil and Fengon were made Governors of the
Province of Ditmarse, and how Horvendil married Geruth,
the daughter to Roderick, chief King of Denmark, by whom
he had Hamlet; and how after his marriage his brother
Fengon slew him traitorously and married his brother's
wife, and what followed.*

You must understand, that long time before the kingdom of
Denmark received the faith of Jesus Christ and embraced
the doctrine of the Christians, that the common people in
those days were barbarous and uncivil and their princes
cruel, without faith or loyalty, seeking nothing but murder
and deposing or at the least offending each other either
in honors, goods, or lives, not caring to ransom such as they
took prisoners but rather sacrificing them to the cruel
vengeance naturally imprinted in their hearts; in such sort
that if there were sometimes a good prince or king among
them who, being adorned with the most perfect gifts of nature, would addict himself to virtue and use courtesy, although the people held him in admiration (as virtue is
admirable to the most wicked) yet the envy of his neighbors
was so great that they never ceased until that virtuous man
were dispatched out of the world.

King Roderick, as then reigning in Denmark, after he
had appeased the troubles in the country and driven the
Swethlanders and Slaveans from thence, he divided the
kingdom into divers provinces, placing governors therein,
who after (as the like happened in France) bare the names
of dukes, marquesses, and earls, giving the government of
Jutie (at this present called Ditmarse), lying upon the country of the Cimbrians in the straight or narrow part of land
that showeth like a point or cape of ground upon the sea
which northward* bordereth upon the country of Norway,
to two* valiant and warlike lords, Horvendil and Fengon,

sons to Gervendil, who likewise had been governor of that
province.

Now the greatest honor that men of noble birth could at
that time win and obtain was in exercising the art of piracy
upon the seas, assailing their neighbors and the countries
bordering upon them; and how much the more they used to
rob, pill,[1] and spoil other provinces and islands far adja-
cent, so much the more their honors and reputation in-
creased and augmented. Wherein Horvendil obtained the
highest place in his time, being the most renowned pirate
that in those days scoured the seas and havens of the north
parts; whose great fame so moved the heart of Collere, King
of Norway, that he was much grieved to hear that Horvendil
surmounted[*2] him in feats of arms, thereby obscuring the
glory by him already obtained upon the seas—honor more
than covetousness of riches in those days being the reason
that provoked those barbarian princes to overthrow and
vanquish one the other, not caring[3] to be slain by the hands
of a victorious person.

This valiant and hardy king having challenged Horvendil
to fight with him body to body, the combat was by him accepted, with conditions that he which should be vanquished
should lose all the riches he had in his ship and that the
vanquisher should cause the body of the vanquished (that
should be slain in the combat) to be honorably buried,
death being the prize and reward of him that should lose
the battle. And to conclude, Collere, King of Norway, although a valiant, hardy, and courageous prince, was in the
end vanquished and slain by Horvendil, who presently
caused a tomb to be erected and therein, with all honorable
obsequies fit for a prince, buried the body of King Collere,
according to their ancient manner and superstitions in
these days and the conditions of the combat, bereaving the
King's ships of all their riches; and, having slain the King's
sister, a very brave and valiant warrior, and overrun all the
coast of Norway and the Northern Islands, returned home
again laden with much treasure, sending the most part
thereof to his sovereign, King Roderick, thereby to procure

1 **pill** plunder   2 **surmounted** excelled   3 **not caring** i.e., not considering it dishonorable

his good liking and so to be accounted one of the greatest favorites about His Majesty.

The King, allured by those presents and esteeming himself happy to have so valiant a subject, sought by a great favor and courtesy to make him become bounden unto him perpetually, giving him Geruth his daughter to his wife, of whom he knew Horvendil to be already much enamored. And, the more to honor him, determined himself in person to conduct her into Jutie, where the marriage was celebrated according to the ancient manner. And, to be brief, of this marriage proceeded Hamlet, of whom I intend to speak, and for his cause have chosen to renew this present history.

Fengon, brother to this prince Horvendil, who, not only* fretting and despiting[4] in his heart at the great honor and reputation won by his brother in warlike affairs but solicited and provoked by a foolish jealousy to see him honored with royal alliance, and fearing thereby to be deposed from his part of the government—or rather desiring to be only governor, thereby to obscure the memory of the victories and conquests of his brother Horvendil—determined, whatsoever happened, to kill him; which he effected in such sort that no man once so much as suspected him, every man esteeming that from such and so firm a knot of alliance and consanguinity there could proceed no other issue than the full effects of virtue and courtesy. But, as I said before, the desire of bearing sovereign rule and authority respecteth neither blood nor amity, nor caring for virtue, as being wholly without respect of laws or majesty divine; for it is not possible that he which invadeth the country and taketh away the riches of another man without cause or reason should know or fear God. Was not this a crafty and subtle counselor? But he might have thought that the mother, knowing her husband's case, would not cast her son into the danger of death.

But Fengon, having secretly assembled certain men, and perceiving himself strong enough to execute his enterprise, Horvendil his brother being at a banquet with his friends,

4 despiting entertaining a grudge

suddenly set upon him, where he slew him as traitorously
as cunningly he purged himself of so detestable a murder to
his subjects; for that before he had any violent or bloody
hands, or once committed parricide upon his brother, he
had incestuously abused his wife, whose honor he ought as
well to have sought and procured as traitorously he pursued and effected his destruction. And it is most certain
that the man that abandoneth himself to any notorious and
wicked action whereby he becometh a great sinner, he
careth not to commit much more heinous and abominable
offenses; and covered his boldness and wicked practice
with so great subtlety and policy, and under a veil of mere
simplicity, that, being favored for the honest love that he
bare to his sister-in-law—for whose sake, he affirmed, he
had in that sort murdered his brother—that his sin found
excuse among the common people and of the nobility was
esteemed for justice. For that Geruth, being as courteous a
princess as any then living in the north parts, and one that
had never once so much as offended any of her subjects,
either commons or courtiers, this adulterer and infamous
murderer slandered his dead brother that he would have
slain his wife,[5] and that he,[6] by chance finding him upon the
point ready to do it, in defense of the lady had slain him,
bearing off the blows which as then he[7] struck at the innocent princess without any other cause of malice whatsoever.
Wherein he wanted[8] no false witnesses to approve[9] his act,
which deposed[10] in like sort as the wicked calumniator himself protested, being the same persons that had borne him
company and were participants of his treason. So that instead of pursuing him as a parricide and an incestuous person, all the courtiers admired and flattered him in his good
fortune, making more account of false witnesses and detestable wicked reporters, and more honoring the calumni-
ators, than they esteemed of those that, seeking to call the
matter in question and admiring the virtues of the murdered prince, would have punished the massacrers and be-
reavers of his life.

---

5 slandered . . . wife i.e., made the slanderous accusation that Horvendil
intended to slay his wife, Geruth   **6 he** i.e., Fengon   **7 he** i.e., Horvendil
8 he wanted i.e., Fengon lacked   **9 approve** confirm   **10 which deposed** who
testified

Which was the cause that Fengon, boldened and encouraged by such impunity, durst venture to couple himself in marriage with her whom he used as his concubine during good Horvendil's life, in that sort spotting his name with a double vice, and charging his conscience with abominable guilt and twofold impiety, as[11] incentuous adultery and parricide murder. And that[12] the unfortunate and wicked woman, that had received the honor to be the wife of one of the valiantest and wisest* princes in the north, embased[13] herself in such vile sort as to falsify her faith unto him and, which is worse, to marry him that had been the tyrannous murderer of her lawful husband; which made divers men think that she had been the causer of the murder, thereby to live in her adultery without control.

But where shall a man find a more wicked and bold woman than a great personage once having loosed the bonds of honor and honesty? This princess, who at the first for her rare virtues and courtesies was honored of all men and beloved of her husband, as soon as she once gave ear to the tyrant Fengon forgot both the rank she held among the greatest names and the duty of an honest wife on her behalf. But I will not stand to gaze and marvel at women, for that there are many which seek to blaze[14] and set them forth, in which their writings they spare not to blame them all for the faults of some one or few women. But I say that either nature ought to have bereaved[15] man of that opinion to accompany[16] with women, or else to endow them with such spirits as that they may easily support the crosses they endure without complaining so often and so strangely, seeing it is their own beastliness that overthrows them. For if it be so that a woman is so imperfect a creature as they make her to be, and that they know this beast to be so hard to be tamed as they affirm, why then are they so foolish to preserve them and so dull and brutish as to trust their deceitful and wanton embracings? But let us leave her in this extremity of lasciviousness, and proceed to show you in what sort the young Prince Hamlet behaved himself to escape the tyranny of his uncle.

---

11 as that is, to wit   **12 And that** i.e., and was the cause that   **13 embased** lowered, debased   **14 blaze** proclaim   **15 bereaved** deprived   **16 accompany** keep company

CHAPTER 2

How Hamlet counterfeited the madman to escape the tyranny of his uncle, and how he was tempted by a woman through his uncle's procurement, who thereby thought to undermine the Prince and by that means to find out whether he counterfeited madness or not; and how Hamlet would by no means be brought to consent unto her, and what followed.

GERUTH having, as I said before, so much forgotten herself, the Prince Hamlet, perceiving himself to be in danger of his life, as being abandoned of his own mother and forsaken of all men, and assuring himself that Fengon would not detract[1] the time to send him the same way his father Horvendil was gone, to beguile[2] the tyrant in his subtleties (that esteemed him to be of such a mind that if he once attained to man's estate[3] he would not long delay the time to revenge the death of his father), counterfeited* the madman with such craft and subtle practices that he made show as if he had utterly lost his wits, and under that veil he covered his pretense and defended his life from the treasons and practices of the tyrant his uncle. And although[4] he had been at the school of[5] the Roman prince who, because he counterfeited himself to be a fool, was called Brutus,[6] yet he imitated his fashions and his wisdom. For, every day being in the Queen's palace (who as then was more careful to please her whoremaster than ready to revenge the cruel death of her husband or to restore her son to his inheritance), he rent and tore his clothes, wallowing and lying in the dirt and mire, his face all filthy and black, running through the streets like a man distraught, not speaking one word but such as seemed to proceed of madness and mere[7] frenzy, all his actions and gestures being no other than the right countenances[8] of a man wholly deprived of all reason and understanding, in such sort that as then he

---

1 detract lengthen   **2 to beguile** in order to beguile   **3 man's estate** manhood   **4 although** inasmuch as   **5 been at the school of** i.e., studied the method of   **6 Brutus** (Lucius Junius Brutus assumed the disguise of idiocy in order to escape the fate of his brother, whom their uncle Tarquinius Superbus had put to death. *Brutus* means "stupid.")
7 mere absolute   **8 right countenances** true demeanor

seemed fit for nothing but to make sport[9] to the pages and ruffling[10] courtiers that attended in the court of his uncle and father-in-law.[11] But the young Prince noted them well enough, minding one day to be revenged in such manner that the memory thereof should remain perpetually to the world. . . .

Hamlet, in this sort counterfeiting the madman, many times did divers actions of great and deep consideration, and often made such and so fit answers that a wise man would soon have judged from what spirit so fine an invention might proceed; for that standing by the fire and sharpening sticks like poniards and pricks, one in smiling manner asked him wherefore he made those little staves so sharp at the points? "I prepare," saith he, "piercing darts and sharp arrows to revenge my father's death." Fools, as I said before, esteemed those his words as nothing; but men of quick spirits and such as had a deeper reach[12] began to suspect somewhat, esteeming that under that kind of folly there lay hidden a great and rare subtlety such as one day might be prejudicial to their prince, saying that under color of such rudeness he shadowed a crafty policy and by his devised simplicity he concealed a sharp and pregnant[13] spirit.

For which cause they counseled the King to try and know, if it were possible, how to discover the intent and meaning of the young Prince. And they could find no better nor more fit invention to entrap him than to set some fair and beautiful woman in a secret place that, with flattering speeches and all the craftiest means she could use, should purposely seek to allure his mind to have his pleasure of her. For the nature of all young men, especially such as are brought up wantonly, is so transported with the desires of the flesh, and entereth so greedily into the pleasures thereof, that it is almost impossible to cover the foul affection, neither yet to dissemble or hide the same by art or industry, much less to shun it. What cunning or subtlety soever they use to cloak their pretense, seeing occasion offered, and that in secret, especially in the most enticing sin that reigneth in man, they cannot choose,

9 make sport serve as the butt of joking   **10 ruffling** swaggering   **11 father-in-law** i.e., stepfather   **12 reach** comprehension   **13 pregnant** fertile, inventive

being constrained by voluptuousness, but fall to natural ef
fect and working.

To this end certain courtiers were appointed to lead Ham
let into a solitary place within the woods, whither they
brought the woman, inciting him to take their pleasures to
gether and to embrace one another—but the subtle practices
used in these our days,[14] not to try if men of great account be
extract[15] out of their wits but rather to deprive them of
strength, virtue, and wisdom by means of such devilish prac
titioners and infernal* spirits, their domestical servants and
ministers of corruption. And surely the poor Prince at this
assault had been[16] in great danger, if a gentleman (that in
Horvendil's time had been nourished with him) had not shown
himself more affectioned to the bringing-up he had received
with Hamlet than desirous to please the tyrant who by all
means sought to entangle the son in the same nets wherein
the father had ended his days. This gentleman bare the cour
tiers (appointed as aforesaid of this treason) company, more
desiring to give the Prince instruction what he should do
than to entrap him, making full account that the least show
of perfect sense and wisdom[17] that Hamlet should make
would be sufficient to cause him to lose his life. And there
fore by certain signs he gave Hamlet intelligence in what dan
ger he was like[18] to fall, if by any means he seemed to obey or
once like the wanton toys[19] and vicious provocations of the
gentlewoman sent thither by his uncle. Which much abashed
the Prince, as then wholly being in affection to the lady;
but by her he was likewise informed of the treason, as being
one that from her infancy loved and favored him and would
have been exceeding sorrowful for his misfortune, and much
more[20] to leave his company without enjoying the pleasure of
his body, whom she loved more than herself. The Prince in
this sort having both deceived the courtiers and the lady's
expectation, that affirmed and swore that he never once of
fered to have his pleasure of the woman, although in sub
tlety[21] he affirmed the contrary, every man thereupon

---

14 but . . . days i.e., machinations used often enough in more recent
times. but only 15 extract extracted, removed 16 had been would
have been 17 the least . . . wisdom (Hamlet's yielding to the lady's
blandishments would be viewed as a proof of sanity and would thus
betray him to his uncle.) 18 like likely 19 toys tricks 20 much more
much more sorrowful 21 in subtlety in private

assured themselves that without all doubt he was distraught of his senses, that his brains were as then wholly void of force and incapable of reasonable apprehension, so that as then[22] Fengon's practice took no effect. But for all that he left not off, still seeking by all means to find out Hamlet's subtlety, as in the next chapter you shall perceive.

CHAPTER 3

How Fengon, uncle to Hamlet, a second time to entrap him in his politic madness, caused one of his counselors to be secretly hidden in the Queen's chamber, behind the arras, to hear what speeches passed between Hamlet and the Queen; and how Hamlet killed him and escaped that danger, and what followed.

AMONG the friends of Fengon there was one that above all the rest doubted of Hamlet's practices in counterfeiting the madman, who for that cause said that it was impossible that so crafty a gallant as Hamlet, that counterfeited the fool, should be discovered with so common and unskillful practices which might easily be perceived, and that to find out his politic pretense it were necessary to invent some subtle and crafty means more attractive whereby the gallant might not have the leisure to use his accustomed dissimulation. Which to effect he said he knew a fit way and a most convenient mean[1] to effect the King's desire and thereby to entrap Hamlet in his subtleties and cause him of his own accord to fall into the net prepared for him, and thereby evidently show his secret meaning.

His devise was thus: that King Fengon should make as though he were to go some long voyage concerning affairs of great importance, and that in the meantime Hamlet should be shut up alone in a chamber with his mother, wherein some other should secretly be hidden behind the hangings, unknown either to him or his mother, there to stand and hear their speeches and the complots[2] by them to be taken[3] con-

---

22 as then as of that time

1 mean means **2 complots** conspiracy **3 taken** undertaken

cerning the accomplishment of the dissembling fool's pretense; assuring the King that if there were any point of wisdom and perfect sense in the gallant's spirit, that without all doubt he would easily discover[4] it to his mother, as being devoid of all fear that she would utter or make known his secret intent, being the woman that had borne him in her body and nourished him so carefully; and withal[5] offered himself to be the man that should stand to hearken and bear witness of Hamlet's speeches with his mother, that he might not be esteemed a counselor in such a case wherein he refused to be the executioner for the behoof and service of his prince.

This invention pleased the King exceeding well, esteeming it as the only and sovereign remedy to heal the Prince of his lunacy, and to that end, making a long voyage, issued out of his palace and rode to hunt in the forest.

Meantime the counselor entered secretly into the Queen's chamber and there hid himself behind the arras not long before the Queen and Hamlet came thither, who, being crafty and politic, as soon as he was within the chamber, doubting[6] some treason and fearing if he should speak severely and wisely to his mother touching his secret practices he should be understood and by that means intercepted, used his ordinary manner of dissimulation and began to come like a cock,[7] beating with his arms (in such manner as cocks use to strike with their wings) upon the hangings of the chamber. Whereby, feeling something stirring under them, he cried, "A rat, a rat!" and presently drawing his sword thrust it into the hangings, which done, pulled the counselor (half dead) out by the heels, made an end of killing him, and, being slain, cut his body in pieces, which he caused to be boiled and then cast it into an open vault or privy that so it might serve for food to the hogs.

By which means having discovered the ambush and given the inventor thereof his just reward, he came again to his mother, who in the meantime wept and tormented herself to see all her hopes frustrate, for that what fault soever she had committed yet was she sore grieved to see her only child made a mere mockery—every man reproaching her with his

---

4 discover reveal   **5 withal** in addition   **6 doubting** suspecting, fearing
7 come like a cock crow like a rooster

folly, one point whereof she had as then seen before her eyes. Which was no small prick to her conscience, esteeming that the gods sent her that punishment for joining incestuously in marriage with the tyrannous murderer of her husband (who likewise ceased not to invent all the means he could to bring his nephew to his end), accusing her* own natural indiscretion, as being the ordinary guide of those that so much desire the pleasures of the body, who, shutting up the way to all reason, respect not what may ensue of their lightness and great inconstancy, and how a pleasure of small moment is sufficient to give them cause of repentance during their lives, and make them curse the day and time that ever any such apprehensions entered into their minds or that they closed their eyes to reject the honesty requisite in ladies of her quality. . . .

And while in this sort she sat tormenting herself, Hamlet entered into the chamber, who, having once again searched every corner of the same, distrusting his mother as well as the rest, and perceiving himself to be alone, began in sober and discreet manner to speak unto her, saying,

"What treason is this, O most infamous woman of all that ever prostrated themselves to the will of an abominable whoremonger, who, under the veil of a dissembling creature, covereth the most wicked and detestable crime that man could ever imagine or was committed! Now may I be assured to trust you that, like a vile wanton adulteress altogether impudent and given over to her pleasure, runs spreading forth her arms joyfully to embrace the traitorous villainous tyrant that murdered my father, and most incestuously receivest the villain into the lawful bed of your loyal spouse, imprudently entertaining him instead of the dear father of your miserable and discomforted son—if the gods grant him not the grace speedily to escape from a captivity so unworthy the degree he holdeth and the race and noble family of his ancestors. Is this the part of a queen and daughter to a king? To live like a brute beast and like a mare that yieldeth her body to the horse that hath beaten her companion away, to follow the pleasure of an abominable king that hath murdered a far more honester and better man than himself in massacring Horvendil, the honor and glory of the Danes? Who are now esteemed of no force nor valor at all since the shining splen-

dor of knighthood was brought to an end by the most wick-
edest and cruelest villain living upon earth.

"I for my part will never account him for my kinsman nor
once know him for mine uncle, nor you my dear mother, for
not having respect to the blood that ought to have united us
so straitly together, and who neither with your honor nor
without suspicion of consent to the death of your husband
could ever have agreed to have married with his cruel enemy.
O, Queen Geruth! It is the part of a bitch to couple with
many and desire acquaintance of divers mastiffs. It is licen-
tiousness only that hath made you deface out of your mind
the memory of the valor and virtues of the good king your
husband and my father. It was an unbridled desire that
guided the daughter of Roderick to embrace the tyrant
Fengon, and not to remember Horvendil (unworthy of so
strange entertainment),[8] neither that he[9] killed his brother
traitorously, and that she being his[10] father's wife betrayed
him, although he[11] so well favored and loved her that for her
sake he utterly bereaved Norway of her riches and valiant
soldiers to augment the treasures of Roderick and make
Geruth wife to the hardiest[12] prince in Europe. It is not the
part of a woman, much less of a princess, in whom all modesty, courtesy, compassion, and love ought to abound, thus to
leave her dear child to fortune in the bloody and murderous
hands of a villain and traitor. Brute beasts do not so, for lions
tigers, ounces,[13] and leopards fight for the safety and defense
of their whelps; and birds that have beaks, claws, and wings
resist such as would ravish them of their young ones. But
you, to the contrary, expose and deliver me to death, whereas
ye should defend me. Is not this as much as if you should
betray me, when you, knowing the perverseness of the tyrant
and his intents (full of deadly counsel as touching the race
and image of his brother), have not once sought nor desired
to find the means to save your child and only son by sending
him into Swethland,[14] Norway, or England, rather than to
leave him as a prey to your infamous adulterer?

"Be not offended, I pray you, madam, if, transported with

---

8 entertainment treatment   **9 neither that he** i.e., nor to remember that he,
Fengon   **10 his** i.e., Hamlet's   **11 although he** i.e., although Horvendil
12 hardiest bravest   **13 ounces** lynxes, wildcats   **14 Swethland** Sweden

dolor and grief, I speak so boldly unto you, and that I respect
you less than duty requireth; for you, having forgotten me
and wholly rejected the memory of the deceased king my
father, must not be abashed if I also surpass the bounds and
limits of due consideration. Behold into what distress I am
now fallen, and to what mischief my fortune and your over-
great lightness[15] and want of wisdom have induced me, that I
am constrained to play the madman to save my life instead of
using and practicing arms, following adventures, and seeking all means to make myself known to be the true and un-
doubted heir of the valiant and virtuous King Horvendil! It
was not without cause and just occasion that my gestures,
countenances, and words seem all to proceed from a madman, and that I desire to have all men esteem me wholly deprived of sense and reasonable understanding, because I am
well assured that he that hath made no conscience to kill his
own brother (accustomed to murders and allured with desire
of government without control in his treasons) will not spare
to save himself with the like cruelty in the blood and flesh
of the loins of his brother by him massacred. . . .

"To conclude, weep not, madam, to see my folly, but rather
sigh and lament your own offense, tormenting your conscience in regard of the infamy that hath so defiled the ancient renown and glory that in times past honored Queen
Geruth; for we are not to sorrow and grieve at other men's
vices but for our own misdeeds and great follies. Desiring
you for the surplus[16] of my proceedings, above all things, as
you love your own life and welfare, that neither the King nor
any other may by any means know mine intent; and let me
alone with the rest, for I hope in the end to bring my purpose
to effect."

[The Queen contritely asks Hamlet's understanding for a
marriage that (she insists) she entered into under duress, im-
plores his forgiveness, and declares that her fondest hope is
to see her son restored to his rights as heir and monarch of
Denmark. Hamlet pledges his faith to her, beseeching her to
put aside her attachment to Fengon, whom Hamlet "will
surely kill, or cause to be put to death, in despite of all the
devils in hell," along with the flatterers who serve him. In

15 lightness wantonness   **16 surplus** what remains still to be done

doing so he will act as the true King of Denmark, he avers, killing a traitor, not a legitimate ruler, and crowning virtue with glory while punishing regicide with ignominious death.]

After this, Fengon, as if he had been out some long journey, came to the court again and asked for him that had received the charge to play the intelligencer to entrap Hamlet in his dissembled wisdom, was abashed to hear neither news nor tidings of him, and for that cause asked Hamlet what was become of him, naming the man. The Prince, that never used lying, and who in all the answers that ever he made during his counterfeit madness never strayed from the truth (as a generous[17] mind is a mortal enemy to untruth), answered and said that the counselor he sought for was gone down through the privy where, being choked by the filthiness of the place, the hogs meeting him had filled their bellies.

CHAPTER 4

How Fengon, the third time, devised to send Hamlet to the King of England with secret letters to have him put to death; and how Hamlet, when his companions slept, read the letters, and instead of them counterfeited others, willing the King of England to put the two messengers to death and to marry his daughter to Hamlet, which was effected; and how Hamlet escaped out of England.

A MAN would have judged anything rather than that Hamlet had committed that murder; nevertheless Fengon could not content himself, but still his mind gave him[1] that the fool would play him some trick of legerdemain, and willingly would have killed him; but he feared King Roderick, his grandfather, and further durst not offend the Queen, mother to the fool, whom she loved and much cherished, showing great grief and heaviness to see him so transported out of his wits. And in that conceit,[2] seeking to be rid of him, he

17 **generous** highborn, noble

1 **gave him** misgave him, made him apprehensive   2 **conceit** frame of mind

determined* to find the means to do it by the aid of a stranger, making the King of England minister of his massacring resolution, choosing rather that his friend should defile his renown with so great a wickedness than himself to fall into perpetual infamy by an exploit of so great cruelty, to whom he purposed to send him and by letters desire him to put him to death.

Hamlet, understanding that he should be sent into England, presently doubted[3] the occasion of his voyage, and for that cause, speaking to the Queen, desired her not to make any show of sorrow or grief for his departure, but rather counterfeit a gladness as being rid of his presence whom, although she loved, yet she daily grieved to see him in so pitiful estate, deprived of all sense and reason; desiring her further that she should hang the hall with tapestry and make it fast with nails upon the walls and keep the brands[4] for him which he had sharpened at the points, then whenas[5] he said he made arrows to revenge the death of his father. Lastly he counseled her that, the year after his departure being accomplished, she should celebrate his funerals, assuring her that at the same instant she should see him return with great contentment and pleasure unto her from that his voyage.

Now, to bear him company were assigned two of Fengon's faithful ministers, bearing letters engraved in wood that contained Hamlet's death, in such sort as he had advertised[6] the King of England. But the subtle Danish Prince, being at sea, whilst his companions slept, having read the letters and known his uncle's great treason, with the wicked and villainous minds of the two courtiers that led him to the slaughter, rased[7] out the letters that concerned his death and instead thereof graved others with commission to the King of England to hang his two companions; and not content to turn the death they had devised against him upon their own necks, wrote further that King Fengon willed him to give his daughter to Hamlet in marriage.

And so arriving in England, the messengers presented

---

3 presently doubted at once suspected   **4 brands** i.e., the staves or sticks that Hamlet sharpened as though in his madness; see Chapter 2. (*A brand* is usually a piece of wood that has been burning on the hearth or is to be used as a torch.)   **5 then whenas** on that occasion when   **6 advertised** given notice to, commanded   **7 rased** erased, or possibly *razed*, scraped

themselves to the King, giving him Fengon's letters, who, having read the contents, said nothing as then, but stayed[8] convenient time to effect Fengon's desire, meantime using the Danes familiarly, doing them that honor to sit at his table (for that kings as then were not so curiously nor solemnly[9] served as in these our days, for in these days mean[10] kings and lords of small revenue are as difficult and hard to be seen as in times past the monarchs of Persia used to be, or as it is reported of the great King of Ethiopia, who will not permit any man to see his face, which ordinarily he covereth with a veil). And as the messengers sat at the table with the King, subtle Hamlet was so far from being merry with them that he would not taste one bit of meat, bread, nor cup of beer whatsoever as then set upon the table, not without great wondering of the company, abashed to see a young man and a stranger not to esteem of the delicate meats and pleasant drinks served at the banquet, rejecting them as things filthy, evil of taste, and worse prepared. The King, who for that time dissembled what he thought, caused his guests to be conveyed into their chamber, willing one of his secret servants to hide himself therein and so to certify him what speeches passed among the Danes at their going to bed.

Now they were no sooner entered into the chamber, and those that were appointed to attend upon them gone out, but Hamlet's companions asked him why he refused to eat and drink of that which he found upon the table, not honoring the banquet of so great a king, that entertained them in friendly sort, with such honor and courtesy as it deserved? Saying further that he did not well but dishonored him that sent him, as if he sent men into England that feared to be poisoned by so great a king. The Prince, that had done nothing without reason and prudent consideration, answered them and said: "What, think you that I will eat bread dipped in human blood, and defile my throat with the rust of iron, and use that meat that stinketh and savoreth of man's flesh already putrified and corrupted, and that scenteth like the savor of a dead carrion long since cast into a vault? And how would you have me to respect the King that hath the countenance of a slave, and the Queen, who instead of great maj-

---

8 stayed awaited   **9 curiously nor solemnly** fastidiously or ceremoniously
10 mean insignificant

esty, hath done three things more like a woman of base parentage and fitter for a waiting-gentlewoman than beseeming a lady of her quality and estate?" And, having said so, used many injurious and sharp speeches as well against the King and Queen as others that had assisted at that banquet for the entertainment of the Danish ambassadors. And therein Hamlet said truth, as hereafter you shall hear, for that in those days, the north parts of the world, living as then under Satan's laws, were full of enchanters, so that there was not any young gentleman whatsoever that knew not something therein sufficient to serve his turn if need required, as yet in those days in Gotland[11] and Biarmy[12] there are many that knew not what the Christian religion permitteth, as by reading the histories of Norway and Gotland you may easily perceive. And so Hamlet, while his father lived, had been instructed in that devilish art whereby the wicked spirit abuseth mankind and advertiseth him (as he can) of things past.

[Hamlet, aided by the devilish power of magic he has learned, amazes the King of England by demonstrating the truth of the riddling and prophetic statements he has just uttered. It turns out that the King's bread is in fact defiled by human blood shed on the battlefield where the grain was grown, that his pork comes from hogs that have fed on a hanged thief, that his beer is brewed from a water supply polluted by rusty armor, and that, more distressingly, the King is the illegitimate son of a slave and the Queen of no less base parentage. The King thereupon treats Hamlet with the respect that such awesome magical powers deserve.]

The King, admiring the young Prince and beholding in him some matter of greater respect than in the common sort of men, gave him his daughter in marriage, according to the counterfeit letters by him devised, and the next day caused the two servants of Fengon to be executed, to satisfy, as he thought, the King's desire. But Hamlet, although the sport[13]

---

11 Gotland an area in what is now southern Sweden **12 Biarmy** a region in northern Lapland **13 the sport** i.e., the execution of his two companions. (Hamlet pretends to be offended at this so that the King will pacify him with a large gift, as he does.)

pleased him well, and that the King of England could not
have done him a greater favor, made as though he had been
much offended, threatening the King to be revenged; but the
King, to appease him, gave him a great sum of gold, which
Hamlet caused to be molten and put into two staves, made
hollow for the same purpose, to serve his turn therewith as
need should require. For of all the King's treasures he took
nothing with him into Denmark but only those two staves,
and as soon as the year began to be at an end, having somewhat before obtained license of the King his father-in-law to
depart, went for Denmark, then with all the speed he could to
return again into England to marry his daughter; and so set
sail for Denmark.

CHAPTER 5

*How Hamlet, having escaped out of England, arrived in
Denmark the same day that the Danes were celebrating his
funerals, supposing him to be dead in England; and how he
revenged his father's death upon his uncle and the rest of
the courtiers; and what followed.*

HAMLET in that sort sailing into Denmark, being arrived in
the country entered into the palace of his uncle the same day
that they were celebrating his funerals, and, going into the
hall, procured no small astonishment and wonder to them
all—no man thinking other but that he had been dead.
Among the which many of them rejoiced not a little for the
pleasure which they knew Fengon would conceive for so
pleasant a loss,[1] and some were sad, as remembering the
honorable King Horvendil, whose victories they could by no
means forget, much less deface out of their memories that
which appertained unto him, who[2] as then greatly rejoiced to
see a false report spread[3] of Hamlet's death and that the tyrant had not as yet obtained his will of the heir of Jutie,[4] but
rather hoped God would restore him to his senses again for

---

1 rejoiced . . . loss i.e., rejoiced greatly to think how Fengon had desired
the loss of Hamlet and how he would now be frustrated   2 who i.e., the
courtiers who admire Hamlet   3 rejoiced . . . spread i.e., rejoiced to
learn that the rumor was false   4 Jutie Jutland, Denmark

the good and welfare of that province. Their amazement at
the last[5] being turned into laughter, all that as then were assistant at the funeral banquet of him whom they esteemed
dead mocked each at other for having been so simply deceived, and, wondering at the Prince, that in his so long a
voyage he had not recovered any of his senses, asked what
was become of them that had borne him company into Great
Britain? To whom he made answer (showing them the two
hollow staves wherein he had put his molten gold that the
King of England had given him to appease his fury concerning the murder of his two companions) and said, "Here they
are both." Whereat many that already knew his humors
presently conjectured that he had played some trick of legerdemain, and to deliver himself out of danger had thrown
them into the pit prepared for him; so that, fearing to follow
after them and light upon some evil adventure, they went
presently out of the court. And it was well for them that they
did so, considering the tragedy acted by him the same day,
being accounted his funeral but in truth their last days that
as then rejoiced for his* overthrow.[6]

For when every man busied himself to make good cheer,
and Hamlet's arrival provoked them more to drink and ca-
rouse, the Prince himself at that time played the butler and a
gentleman attending on the tables, not suffering the pots nor
goblets to be empty, whereby he gave the noblemen such
store of liquor that all of them, being full laden with wine
and gorged with meat, were constrained to lay themselves
down in the same place where they had supped, so much
their senses were dulled and overcome with the fire of over-
great drinking (a vice common and familiar among the Almains[7] and other nations inhabiting the north parts of the
world). Which when Hamlet perceiving, and finding so good
opportunity to effect his purpose and be revenged of his enemies, and, by the means to abandon the actions, gestures,
and apparel of a madman, occasion so fitly finding his turn
and as it were effecting itself, failed not to take hold thereof;[8]
and, seeing those drunken bodies filled with wine, lying like

5 at the last finally   **6 but in truth . . . overthrow** i.e., a day that was
supposed to have been for Hamlet's funeral but that in truth became
the day of doom for those who had rejoiced in his overthrow
7 Almains Germans   **8 take hold thereof** seize the opportunity

hogs upon the ground, some sleeping, others vomiting the
over-great abundance of wine which without measure they
had swallowed up, made the hangings about the hall to fall
down and cover them all over, which he nailed to the ground,
being boarded, and at the ends thereof he stuck the brands
whereof I spake before, by him sharpened, which served for
pricks,[9] binding and tying the hangings in such sort that,
what force soever they used to loose themselves, it was un-
possible to get from under them. And presently he set fire to
the four corners of the hall in such sort that all that were as
then therein not one escaped away, but were forced to purge
their sins by fire and dry up the great abundance of liquor by
them received into their bodies, all of them dying in the inevitable[10] and merciless flames of the hot and burning fire.

Which the Prince, perceiving, became wise; and knowing
that his uncle, before the end of the banquet, had withdrawn
himself into his chamber, which stood apart from the place
where the fire burnt, went thither and, entering into the
chamber, laid hand upon the sword of his father's murderer,
leaving his own in the place (which, while he was at the banquet, some of the courtiers had nailed fast into the scabbard); and going to Fengon said: "I wonder, disloyal king,
how thou canst sleep here at thine ease, and all thy palace is
burnt, the fire thereof having burnt the greatest part of thy
courtiers and ministers of thy cruelty and detestable tyran-
nies. And, which is more, I cannot imagine how thou
shouldst well assure thyself and thy estate[11] as now to take thy
ease, seeing Hamlet so near thee armed with the shafts by
him prepared long since, and at this present is ready to revenge the traitorous injury by thee done to his lord and
father."

Fengon, as then knowing the truth of his nephew's subtle
practice, and hearing him speak with staid[12] mind, and,
which is more, perceived a sword naked in his hand which he
already lifted up to deprive him of his life, leaped quickly out
of the bed, taking hold of Hamlet's sword that was nailed
into the scabbard, which, as he sought to pull out, Hamlet
gave him such a blow upon the chine[13] of the neck that he cut
his head clean from his shoulders, and, as he fell to the

9 **pricks** skewers   10 **inevitable** irresistible   11 **assure . . . estate** feel confident about your situation   12 **staid** steady   13 **chine** back

ground, said, "This just and violent death is a just reward for
such as thou art. Now go thy ways, and when thou comest in
hell, see thou forget not to tell thy brother whom thou traitorously slewest that it was his son that sent thee thither
with the message, to the end that, being comforted thereby,
his soul may rest among the blessed spirits and quit[14] me of
the obligation that bound me to pursue his vengeance upon
mine own blood, that seeing it was by thee that I lost the
chief thing that tied me to this alliance and consanguinity."

A man, to say the truth, hardy, courageous, and worthy of
eternal commendation, who, arming himself with a crafty,
dissembling, and strange show of being distract out of his
wits, under that pretense deceived the wise, politic, and crafty,
thereby not only preserving his life from the treasons and
wicked practices of the tyrant, but, which is more, by a new
and unexpected kind of punishment revenged his father's
death many years after the act committed, in such* sort that,
directing his courses with such prudence and effecting his
purposes with so great boldness, and constancy, he left a
judgment to be decided among men of wisdom, which[15] was
more commendable in him, his constancy, or magnanimity,
or his wisdom in ordering his affairs according to the pre-
meditable determination he had conceived. . . .

Hamlet, having in this manner revenged himself, durst not
presently declare his action to the people, but to the contrary
determined to work by policy, so to give them intelligence
what he had done and the reason that drew him thereunto; so
that, being accompanied with such of his father's friends
that then were rising,[16] he stayed to see what the people
would do when they should hear of that sudden and fearful
action. The next morning, the towns bordering thereabouts,
desiring to know from whence the flames of fire proceeded
the night before they had seen, came thither, and, perceiving
the King's palace burnt to ashes and many bodies (most part
consumed) lying among the ruins of the house, all of them
were much abashed, nothing being left of the palace but the
foundation. But they were much more amazed to behold the
body of the King all bloody, and his head cut off lying hard
by him; whereat some began to threaten revenge, yet not

14 quit acquit, free   15 which as to which   16 rising arising

knowing against whom; others, beholding so lamentable a spectacle, armed themselves; the rest rejoicing, yet not daring to make any show thereof, some detesting the cruelty, others lamenting the death of their prince but the greatest part, calling Horvendil's murder to remembrance, acknowledging a just judgment from above that had thrown down the pride of the tyrant. And in this sort, the diversities of opinions among that multitude of people being many, yet every man ignorant what would be the issue of that tragedy, none stirred from thence, neither yet attempted to move[17] any tumult, every man fearing his own skin and distrusting his neighbor, esteeming each other to be consenting to the massacre.

[In the last three chapters of the story, Hamlet makes an oration to the Danes in defense of his conduct, wins the loyalty of one and all, and makes good his promise to return to England. There, threatened with a secret plot on the part of the King of England to avenge the death of Fengon, Hamlet slays the English king and returns to Denmark with two wives. He is betrayed by his second wife, Hermetrude, Queen of Scots, in league with his uncle Wiglerus, and is slain.]

———————

Text based on *The History of Hamlet* [spelled *Hamblet* in the original]. *London: Imprinted by Richard Bradocke for Thomas Pavier, and are to be sold at his shop in Cornhill near to the Royal Exchange. 1608.*

In the following, departures from the original text appear in boldface; original readings are in roman.

p. 165 ***northward** neithward   ***to two** two   p. 166 ***surmounted** surmounting
p. 167 ***not only** onely   p. 169 ***wisest** wiseth   p. 170 ***counterfeited** counterfeiting
p. 172 ***infernal** intefernal   p. 175 ***accusing her** accusing his   p. 179 ***he determined** determined   p. 183 ***his** their   p. 185 ***in such** in no such

———————

17 move set in motion, instigate

Further Reading

Alexander, Nigel. *Poison, Play, and Duel: A Study in "Hamlet."* London: Routledge and Kegan Paul, 1971. Alexander argues that the play's representation of complex moral and psychological problems depends upon three dominant symbols—poison, play, and duel—that structure the play's action and language. Through these powerful images, which come together in the play's final scene, Shakespeare conveys a sense of the inescapable difficulties of moral choice and action.

Bevington, David. "'Maimed Rites': Violated Ceremony in *Hamlet.*" *Action Is Eloquence: Shakespeare's Language of Gesture.* Cambridge and London: Harvard Univ. Press, 1984. Bevington traces how Shakespeare shapes our responses to the play through visual means. *Hamlet,* he argues, is a play of "maimed rites," perversions of ceremony that reflect the moral and social disruptions in Denmark. In the final scene, the solemnity with which Hamlet is borne offstage serves to rehabilitate ceremony, restoring "some hope of perceivable meaning in the ceremonial meanings that hold together the social and moral order."

Bohannan, Laura. "Shakespeare in the Bush." *Natural History* 75 (1966): 28–33. Rpt. in *Every Man His Way: Readings in Cultural Anthropology,* ed. Alan Dundes. Englewood Cliffs, N.J.: Prentice-Hall, 1968. Bohannan, a cultural anthropologist, narrates the response of the elders of the Tiv tribe of West Africa to her retelling of the story of *Hamlet.* Her lively essay is a lesson in cultural relativity: familiar critical issues like the ghost, the incestuous marriage, Ophelia's madness, and Hamlet's revenge are freshly viewed from the perspective of a culture with non-Western ethical values and practices.

Booth, Stephen. "On the Value of *Hamlet.*" In *Reinterpretations of Elizabethan Drama,* ed. Norman Rabkin. New York: Columbia Univ. Press, 1969. Booth focuses on the audience's experience of the play. His patient analysis of the opening scene sets forth the process whereby Hamlet's frustrated desire for certainty and coherence be-

comes the audience's own. The result for Booth is that
"*Hamlet* is a tragedy of an audience that cannot make up
its mind."

Bowers, Fredson. "Hamlet as Minister and Scourge."
PMLA 70 (1955): 740–749. When Hamlet calls himself a
"scourge and minister," Bowers argues, he signals his
awareness of a conflict between his roles as private
avenger and agent of providential design. By locating
Hamlet within the moral and dramatic traditions of
Elizabethan revenge tragedy, Bowers discovers the cause
of the hero's delay in Hamlet's desire for Heaven to define and facilitate his complex responsibility.

Bradlay, A. C. "Hamlet." *Shakespearean Tragedy*, 1904.
Rpt., New York: St. Martin's, 1985. Bradley explores the
sources of Hamlet's delay, locating it not in a temperament characteristically resistant to action but in a
"violent shock to his moral being" that produces an ener-
vating melancholy. The Ghost's revelation and demand
for revenge is "the last rivet in the melancholy which
holds him bound," and the play presents "his vain efforts
to fulfill this duty, his unconscious self-excuses and unavailing self-reproaches, and the tragic results of his
delay."

Calderwood, James L. *To Be and Not to Be: Negation and
Metadrama in "Hamlet."* New York: Columbia Univ.
Press, 1983. Calderwood's metadramatic reading pro-
vocatively examines the tensions between illusion and
reality, absence and presence, negation and assertion,
inscribed into a play that relentlessly proliferates uncer-
tainties and contradictions, but that, as Calderwood's title suggests, ultimately accepts and contains them.

Charney, Maurice. *Style in "Hamlet."* Princeton, N.J.:
Princeton Univ. Press, 1969. Charney provides an extensive analysis of verbal and visual style in the play. He
moves from an analysis of *Hamlet*'s dominant patterns of
imagery to an examination of the play in performance,
concluding with an extended rhetorical analysis of the
characters of Polonius, Claudius, and Hamlet.

Coleridge, Samuel Taylor. "Hamlet." *Coleridge's Writings
on Shakespeare*, ed. Terence Hawkes. New York: G. P.
Putnam's Sons, 1959. Coleridge, along with other early

nineteenth-century intellectuals, was strongly drawn to Hamlet ("I have a smack of Hamlet myself") and saw him as an agonizing intellectual, endlessly reasoning and hesitating, detached from the world of events. In Coleridge's influential psychological reading, Hamlet is a man both "amiable and excellent" who is defeated by his "aversion to action, which prevails among such as have a world in themselves."

Eliot, T. S. "Hamlet and His Problems." *Selected Essays, 1917–1932.* New York: Harcourt, Brace and Co., 1932. The "problems" Eliot identifies in his influential essay are not in Hamlet's character but in the play itself. Eliot believes that *Hamlet* is Shakespeare's revision of a lost revenge play onto which Shakespeare's main theme—the effect of a mother's guilt upon her son—is unsuccessfully grafted. Hamlet's emotions are "in excess of the facts as they appear," Eliot finds; Hamlet can neither understand nor objectify them, since Shakespeare himself is unable to find any "objective correlative" in his play for Hamlet's complex psychological state.

Ewbank, Inga-Stina. "*Hamlet* and the Power of Words." *Shakespeare Survey* 30 (1977): 85–102. Rpt. in *Aspects of "Hamlet": Articles Reprinted from "Shakespeare Survey,"* ed. Kenneth Muir and Stanley Wells. Cambridge: Cambridge Univ. Press, 1979. Examining how language functions as a major thematic concern in *Hamlet,* Ewbank explores the possibilities and limitations of verbal communication in the play. Speaking is the play's dominant mode of action, as characters stretch and shape words to the mysterious realities that they confront. For Ewbank, the play's greatness rests on its ability to express so much, even if what is finally expressed is the presence of something inexpressible at its heart.

Forker, Charles. "Shakespeare's Theatrical Symbolism and Its Function in *Hamlet.*" *Shakespeare Quarterly* 14 (1963): 215–229. Rpt. in *Essays in Shakespearean Criticism,* ed. James L. Calderwood and Harold E. Toliver. Englewood Cliffs, N.J.: Prentice-Hall, 1970. Forker examines Shakespeare's complex handling of the theatrical symbolism that pervades the play. Throughout, characters alternating between the roles of spectator and actor play to each other; Hamlet emerges as the consummate performer, whose role-playing embodies all the ambiguities and paradoxes of what it means to act.

Frye, Roland Mushat. *The Renaissance "Hamlet."* Princeton, N.J.: Princeton Univ. Press, 1984. Drawing upon a rich array of historical, literary, and pictorial evidence, Frye seeks to reconstruct the challenges and excitement that *Hamlet* offered to Shakespeare's Elizabethan audience. The rich specificity of the background that Frye reconstructs acknowledges "the complex and sophisticated concerns of Elizabethan minds" and the complexity of the play itself.

Goldman, Michael. " 'To Be or Not to Be' and the Spectrum of Action." *Acting and Action in Shakespearean Tragedy.* Princeton, N.J.: Princeton Univ. Press, 1985. Goldman argues that the challenges the role of Hamlet poses to an actor are analogous to the challenges the play poses to an audience. Each must engage in an act of interpretation that will discover unity and coherence in the multiple and often contradictory evidence of language and action.

Granville-Barker, Harley. *Preface to "Hamlet."* Princeton, N.J.: Princeton Univ. Press, 1946. This book-length "Preface" draws upon Granville-Barker's insights as a theatrical director and literary critic in its focus on the structure and tone of *Hamlet*. The first half of the study contains a detailed analysis of the three distinct movements (rather than the imposed five-act structure) that govern the play's action. Granville-Barker concludes with a discussion of the characters in this "tragedy of thwarted thought and tortured spirit."

Jones, Ernest. *Hamlet and Oepidus.* New York: Norton, 1949; published in 1910 in an earlier essay form. Jones, a student of Freud, considers the personality of Hamlet from a psychoanalytic perspective and diagnoses his delay as symptomatic of an Oepidal complex. Hamlet is incapable of revenge because of his unconscious identification with Claudius, who has enacted Hamlet's unconscious wish to kill his father and marry his mother. Jones extends his provocative argument with the suggestion that the play's Oedipal aspects have their origin in

Shakespeare's own psychology in 1601, the year the play was written and in which Shakespeare's father died.

Levin, Harry. *The Question of "Hamlet."* New York: Oxford Univ. Press, 1959. Levin's rhetorical analysis of the play's tone and action focuses on three dominant figures of speech (which are simultaneously modes of thought): interrogation, doubt, and irony. These, Levin finds, are organized dialectically, with the play's and Hamlet's own pervasive irony serving as a synthesis that permits us to face—though never to solve—the contradictions that the play's questions and unexpected answers expose.

Lewis, C. S. "Hamlet: The Prince or the Poem?" *Proceedings of the British Academy* 28 (1943 for 1942): 11–18. Rpt. in *They Asked for a Paper.* London: Bles, 1962; and in part as "Death in *Hamlet*" in *Shakespeare, the Tragedies: A Collection of Critical Essays,* ed. Alfred Harbage. Englewood Cliffs, N.J.: Prentice-Hall, 1964. Lewis takes issue with the focus on Hamlet's character that has dominated critical discussion of the play since the nineteenth century. He argues that the true subject of the play is death. The fear of being dead, born of a failure to understand human nature or the nature of the universe, is, for Lewis, the source of the play's powerful presentation of doubt and dread.

Mack, Maynard. "The World of *Hamlet.*" *Yale Review* 41 (1952): 502–523. Rpt. in *Shakespeare, the Tragedies: A Collection of Critical Essays,* ed. Alfred Harbage. Englewood Cliffs, N.J.: Prentice-Hall, 1964. Mack's sensitive account of the play's verbal texture establishes the "imaginative environment" of *Hamlet* that is dominated both by a deep and disabling inscrutability and by an overriding sense of morality. In the final act, Mack argues, Hamlet comes to understand what it means to live in such a world and to accept the mysterious condition of being human.

Nietzsche, Friedrich. "The Birth of Tragedy or: Hellenism and Pessimism" (1872). In *The Birth of Tragedy and the Case of Wagner,* trans. Walter Kaufmann. New York: Vintage, 1967. Nietzsche rejects the common nineteenth-century notion that Hamlet fails to act because he is paralyzed by excessive thought in favor of a view of Hamlet's "nausea" induced by looking "truly into the nature of things." What inhibits Hamlet is his tragic knowledge of the futility and folly of action in a world that is out of joint. "Knowledge kills action," Nietzsche asserts; "action requires the veil of illusion."

Prosser, Eleanor. *Hamlet and Revenge*. Stanford, Calif.: Stanford Univ. Press, 1967. Surveying Renaissance ethical codes and dramatic conventions, Prosser examines *Hamlet* in light of the Elizabethan understanding of revenge and ghosts. She contends that once we accept that the moral universe of the play (as well as of the audience) is Christian, we must see the Ghost as "demonic" and Hamlet's commitment to revenge as immoral and appalling.

Memorable Lines

A little more than kin, and less than kind. (HAMLET 1.2.65)

O, that this too too sullied flesh would melt . . .
(HAMLET 1.2.129)

How weary, stale, flat, and unprofitable
Seem to me all the uses of this world!
(HAMLET 1.2.133–134)

Frailty, thy name is woman! (HAMLET 1.2.146)

'A was a man. Take him for all in all,
I shall not look upon his like again. (HAMLET 1.2.187–188)

Neither a borrower nor a lender be. (POLONIUS 1.3.75)

This above all: to thine own self be true. (POLONIUS 1.3.78)

But to my mind, though I am native here
And to the manner born, it is a custom
More honored in the breach than the observance.
(HAMLET 1.4.14–16)

Something is rotten in the state of Denmark.
(MARCELLUS 1.4.90)

Murder most foul, as in the best it is . . . (GHOST 1.5.28)

O, my prophetic soul! (HAMLET 1.5.42)

There are more things in heaven and earth, Horatio,
Than are dreamt of in your philosophy.
(HAMLET 1.5.175–176)

The time is out of joint. O cursèd spite
That ever I was born to set it right! (HAMLET 1.5.197–198)

Brevity is the soul of wit. (POLONIUS 2.2.90)

More matter, with less art.   (QUEEN   2.2.95)

That he's mad, 'tis true; 'tis true 'tis pity,
And pity 'tis 'tis true.   (POLONIUS   2.2.97–98)

Words, words, words.   (HAMLET   2.2.193)

Though this be madness, yet there is method in 't.
     (POLONIUS   2.2.205–206)

There is nothing either good or bad but thinking makes it so.
     (HAMLET   2.2.250–251)

What a piece of work is a man!   (HAMLET   2.2.304–305)

What's Hecuba to him, or he to Hecuba,
That he should weep for her?   (HAMLET   2.2.559–560)

     The play's the thing
Wherein I'll catch the conscience of the King.
     (HAMLET   2.2.605–606)

To be, or not to be, that is the question.   (HAMLET   3.1.57)

Whether 'tis nobler in the mind to suffer
The slings and arrows of outrageous fortune,
Or to take arms against a sea of troubles
And by opposing end them.   (HAMLET   3.1.58–61)

     To die, to sleep;
To sleep, perchance to dream. Ay, there's the rub.
     (HAMLET   3.1.65–66)

Thus conscience does make cowards of us all.
     (HAMLET   3.1.84)

Get thee to a nunnery.   (HAMLET   3.1.122)

The glass of fashion and the mold of form,
Th' observed of all observers ...   (OPHELIA   3.1.156–157)

I would have such a fellow whipped for o'erdoing Termagant.
It out-Herods Herod.   (HAMLET   3.2.12–14)

Suit the action to the word, the word to the action, with this
special observance, that you o'erstep not the modesty of nature.   (HAMLET   3.2.17–19)

. . . the purpose of playing, whose end, both at the first and
now, was and is to hold as 'twere the mirror up to nature.
                                        (HAMLET   3.2.20–22)

. . . for thou hast been
As one, in suffering all, that suffers nothing,
A man that Fortune's buffets and rewards
Hast ta'en with equal thanks.   (HAMLET   3.2.64–67)

OPHELIA   'Tis brief, my lord.
HAMLET   As woman's love.   (3.2.151–152)

The lady doth protest too much, methinks.   (QUEEN   3.2.228)

'Tis now the very witching time of night.   (HAMLET   3.2.387)

           The cess of majesty
Dies not alone, but like a gulf doth draw
What's near it with it.   (ROSENCRANTZ   3.3.15–17)

For 'tis the sport to have the enginer
Hoist with his own petard.   (HAMLET   3.4.213–214)

How all occasions do inform against me
And spur my dull revenge!   (HAMLET   4.4.33–34)

           Rightly to be great
Is not to stir without great argument,
But greatly to find quarrel in a straw
When honor's at the stake.   (HAMLET   4.4.54–57)

When sorrows come, they come not single spies,
But in battalions.   (KING   4.5.79–80)

There's rosemary, that's for remembrance . . . And there is
pansies; that's for thoughts.   (OPHELIA   4.5.179–181)

Alas, poor Yorick! I knew him, Horatio, a fellow of infinite
jest, of most excellent fancy.   (HAMLET   5.1.183–185)

The cat will mew, and dog will have his day.
                                      (HAMLET   5.1.295)

There's a divinity that shapes our ends,
Rough-hew them how we will.   (HAMLET   5.2.10–11)

Not a whit, we defy augury. There is special providence in
the fall of a sparrow. If it be now, 'tis not to come; if it be not
to come, it will be now; if it be not now, yet it will come. The
readiness is all.   (HAMLET   5.2.217–220)

A hit, a very palpable hit.   (OSRIC   5.2.282)

              Good night, sweet prince,
And flights of angels sing thee to thy rest!
                                      (HORATIO   5.2.361–362)